触动心灵的经典
— Heart-Touching Essay Series —

中英对照·双语典藏

追忆 逝水年华

回忆篇

Remembrance Of Things Past

希望这些散文能在提高你英语水平的同时，也能勾起你一份淡淡而美好的回忆。

如果你是一名学生，
阅读它可以增强文学素养，开阔视野
如果你是一位英语爱好者，
阅读它可以一览名家杰作的熠然风采，丰富思想
如果你是一位文学爱好者，
阅读它你可以细品文字的优美，怡情益智。

丛书主编／戴艳萍　主编／王婧　副主编／许剑楠　王星宇

大连理工大学出版社

图书在版编目(CIP)数据

追忆逝水年华:回忆篇:英汉对照 / 王婧主编.
— 大连:大连理工大学出版社,2012.8
　　(触动心灵的经典)
ISBN 978-7-5611-7191-2

Ⅰ.①追… Ⅱ.①王… Ⅲ.①英汉—汉语—对照读物
②散文集—世界 Ⅳ.①H319.4:I

中国版本图书馆CIP数据核字(2012)第182773号

大连理工大学出版社出版

地址:大连市软件园路80号　　邮政编号:116023
发行:0411-84708842　邮购:04411-84703636　传真:0411-84701466
E-mail: dutp@dutp.cn　　DRL:http://www.dutp.cn
辽宁星海彩色印刷有限公司印刷　　大连理工大学出版社发行

幅面尺寸:168mm×235mm	印张:14.75	字数:233千

印数:1~6000

2012年8月第1版	2012年8月第1次印刷

责任编辑:李玉霞	责任校对:刁婷婷

封面设计:王付青

ISBN 978-7-5611-7191-2　　　　　　　定　价:25.00元

前言
preface

怀旧是对过往岁月的点点追忆。

黄昏里一段沙哑的老歌，老屋墙壁上几张泛黄的照片，小时候百玩不厌的几个玻璃球，百看不厌的几本小人书……都是装裱在镜框里凝固的风景，是我们心中永远挥之不去的记忆。即使在科技非常发达、生活非常便利、生活节奏特别快捷的今天，我们也会在不经意间停下匆匆的脚步，想起我们生命中曾经穿越而过的人、事、物。回忆往事，使我们仿佛一下子又找回了真实的自己，脸上洋溢出久违的笑容，心头荡漾起温暖的涟漪。怀旧是我们曾经历过和拥有过的一种证明，怀旧是一种幸福的体验。

有人说怀旧是沉湎故往、不思进取，它其实是一种人生美好情愫的积淀，是心灵憩息的港湾，它让我们反思过往的心路历程，珍惜拥有的美好瞬间，感念帮助我们的那些好人，并由此获取前行的信念与力量。

人不能生活在对往日的回忆中，但不意味着就不能怀旧。羁鸟还恋旧林，池鱼还思故渊呢！享尽繁华，感觉麻木，心灵空虚时，需要怀旧，以便给自己空虚的灵魂找一个能激发斗志的栖息地；身处逆境，望尽天涯，皆无归路时，需要怀旧，以便给自己脆弱的心灵找一个有力的支撑点。怀旧能让我们蓦然明白一些是是非非，怀旧能让我们回首过往，心存感激。

本书收录的是英美散文中的怀旧名作，文章雅致，字字珠玉。有对故园故土的怀念，有对故人故事的追忆，也有对今时今世的感慨。无论是故园故土，还是故人故事，都是情溢笔端，感人至深。让我们不仅能体会名家的细腻情怀，领略作者独特的艺术匠心和人生智慧，还让我们感受到英语是如何在各位语言大师手下妙笔生花的。所配优美流畅的译文，为品读英汉两种语言提供了便利，让读者在阅读中感受不同的语言

魅力。作家介绍、选文简析让读者在体味名家怀旧情怀的同时，增添文化知识，提高文化素养，促进英语水平的整体提升。

　　如果你是一名大、中学生，阅读怀旧经典，可以让你在丰富英语知识的同时，感受到成长的美好和快乐；如果你是一位文学爱好者，阅读怀旧经典不仅可以让你饱览名家杰作的熠然风采，而且可以丰富思想，怡情益智；如果你是一位历经沧桑的智者，阅读怀旧经典能勾起你一份或遥远或苍凉或刻骨铭心或淡淡而美好的追忆，但无论着以什么样的色彩，都是你人生宝贵的财富。

　　愿你经常翻开怀旧经典，在阅读中感受他人的成长，回顾自己的青春年华，把自己内心深处最柔软、最美好的瞬间定格成永恒的记忆。

　　本册书主编为王婧，副主编为许剑楠、王星宇，参与本书编写的还有：刘晓琳、王宁、王欣、王丽丽、余双全、周迈、汪露秋、项丹凤、王晓英、庄欣、孙礼中、刘瑜、宋沈黎、李雪等老师，在此表示感谢。

编者

2012. 8

Contents

目录

目录

目录

故园回望

My Boyhood's Home
我童年时代的家

I Observe
我的回忆

The Legend of Sleep Hollow
睡谷传说

Going Home Again
再访故居

Mark Twain
马克·吐温

马克·吐温（1835—1910），原名塞缪尔·朗赫恩·克莱门斯（*Samuel Langhorne Clemens*），美国批判现实主义文学的奠基人，世界著名的短篇小说大师。他经历了美国从"自由"资本主义到帝国主义的发展过程，其思想和创作也表现为从轻快调笑到辛辣讽刺再到悲观厌世的发展阶段。代表作有短篇小说《竞选州长》（*Running For Governor, 1870*）、《哥尔斯密的朋友再度出洋》（*Goldsmith's Friend Abroad Again, 1870*）等，中篇小说《镀金时代》（*The Gilded Age, 1873*，与查尔斯·特德雷·华纳）、《哈克贝里·费恩历险记》（*Huckleberry Finn, 1885*）及《傻瓜威尔逊》（*The innocents abroad, 1893*）等。19世纪末，随着美国进入帝国主义发展阶段，马克·吐温的一些游记、杂文、政论等的批判揭露意义逐渐减弱，而绝望神秘情绪则有所增长。他被誉为"美国文学中的林肯"（"*Lincoln of American literature*"）。

My Boyhood's Home

At seven in the morning we reached Hannibal[1], Missouri where my boyhood was spent. I had had a glimpse of it fifteen years ago, and another glimpse six years earlier, but both were so brief that they hardly counted. The only notion of the town that remained in my mind was the memory of it as I had known it when I first quitted it twenty-nine years ago. That picture of it was still as clear and vivid to me as a photograph. I stepped ashore with the feeling of one who returns out of a dead-and-gone generation. I had a sort of realizing sense of what the Bastille[2] prisoners must have felt when they used to come out and look upon Paris after years of captivity[3], and note how curiously the familiar and the strange were mixed together before them. I saw the new houses — saw them plainly enough — but they did not affect the older picture in my mind, for through their solid bricks and mortar[4] I saw the vanished houses, which had formerly stood there, with perfect distinctness.

It was Sunday morning, and everybody was abed[5] yet. So I passed through the vacant

我童年时代的家

早上七点，我们抵达密苏里州的汉尼拔，我曾在这儿度过了我的童年时光。十五年前我回此地匆匆地看了它一眼，六年前又来这儿匆忙一瞥，但那两次都为时过短，没留下什么印象。在我心中关于小镇的一切还和我二十九年前离开它时的记忆一样。对我来说，它的图景仍然像一幅照片那样清晰，那么栩栩如生。我向岸边走去，感觉自己从已经死去好久了的一代人中回来；好似巴士底狱中的囚徒，在被囚禁多年之后，离开监狱仰望巴黎面貌时，发现眼前那些混淆在一起的既熟悉又陌生的东西，心头是多么的惊奇。我看到新的房屋——看得分外清晰——但它们没有影响我脑中那张小镇的旧图景，我却从它们坚实的砖泥当中看到了那些化为乌有的老房子，它们站在那儿，轮廓十分清晰。

星期天早晨，大家都还没有起床。我走在空荡无人的街道

---

1 **Hanniba** *n.*   汉尼拔，美国密苏里州东北部的一个城镇，马克·吐温在此度过童年
2 **Bastille** *n.*   巴士底狱，法国专制王朝的象征，关押了许多反对封建制度的著名人物。1789年7月3日，巴黎人民愤然起义，14日攻占了巴士底狱，史称法国大革命，标志着法国资产阶级革命的开始
3 **captivity** /kæp'tivəti/ *n.* 囚禁，关押
4 **mortar** /'mɔːtə(r)/ *n.* 灰泥
5 **abed** /ə'bed/ *adv.* 在床上

streets, still seeing the town as it was, and not as it is, and recognizing and metaphorically shaking hands with a hundred familiar objects which no longer exist; and finally climbed Holiday's Hill to get a comprehensive view. The whole town lay spread out below me then, and I could mark and fix every locality, every detail. Naturally, I was a good deal moved. I said, "Many of the people I once knew in this tranquil[1] refuge[2] of my childhood are now in heaven; some, I trust, are in the other place." The things about me and before me made me feel like a boy again — convinced me that I was a boy again, and that I had simply been dreaming an unusually long dream; but my reflections spoiled all that; for they forced me to say, "I see fifty old houses down yonder, into each of which I could enter and find either a man or a woman who was a baby or unborn when I noticed those houses last, or a grandmother who was a plump[3] young bride at that time."

From this vantage ground[4] the extensive view up and down the river, and wide over the wooded expanses of Illinois[5], is very beautiful — one of the most beautiful on the Mississippi, I think; which is a hazardous[6] remark to make, for the eight hundred miles of river between St. Louis[7] and St. Paul[8] afford an unbroken succession of

上，看到的仍是小镇的旧貌，而非新颜。我的头脑中映出了上百个熟悉的事物，我和它们一一握手，虽然它们已经不复存在。最后我登上了假日山，得以鸟瞰小镇全景。整个镇子在我脚下延伸开来，而我则能够细致地标记每个地方，给它们定下方位。自然地，此情此景使我深受感动。我说道："我童年时静谧的住处，当年我认识的人们中，有许多已经进入了天堂；而我相信，另一些则在别的什么地方。"周围和眼前的事物让我觉得自己又回到了童年——让我深信自己又回到了童年，而这种感觉恰恰是我长久以来希冀的梦想，但我的思绪却破坏了它，因为它们让我不得不说："我看到的五十幢老房子，走进他们中的任何一家，都找到一个成年男子或妇女，当我最后看到那些房子时他们不过是婴儿甚至还未出世，而那时丰满年轻的新娘如今也已经变成了孩子的祖母。"

从这一有利地形可以俯瞰小河绵长的流域，并能一直看到伊利诺伊州辽阔的森林，景致十分优美——我认为它是密

---

1 tranquil /ˈtræŋkwɪl/ adj. 安静的
2 refuge /ˈrefjuːdʒ/ n. 避难所
3 plump /plʌmp/ adj. 丰满的
4 vantage ground /ˈvaːntɪdʒ/ 有利地形，优越地位
5 Illinois 美国伊利诺伊州
6 hazardous /ˈhæzədəs/ adj. 有争议的，有待商榷的
7 St.Louis 圣·路易斯，美国密苏里州最大的城市，位于密西西比河西岸
8 St. Paul 圣·保罗，美国明尼苏达州首府，位于密西西比河东岸

lovely pictures. It may be that my affection for the one in question biases my judgment in its favor; I cannot say as to that. No matter, it was satisfyingly beautiful to me, and it had this advantage over all the other friends whom I was about to greet again: it had suffered no change; it was as young and fresh and comely[1] and gracious as ever it had been; whereas, the faces of the others would be old, and scarred with the campaigns of life, and marked with their grieves and defeats, and would give me no uplifting of spirit.

An old gentleman, out on an early morning walk, came along, and we discussed the weather, and then drifted into other matters. I could not remember his face. He said he had been living here twenty-eight years. So he had come after my time, and I had never seen him before. I asked him various questions; first about a mate of mine in Sunday[2] school — what became of him?

"He graduated with honor in an Eastern[3] college, wandered off into the world somewhere, succeeded at nothing, passed out of knowledge and memory years ago, and is supposed to have gone to the dogs[4]."

"He was bright, and promised[5] well when he was a boy."

1 comely /'kʌmli/ adj. 清秀的，标致的
2 Sunday 主日学校，基督教教会为了向儿童灌输宗教思想，在星期天开办的儿童班
3 Eastern /'iːst(ə)n/ adj. 罗马东正教的
4 dogs 每况愈下
5 promised /'prɒmɪst/ adj. 有希望的

西西比河上最美丽的景致之一。这是个危险的评论，因为密西西比河在圣·路易斯和圣·保罗之间的八百英里中，可爱美丽的图景延绵不断。可能是我颇具争议的情感，让我的判断偏向于对它的喜爱；对于这偏爱我也说不出什么。不过没关系，对我来说，它是如此令人心旷神怡的美丽，我想再见它的欲望胜过我想见任何一位老朋友。它没有经受任何改变；它还像原本那样生气勃勃、清新秀丽、优美亲切。然而，其他人的面容将会变老，留下岁月磨难的痕迹，带着悲伤和失败的标志，它们不会带给我高涨的心绪。

一位早上出去散步的老先生走了过来，我们从天气一直谈到了其他一些事情。我已经记不得他的长相。他说自己已经在这居住二十八年了。所以他是我离开之后才来的，之前我从没见过他。我问了他许多问题，首先问及了一个我在主日学校的伙伴——他过得怎样？

"他是一所东正教学院的荣誉毕业生，在这个世界的某个地方徘徊游荡，一事无成，几年前他满带着学识和记忆去世了。大家觉得他堕落了。"

"Yes, but the thing that happened is what became of it all."

I asked after another lad, altogether the brightest in our village school when I was a boy.

"He, too, was graduated with honors, from an Eastern college; but life whipped him in every battle, straight along, and he died in one of the Territories, years ago, a defeated man."

I named three school-girls.

"The first two live here, are married and have children; the other is long ago dead — never married."

The answer to several other inquiries was brief and simple —

"Killed in the war."

I named another boy.

"Well, now, his case is curious! There wasn't a human being in this town but knew that that boy was a perfect chucklehead[1]; perfect dummy[2]; just a stupid ass, as you may say. Everybody knew it, and everybody said it. Well, if that very boy isn't the first lawyer in the State of Missouri to-day, I'm a Democrat[3]!"

"Is that so?"

"It's actually so. I'm telling you the truth."

"How do you account for it?"

---

1 chucklehead /'tʃʌk(ə)lhed/ n. 傻子
2 dummy /'dʌmi/ n. （口语）傻瓜，笨蛋，蠢货
3 Democrat /'deməkræt/ n. 美国民主党

"他过去很聪明啊，小的时候很有希望呢。"

"没错，可是这就是已经发生了的事实。"

我问到另一位老朋友，我小时候，他简直是我们村庄上最聪明的孩子。

"他也一样，从一所东正教学院荣誉毕业；但是生活在每一次搏斗中都直面鞭打了他。几年前，他在其中一次战斗中死了，一个失败的人。"

我又说了三个女同学的名字。

"前两个生活在这，已经结婚生子了；另一个很久以前就死了，还没结婚呢。"

对另一些询问的回答则简单明了——

"在战争中死了。"

我问了另一个男同学的情况。

"嗯，好吧，他的情况倒是很不寻常！这个镇上没人不知道那小子是个十足的傻瓜，十足的笨蛋，或者你会说，完全是个蠢驴。每个人都知道，并且每个人都这么说。可是，如果那小子不是现如今密苏里州的首席律师，那我就是民主党人了！"

"真的吗？"

"确实是这样，我告诉你的都是实事。"

"那你怎么解释这事儿

"Account for it? There ain't any accounting for it, except that if you send a damned fool to St. Louis, and you don't tell them he's a damned fool they'll never find it out. There's one thing sure — if I had a damned fool I should know what to do with him: ship him to St. Louis — it's the noblest market in the world for that kind of property. Well, when you come to look at it all around, and chew at it and think it over, don't it just bang[1] anything you ever heard of?"

"Well, yes, it does seem to. But don't you think maybe it was the Hannibal people who were mistaken about the boy, and not the St. Louis people."

"Oh, nonsense! The people here have known him from the very cradle[2] — they knew him a hundred times better than the St. Louis idiots could have known him. No, if you have got any damned fools that you want to realize[3] on, take my advice — send them to St. Louis."

I mentioned a great number of people whom I had formerly known. Some were dead, some were gone away, some had prospered, some had come to naught[4]; but as regarded a dozen or so of the lot, the answer was comforting:

---

1 **bang** /bæŋ/　*vt.*　重敲，猛撞
2 **cradle** /'kreɪdl/　*n.*　婴儿时期
3 **realize on** /'riːəlaiz/　变卖
4 **naught** /nɔːt/　*n.*　零

呢？"

"解释？这件事没什么可解释的，除了说，如果你把一个该死的蠢货送到圣·路易斯去，并不告诉他们他是个该死的蠢货，那他们就永远也发现不了他蠢。有件事我很确定——要是我生了个该死的蠢货，我可知道该把他怎么办：让他坐船去圣·路易斯——那儿是这世界上有着那种货色最著名的市场。好吧，你好好看看这事，反复考虑一下，它不比你听到的任何事情都震撼吗？"

"嗯，是的，好像确实是这样。但你不认为，也许错看他的是汉尼拔人，而非圣·路易斯人呢？"

"噢，一派胡言！这儿的人从他还是婴儿的时候就认识他了——他们要比圣·路易斯那些白痴了解他一百倍。不，如果你生了该死的蠢货，并想用他们换点钱的话，听我的话，把他们送到圣·路易斯去。"

我提到了我之前认得的一大群人。一些已经死了，还有一些去了其他地方；有一些人成功了，另一些人一无所获；但是这些人里大约对于十二个人的回答令人满意：

"Prosperous — live here yet — town littered with their children."

After asking after such other folk as I could call to mind, I finally inquired about MYSELF:

"Oh, he succeeded well enough — another case of damned fool. If they'd sent him to St. Louis, he'd have succeeded sooner."

It was with much satisfaction that I recognized the wisdom of having told this candid[1] gentleman, in the beginning, that my name was Smith.

"很成功，还住在这儿，在镇上生了很多孩子。"

问过了所有我能想起的人以后，最终，我问到了关于我自己的事情：

"噢，他相当成功——另一个该死的蠢货的实例。如果他被送去圣·路易斯，那他早就成功了。"

我对自己的小聪明十分满意，因为一开始我就告诉这位公正的先生，我的名字叫史密斯。

---

1 candid /ˈkændɪd/　*adj.* 　无偏见的，公正的

含英咀华

本文选自马克·吐温的《密西西比河》（Life on the Mississippi, 1875），写的是作者多年后再次回到童年时生活的小镇时的见闻，以及与一位多年生活在这个镇上的老人的谈话。文章写景优美动人，对话生动诙谐，流露出作者对故乡小镇的美好眷恋之情。

Charles Dickens

查尔斯·狄更斯

查尔斯·狄更斯(1812—1870)，十九世纪英国批判现实版作家的代表。通常被认为英国维多利亚时代（1837~1901）最伟大的小说家。他出身贫寒，十五岁在法律事务所工作，后成为新闻记者，从此走上文学之路。其作品广泛而深刻地描写了英国由半封建社会向工业资本主义社会的过渡时期，鲜明而生动地刻画了各阶层的代表人物形象。艺术上以妙趣横生的幽默、细致入微的心理分析，以及现实主义描写与浪漫主义气氛的有机结合著称。狄更斯一生共创作了十四部长篇小说，其中最著名的作品是描写劳资矛盾的长篇代表作《艰难时期》（*Hard Times, 1854*）和描写1789年法国革命的另一篇代表作《双城记》（*A Tale of Two Cities, 1859*）。

I Observe

我的回忆

From "David Copponfied"

The first objects that assume a distinct presence before me, as I look far back, into the blank of my infancy, are my mother with her pretty hair and youthful shape, and Peggotty[1] with no shape at all, and eyes so dark that they seemed to darken their whole neighbourhood in her face, and cheeks and arms so hard and red that I wondered the birds didn't peck her in preference to[2] apples.

I believe I can remember these two at a little distance apart, dwarfed[3] to my sight by stooping downor[4] kneeling on the floor, and I going unsteadily from the one to the other. I have an impression on my mind which I cannot distinguish from[5] actual remembrance, of the touch of Peggotty's forefinger as she used to hold it out to me, and of its being roughened by needlework, like a pocket nutmeg-grater[6].

This may be fancy, though I think the memory of most of us can go farther back into such times than many of us suppose; just as I

当我回忆起幼年的模糊岁月时，首先清晰地浮现在眼前的便是我的母亲，她秀发飘飘，相貌年轻。然后就是皮高提，她实在没有模样可言，她的眼睛黑黑的，以至于眼周的皮肤也黯淡无光。她的脸颊和手臂硬邦邦、红彤彤的，我常为鸟儿们不来啄她却去啄苹果而感到奇怪。

我相信，我记得这两个人在我不远处弯下腰来或跪在地上，于是在我眼里她们变得矮小了，然后我摇摇晃晃地从一个走到另一个身边。我往往分不清这是印象还是确实存在的记忆——皮高提常常用她那被针线活磨粗糙了的食指抚摸我，那感觉像是一个小小的用来磨肉豆蔻的擦子摩擦一样。

这也许只是幻觉，但是我相信，我们大多数人能够回忆起的岁月远比我们许多人所认为的久远；正如我相信，许多幼儿精准贴切的观察力会让人赞叹不已。说实在的，有许多成年人在这方面卓越超群，

1 Peggotty: 皮高提，大卫幼年时在母亲及女仆皮高提的照顾下长大
2 in preference to /'prefrəns/ 优先于
3 dwarf /dwɔːf/ vt. （由于距离或对比）使显得矮小
4 stooping down /ˌstuːpɪŋ/ 屈身，弯腰
5 distinguish from /dɪˈstɪŋgwɪʃ/ 区分，辨别
6 nutmeg-grater /ˈnʌtmeɡˈɡreɪtə/ n. 磨肉豆蔻的磨碎机

believe the power of observation in numbers of very young children to be quite wonderful for its closeness and accuracy. Indeed, I think that most grown men who are remarkable in this respect, may with greater propriety[1] be said not to have lost the faculty, than to have acquired it; the rather, as I generally observe such men to retain a certain freshness, and gentleness, and capacity of being pleased, which are also an inheritance[2] they have preserved from their childhood.

Looking back, as I was saying, into the blank of my infancy, the first objects I can remember as standing out by themselves from a confusion of things, are my mother and Peggotty. What else do I remember? Let me see.

There comes out of the cloud, our house — not new to me, but quite familiar, in its earliest remembrance. On the ground-floor is Peggotty's kitchen, opening into a back yard; with a pigeon-house on a pole, in the centre, without any pigeons in it; a great dog-kennel[3] in a corner, without any dog; and a quantity of fowls that look terribly tall to me, walking about, in a menacing[4] and ferocious[5] manner. There is one cock who gets upon a post to crow, and seems to take particular notice of me as I look at him through the kitchen window, who makes me shiver, he is so fierce. Of the geese outside the side-gate who

---

1 with propriety: /prəˈpraɪəti/ 适当
2 inheritance /inˈheritəns/ n. 遗产，遗留的财富
3 kennel /ˈkenl/ n. 狗舍
4 menacing /ˈmenəsiŋ/ adj. 威胁的
5 ferocious /fəˈrəʊʃəs/ adj. 凶猛的，残忍的

我认为与其说他们获得了这种能力，不如说他们还没有丧失这种能力；尤其是，我大致观察过那些仍旧保持蓬勃朝气、温文尔雅和乐观精神的人，更觉得这也是他们童年留下的财富。

正如我说过的，回顾幼年的模糊岁月，在一片纷纭杂乱之中首先浮现在我眼前的是母亲和皮高提。我还记得别的什么呢？让我想想看。

云雾中出现了我们的房子——在我看来它并不新，但非常熟悉，还是早年记忆中的模样。一楼是皮高提的厨房，厨房门通向后院；在院子中间的一根柱子上有一个鸽笼，里面一只鸽子也没有；角落里有一个硕大的狗窝，里面没有一条狗；还有一大群在我看来个头高得可怕的家禽，趾高气扬、气势汹汹地走来走去。有一只公鸡总是跳上柱子鸣叫，每当我从厨房的窗子看它时，它似乎格外注意我，样子很凶，吓得我发抖。院门旁边有一群鹅，每当我从那边走，它们都会伸长脖子摇摇摆摆地追我，我睡觉也会梦到这群鹅，就好像一个曾被野兽围

come waddling after me with their long necks stretched out when I go that way, I dream at night: as a man environed[1] by wild beasts might dream of lions.

Here is a long passage — what an enormous perspective I make of it! — leading from Peggotty's kitchen to the front door. A dark store-room opens out of it, and that is a place to be run past at night; for I don't know what may be among those tubs and jars and old tea-chests, when there is nobody in there with a dimly-burning light, letting a mouldy[2] air come out of the door, in which there is the smell of soap, pickles[3], pepper, candles, and coffee, all at one whiff[4]. Then there are the two parlours: the parlour in which we sit of an evening, my mother and I and Peggotty — for Peggotty is quite our companion, when her work is done and we are alone — and the best parlour[5] where we sit on a Sunday; grandly, but not so comfortably. There is something of a doleful[6] air about that room to me, for Peggotty has told me — I don't know when, but apparently ages ago — about my father's funeral, and the company having their black cloaks put on.

There is nothing half so green that I know anywhere, as the grass of that churchyard; nothing half so shady as its trees; nothing half so

---

1 **environ** /in'vaiərən/ *vt.* 包围
2 **mouldy = moldy** /'məuldi/ *adj.* 发霉的，陈腐的，乏味的
3 **pickle** /'pɪkl/ *n.* （复数）泡菜
4 **whiff** /wɪf/ *n.* 一阵（微弱的）气味
5 **parlour** /'pɑːlə(r)/ *n.* 客厅
6 **doleful** /'dəulfl/ *adj.* 阴沉的，悲哀的

攻的人会梦到狮子一样。

有一条长廊从皮高提的厨房一直通向前门——在我看来它真是悠长啊！一间幽暗的储藏室就对着这条长廊上开了个门，晚上从那里经过非跑着过去不可；因为要是没有人拿着盏光线暗淡的灯站在那儿，我就会担心从那些木桶啊、罐子啊或是旧茶叶箱子里会蹦出什么东西来。门里透出一股发霉的气味，其中有肥皂味、泡菜味、胡椒味、蜡烛味、咖啡味，全部混杂在一起。再还有两间客厅：一间是我们——母亲、我、皮高提晚上坐的客厅——当皮高提做完了活，我们又很孤独时，她更是我们的伙伴。另一间是我们在周日才坐的那间最好的客厅，这间虽然气派，但却不怎么舒服。我觉得那间屋子阴森森的，因为皮高提曾经告诉我——不知道是什么时候，反正显然是很久很久以前——关于我父亲葬礼的事，还有那群穿黑色丧服的人。

我不知道还有什么赶得上墓地的草地一半翠绿，赶得上那的树木一半阴凉，赶得上那的墓碑一半静谧。清晨，我跪在母亲卧室里我那个小套间

quiet as its tombstones. The sheep are feeding there, when I kneel up, early in the morning, in my little bed in a closet within my mother's room, to look out at it; and I see the red light shining on the sun-dial[1], and think within myself, 'Is the sun-dial glad, I wonder, that it can tell the time again?'

Here is our pew[2] in the church. What a high-backed pew! With a window near it, out of which our house can be seen, and is seen many times during the morning's service[3], by Peggotty, who likes to make herself as sure as she can that it's not being robbed, or is not in flames. But though Peggotty's eye wanders, she is much offended if mine does, and frowns to me, as I stand upon the seat, that I am to look at the clergyman[4]. But I can't always look at him — I know him without that white thing on, and I am afraid of his wondering why I stare so, and perhaps stopping the service to inquire — and what am I to do? It's a dreadful thing to gape[5], but I must do something. I look at my mother, but she pretends not to see me. I look at a boy in the aisle, and he makes faces[6] at me. I look at the sunlight coming in at the open door through the porch, and there I see a stray sheep[7] — I don't mean a sinner, but mutton[8] — half making up his mind to come into the church. I feel that if

1　sun-dial /ˈsʌndaɪəl/　日晷
2　pew /pjuː/　n.　教堂内的靠背长椅
3　service /ˈsɜːvɪs/　n.　礼拜
4　clergyman /ˈklɜːdʒɪmən/　n.　神职人员，牧师，教士
5　gape /ɡeɪp/　vi.　瞪着眼睛，直直地看
6　make faces　做鬼脸
7　stray sheep /streɪ/　迷途的羔羊
8　I don't mean a sinner, but mutton　基督教把"迷途的羊"比作误入歧途的罪人

的小床上向外望去，看见羊儿在那吃草；看见日晷上闪着红光，心里想着，"日晷又能报时了，它会高兴吗？"

我们在教堂的座位上。多高的椅背啊！附近有扇窗，从那儿可以看见我们的房子。早上做礼拜的时候，皮高提会看房子好多次，要尽可能地确保我们的房子没有被劫，或是着火。可虽然皮高提自己四处张望，而我要是也到处看，她就会很不高兴，我站在座位上时，她就向我皱眉头，示意我要看牧师。可我不能老是看着他呀——他就是没穿那身白袍子我也认得他，我还怕他会因为我那样盯着他看而觉着奇怪呢，说不定他会停下讲道来问我——那我干点什么呢？干瞪眼睛实在太无聊了，我总得找点事做啊。我看看母亲，但是她装作没看见我。我又看看过道里的一个男孩，他朝我做鬼脸。我朝从门口照射进来并穿过门廊的阳光看去，竟看到了一只迷途羔羊——我不是指罪人，而是长着羊肉的羊——好像有点想进教堂来的意思。我觉得我要再朝它看就会忍不住大声喊出来；那时我可怎么办呀！我又抬头朝墙上的灵牌望

I looked at him any longer, I might be tempted to say something out loud; and what would become of[1] me then! I look up at the monumental tablets on the wall, and try to think of Mr. Bodgers' late of this parish, and what the feelings of Mrs. Bodgers must have been, when affliction sore, long time Mr. Bodgers bore, and physicians were in vain.

And now I see the outside of our house, with the latticed[2] bedroom-windows standing open to let in the sweet-smelling air, and the ragged old rooks'[3]-nests still dangling in the elm-trees at the bottom of the front garden. Now I am in the garden at the back, beyond the yard where the empty pigeon-house and dog-kennel are — a very preserve of butterflies, as I remember it, with a high fence, and a gate and padlock[4]; where the fruit clusters[5] on the trees, riper and richer than fruit has ever been since, in any other garden, and where my mother gathers some in a basket, while I stand by, bolting furtive[6] gooseberries[7], and trying to look unmoved. A great wind rises, and the summer is gone in a moment. We are playing in the winter twilight, dancing about the parlour. When my mother is out of breath and rests herself in an elbow-chair, I watch her

去，努力怀想我们这个教区已故的伯杰斯先生，想象他久病不愈，饱受折磨，而医生又回天乏术时，伯杰斯太太会是怎样的心情啊。

现在，我看见了我们房子的外部，卧室的格子窗敞开着好让清新宜人的空气吹进来，粗糙老旧的白嘴鸭巢还在前花园尽头那些老榆树上荡来荡去。现在，我在后面园子里，院子远处的空鸽子笼和空狗窝，是蝴蝶们绝妙的庇护地。我记得，园子周围有高高的篱笆，一个大门和一把锁头；园子里的树上挂着累累果实，没有哪个果园里的果实会有那么熟，那么多，妈妈往篮子里摘一些果实，而我站在旁边，偷偷摸摸地紧紧握着醋栗，还装着做出没动过的样子。一阵大风吹过，夏天一转眼就过去了。冬日黄昏的余晖里，我们在客厅玩耍、跳舞。母亲累得喘不过气来时就坐在扶手椅里休息，我看到她用手指绕着她

---

1 become of　发生于，发生……情况
2 latticed /'lætɪst/　adj.　格子状的
3 rook /rʊk/　n.　白嘴鸭
4 padlock /'pædlɒk/　n.　挂锁
5 cluster /'klʌstə(r)/　vi.　丛生
6 furtive /'fɜːtɪv/　adj.　偷偷摸摸的
7 gooseberry /'guzbəri/　n.　醋栗

winding her bright curls round her fingers, and straitening her waist, and nobody knows better than I do that she likes to look so well, and is proud of being so pretty. That is among my very earliest impressions.

漂亮的发卷，并挺直了腰。我比任何人都清楚的是，她喜欢看上去很棒，并为自己有着如此姣好的面容感到骄傲。这就是我最早的回忆中的一部分。

含英咀华

本文节选自狄更斯自传体小说《大卫·科波菲尔》（David Copperfield, 1849），描写的是主人公大卫·科波菲尔对幼年时代温馨美满的家庭生活的回忆，表达了他对快乐无忧的童年生活的无限眷恋。作者生动细致地描绘了大卫的生活环境和对母亲以及女仆皮提高的深深依恋。本文从一个幼儿的视角观察周围的事物，语言诙谐。

Washington Irving

华盛顿·欧文

华盛顿·欧文（1783—1859），十九世纪美国最著名的作家，被誉为"美国文学之父"，是第一个为美国文学赢得欧洲乃至世界声誉的作家。他一生著述颇多，体裁多样，包括散文、短篇小说、传记、和历史书籍等，代表作有《见闻札记》（*The Sketch Book, 1820*）、《布雷斯勃列奇田庄》（*Bracebridge Hall, 1822*）和《阿尔汗伯拉》（*The Alhambra, 1832*）。他开创了自己"欧文式风格"，其笔调自然清新、细腻委婉、优雅动人且富于活力。他与生俱来的幽默和多愁善感相辅相成、相得益彰。

The Legend of Sleep Hollow

睡谷传说

In the bosom of one of those spacious coves[1] which indent[2] the eastern shore of the Hudson[3], at that broad expansion of the river denominated[4] by the ancient Dutch[5] navigators the Tappan Zee, and where they always prudently shortened sail[6] and implored the protection of St. Nicholas[7] when they crossed, there lies a small market town[8] or rural port, which by some is called Greensburgh, but which is more generally and properly known by the name of Tarry Town[9]. This name was given, we are told, in former days, by the good housewives of the adjacent[10] country, from the inveterate[11] propensity[12] of their husbands to linger about the village tavern[13] on market days. Be that as it may[14], I do not vouch for[15] the fact, but merely advert to[16] it, for the sake of[17] being precise

在哈得逊河东岸的那些宽阔的峡谷之中，坐落着一个集市小镇，也可以说是乡间码头，河道在此放宽，古代的荷兰航海家将其命名为塔班湖。当他们航行至此，总是会谨小慎微地收起船帆，并祈求圣尼古拉斯的庇护。这小镇，有人叫它格林斯堡，但是更通行更合适的叫法是流连镇。据说这名字是以前邻乡的好主妇们给取的。那时，她们的丈夫在赶集的日子总会在镇上的小酒馆里流连忘返。话虽如此，为了精准可信，我并不保证这就是事实，而只是留意到有此一

1 cove /kəuv/   n.   峡谷
2 indent /ɪn'dent/   vi.   排列
3 Hudson   美国纽约州东部的一条河流
4 denominate /dɪ'nɒmɪneɪt/   vt.   命名
5 Dutch /dʌtʃ/   n.   荷兰人
6 shorten sail   收起船帆
7 St. Nicholas   圣·尼古拉斯，公元4世纪初小亚细亚的一个主教，是天主教中旅行者的守护神
8 market town   集镇
9 Tarry Town   荷兰殖民者所建的哈德逊河畔最早的聚居地之一
10 adjacent /ə'dʒeɪsnt/   adj.   邻近的
11 inveterate /ɪn'vetərət/   adj.   成癖的
12 propensity /prə'pensəti/   n.   倾向
13 tavern /'tævən/   n.   酒馆
14 be that as it may   尽管是这样
15 vouch for /vautʃ/   担保
16 advert to /'ædvɜ:t/   留意到
17 for the sake of   为了

and authentic. Not far from this village, perhaps about two miles, there is a little valley or rather lap of land among high hills, which is one of the quietest places in the whole world. A small brook[1] glides[2] through it, with just murmur enough to lull[3] one to repose[4]; and the occasional whistle of a quail[5] or tapping of a woodpecker[6] is almost the only sound that ever breaks in upon the uniform tranquility[7].

I recollect that, when a stripling[8], my first exploit in squirrel-shooting was in a grove[9] of tall walnut-trees[10] that shades one side of the valley. I had wandered into it at noontime, when all nature is peculiarly[11] quiet, and was startled by the roar of my own gun, as it broke the Sabbath[12] stillness around and was prolonged and reverberated[13] by the angry echoes. If ever I should wish for a retreat[14] whither[15] I might steal from the world and its distractions, and dream quietly away the remnant[16] of a troubled life, I know of none more promising than this little valley.

说。离镇子不远，大概两英里吧，有一个小山谷，其实也就是群山环绕的一个小盆地，这是世界上最幽静的地方之一。一条小溪平缓滑过，喃喃的水声恰好可以催人入眠；除了鹌鹑偶尔的鸣声或是啄木鸟啄树干时的嗒嗒声外，就再没有什么打破这一贯的静谧。

我还记得年轻时第一次打松鼠，是在高大的胡桃树林里，它的绿荫遮蔽了半边山谷。那是正午时分，漫步于林中，万籁俱静，我被自己的枪声吓了一跳，打破了有如安息日时的寂静，愤怒的回声激荡不已。要是有一天我想隐退，躲到任何可以远离尘世烦扰的地方，如梦般宁静地度过残生，我真不知道有比这小山谷更好的地方了。

1 brook /brʊk/ n. 小溪
2 glide /glaɪd/ vi. 滑过
3 lull /lʌl/ vt. 使平静
4 repose /rɪˈpəʊz/ vi. 睡眠
5 quail /kweɪl/ n. 鹌鹑
6 woodpecker /ˈwʊdpekə(r)/ n. 啄木鸟
7 tranquility /træŋˈkwɪləti/ n. 安静
8 stripling /ˈstrɪplɪŋ/ n. 年轻人
9 grove /grəʊv/ n. 小树林
10 walnut-tree /ˈwɔːlnʌt triː/ n. 胡桃树
11 peculiarly /pɪˈkjuːliəli/ adv. 特别地
12 Sabbath /ˈsæbəθ/ n. 安息日
13 reverberate /rɪˈvɜːbəreɪt/ vt. 反响
14 retreat /rɪˈtriːt/ n. 隐退
15 whither /ˈwɪðə/ n. 地方
16 remnant /ˈremnənt/ n. 剩余

From the listless[1] repose[2] of the place, and the peculiar character of its inhabitants[3], who are descendants[4] from the original Dutch settlers, this sequestered[5] glen[6] has long been known by the name of SLEEPY HOLLOW, and its rustic[7] lads are called the Sleepy Hollow Boys throughout all the neighboring country. A drowsy[8], dreamy influence seems to hang over the land, and to pervade[9] the very atmosphere. Some say that the place was bewitched by a High German[10] doctor, during the early days of the settlement; others, that an old Indian chief[11], the prophet[12] or wizard[13] of his tribe, held his powwows[14] there before the country was discovered by Master Hendrick Hudson[15]. Certain it is, the place still continues under the sway of some witching power that holds a spell over the minds of the good people, causing them to walk in a continual reverie[16]. They are given to all kinds of marvellous beliefs, are subject to trances[17] and visions, and frequently see strange sights, and

就凭这地方懒洋洋的安闲和身为古老荷兰殖民者后裔的居民的性格，这块幽僻的峡谷向来就有"睡谷"之称，而这村子里的孩子也被附近一带人称做"睡谷娃"。仿佛睡意蒙眬，恬恬酣梦笼罩着这片土地，弥漫于空气中。有些人说，在移民初期一个德国南部的医生给这地方施了魔法；另一些则说，在亨利·哈得逊船长发现这片村落之前，一个印第安酋长，即他的部落里的先知或巫师，会在那里举行各种仪式。确信无疑的是，这地方仍被某种魔力所控制，迷惑当地善良人们的思想，使他们游走于迷惘幻想之间。他们喜欢相信各种神奇的传说，易于神情恍惚，产生幻觉，经常会看见

1 **listless** /ˈlistləs/ *adj.* 懒洋洋的
2 **repose** /rɪˈpəʊz/ *n.* 安闲
3 **inhabitant** /inˈhæbitənt/ *n.* 居民
4 **descendant** /diˈsendənt/ *n.* 后代
5 **sequestered** /sɪˈkwestəd/ *adj.* 静僻的
6 **glen** /glen/ *n.* 幽谷
7 **rustic** /ˈrʌstik/ *adj.* 乡村的
8 **drowsy** /ˈdraʊzi/ *adj.* 睡意蒙眬的
9 **pervade** /pəˈveid/ *vt.* 遍及
10 **High German** 德意志南部和中部
11 **chief** /tʃiːf/ *n.* 酋长
12 **prophet** /ˈprɒfit/ *n.* 先知
13 **wizard** /ˈwizəd/ *n.* 巫师
14 **powwow** /ˈpaʊwaʊ/ *n.* 仪式
15 **Hendrick Hudson** 即Henry Hudson亨利·哈得逊，英国航海家，纽约的哈得逊河与加拿大的哈得逊海湾以他的名字命名
16 **reverie** /ˈrevəri/ *n.* 幻想
17 **trance** /traːns/ *n.* 恍惚

hear music and voices in the air. The whole neighborhood abounds with local tales, haunted spots, and twilight[1] superstitions; stars shoot and meteors[2] glare oftener across the valley than in any other part of the country, and the nightmare, with her whole ninefold[3], seems to make it the favorite scene of her gambols[4].

The dominant spirit, however, that haunts this enchanted region, and seems to be commander-in-chief[5] of all the powers of the air, is the apparition[6] of a figure on horseback, without a head. It is said by some to be the ghost of a Hessian[7] trooper[8], whose head had been carried away by a cannon-ball[9], in some nameless battle during the Revolutionary War[10], and who is ever and anon[11] seen by the country folk hurrying along in the gloom of night, as if on the wings of the wind. His haunts are not confined to the valley, but extend at times to the adjacent roads, and especially to the vicinity[12] of a church at no great distance. Indeed, certain of the most authentic historians of those parts, who have been careful in collecting and collating[13]

奇异的图景，听到凭空传来的音乐与声音。整个这一带多的是地方神话、鬼神出没之地和朦胧的迷信；恒星闪耀、流星划过山谷的次数也比其他地方多，噩梦妖女带着她的九头小马，似乎也把这当做由衷喜爱的嬉戏场地。

然而，在这片魔法之地上出没的精灵中，最有权威的当属骑着马的无头鬼，他像是空中所有魔力的总司令。据说他是黑森骑兵的灵魂，在美国独立战争的某个无名战役中，他的脑袋被炮弹打掉了，自此村民时常能看见他在昏暗的夜色中匆匆而过，仿佛乘风而行。他不止出没于山谷之中，也会时常出现在邻近的道路上，尤其是离这儿不远的一座教堂附近。确有几位在那些方面最具权威的历史学家，在仔细地搜集整理了有关此鬼的传说之

1 twilight /'twaɪlaɪt/ *adj.* 朦胧的
2 meteor /'miːtɪə, -tɪɔː/ *n.* 流星
3 the nightmare, with her whole ninefold /'naɪnfəʊld/ 噩梦妖女和她的九头小马，是传说中噩梦妖女和她的孩子
4 gambol /'gæmbl/ *n.* 嬉戏
5 commander-in-chief /kə'mɑːndə(r) ɪn tʃiːf/ *n.* 总司令
6 apparition /æpə'rɪʃn/ *n.* 鬼怪
7 Hessian /'hesɪən/ 德国黑森州
8 trooper /'truːpə(r)/ *n.* 骑兵
9 cannon-ball /'kænənbɔːl/ *n.* 古炮炮弹
10 Revolutionary War /revə'luːʃnəri/ 独立战争
11 ever and anon /ə'nɒn/ （古英语）不时地
12 vicinity /və'sinəti/ *n.* 附近
13 collate /kə'leɪt/ *vt.* 整理

the floating facts concerning this spectre[1], allege[2] that the body of the trooper having been buried in the churchyard, the ghost rides forth to the scene of battle in nightly quest of[3] his head, and that the rushing speed with which he sometimes passes along the Hollow, like a midnight blast, is owing to his being belated[4], and in a hurry to get back to the churchyard before daybreak.

Such is the general purport[5] of this legendary superstition, which has furnished materials for many a wild story in that region of shadows; and the spectre is known at all the country firesides, by the name of the Headless Horseman of Sleepy Hollow.

It is remarkable[6] that the visionary propensity I have mentioned is not confined to the native inhabitants of the valley, but is unconsciously imbibed[7] by every one who resides there for a time. However wide awake they may have been before they entered that sleepy region, they are sure, in a little time, to inhale[8] the witching influence of the air, and begin to grow imaginative, to dream dreams, and see apparitions.

I mention this peaceful spot with all possible laud[9], for it is in such little retired Dutch valleys,

1　spectre /ˈspektə(r)/　n.　鬼
2　allege /əˈledʒ/　vt.　认定
3　in quest of　　为了寻找
4　belated /bɪˈleɪtɪd/　adj.　迟了的
5　purport /pəˈpɔːt/　n.　要义
6　remarkable /rɪˈmɑːkəbl/　adj.　不寻常的
7　imbibe /ɪmˈbaɪb/　vt.　吸收
8　inhale /ɪnˈheɪl/　vt.　吸气
9　laud /lɔːd/　n.　赞美

后，认定这位骑士的尸体就埋葬在教堂墓场，他的魂魄每晚都驰骋疆场，寻找他的头颅，有时他像是午夜飓风，疾驰掠过山谷，那是因为他已耽搁了太久，并且要在黎明前赶回教堂墓场。

这流传已久的传说，内容大致如此。在那个鬼神出没之地，它为许多怪异的故事提供了素材。乡下人围炉夜话的时候，都称这鬼为"睡谷的无头骑士"。

不寻常的是，我刚才提到的幻境倾向，不仅山谷的本地居民有，任何人只要在这儿住上一段时间，也会不知不觉地滋生这种倾向。不论他们在进入这睡意浓浓的地方之前多么清醒，不一会儿，他们就一定会吸入带有魔魇影响的空气，开始浮想联翩，梦见梦幻，看见鬼怪幻影。

提到这宁静的地方，我充满了赞美之情，因为它处于这偏僻的荷兰式风格山谷中，在广大的纽约州偶尔也可以找见它们，它的人口、礼仪、风俗还都保持未变。然而，在这片不安定的国土上，移民与发展的洪流在别处不断引起各种变化，在这儿任其冲刷却不引起

found here and there embosomed[1] in the great State of New York, that population, manners, and customs remain fixed, while the great torrent[2] of migration and improvement, which is making such incessant[3] changes in other parts of this restless country, sweeps by them unobserved. They are like those little nooks of still water[4], which border a rapid stream, where we may see the straw and bubble riding quietly at anchor[5], or slowly revolving in their mimic[6] harbor, undisturbed by the rush of the passing current. Though many years have elapsed[7] since I trod[8] the drowsy shades of Sleepy Hollow, yet I question whether I should not still find the same trees and the same families vegetating[9] in its sheltered bosom.

任何风浪。它们像是那些死水潭，挨着的是湍急的溪流，在那儿稻草和水泡抛了锚似的安静地浮在水面上，或是在那似是港湾的地方徐徐打转，湍急的水流经过时，它们也不受打扰。虽然自从我漫步于睡谷静谧的绿荫下，许多年岁已经流逝，然而我相信，我仍能找到同样的树和同样的家，在这儿的荫蔽下生活。

1 embosomed /ɪmˈbʊzəmd/ adj. 在……之中的
2 torrent /ˈtɒrənt/ n. 湍流
3 incessant /inˈsesnt/ adj. 不停的
4 nook of still water /nʊk/ 死水潭
5 at anchor /ˈæŋkə(r)/ n. 抛锚
6 mimic /ˈmɪmɪk/ adj. 假设的
7 elapse /ɪˈlæps/ vi. 流逝
8 tread /tred/ vi. 行走
9 vegetate /ˈvedʒɪteɪt/ vi. 生活，生长

含英咀华

本文选自欧文的《见闻札记》。《睡谷传说》取材于欧文所熟悉的环境哈德逊河，他以诙谐幽默、略带乡愁感伤的笔调，书写旧日的传奇故事和古朴的民风，表现了浓重的怀旧感。虽然此文体裁为小说，但文笔清新自然，优美生动，对奇闻轶事和风俗习惯的描述极富随笔特点。

Teresa Strasser

特里萨·斯特拉瑟

特里萨·斯特拉瑟（1970— ），作家、美国电台节目主持人。主持的有名的
节目有"当你外出时"（*While You Were Out*）和"亚当·卡洛拉秀"（*The Adam
Carolla Show*），著有《掷硬币的101种赢法》(*101 Ways to Win a Coin Toss, 2008*)一书。

Going Home Again

They say you can never go home again.

Well, you can. Only you might find yourself staying at a travel lodge[1], driving a rented Ford Contour and staking[2] out your childhood home like some noir[3] private eye just trying to catch a glimpse of the Johnny-come-latelys[4] that are now living in YOUR HOUSE.

It's a familiar story. Kids grow up; parents sell the family home and move to some sunnier climate, some condo[5] somewhere, some smaller abode[6]. We grown-up kids boxed up all the junk from our childhoods — dusty ballet shoes, high school text books, rolled up posters of Adam Ant — and wonder where home went.

I'm not a sentimental[7] person, I told myself. I don't need to see old 3922 26th Street before we sell the place. I even skipped the part where I return home to salvage[8] my mementos[9] from the garage. I let my parents box up the stuff which arrived from San Francisco[10] like the little package you get when

再 访 故 居

人们说你再也不能回家了。

其实你可以。只是你会发现，自己将住进汽车旅馆，开一辆租来的福特康拓，在你童年的家门口徘徊，像是黑色电影里的私家侦探那样，总想窥探那些占了你"老家"的到底是什么人。

这是个熟悉的故事。孩子们长大了，父母卖掉老房子，搬去气候更宜人的地方，住公寓或是更小的房子。我们这些长大了的孩子，把童年那些破烂玩意儿装箱收拾好——布满灰尘的芭蕾舞鞋、高中时期的课本和已经卷好的亚当·恩特的海报——心里想着，家要搬去哪儿。

我对自己说，我并不是个多愁善感的人。我们卖掉26街3922号那栋老房子之前，我并没有要去多看它一眼，甚至没有回去打捞车库里的纪念品，而让父母帮我打包后从旧金山寄给我。那包裹就像出狱时发还给你的个人物品包一样，你知道的，这是你的手表，你在这儿穿过的衣服，一些现金。

1 travel lodge /lɒdʒ/　汽车旅馆
2 stake /steɪk/　vi.　徘徊
3 noir /'nwɑː/　adj.　原是法语词，常用词组为film noir，黑色电影，黑暗侦探电影
4 Johnny-come-lately　n.　新人
5 condo=condominium /'kɒndəu/　公寓
6 abode /ə'bəud/　n.　住处
7 sentimental /ˌsenti'mentl/　adj.　多愁善感的
8 salvage /'sælvɪdʒ/　vt.　打捞
9 memento /mɪ'mentəu/　n.　纪念品
10 San Francisco /ˌsæn fræn'sɪskəu/　旧金山，美国加利福尼亚西部港口城市

released from jail. You know, here's your watch, the outfit you wore in here, some cash. Here's the person you once were.

After a year, San Francisco called me home again. I missed it. High rents had driven all my friends out of the city to the suburbs so I made myself a reservation at a motel and drove there in a rented car.

The next day, I cruised[1] over to my old neighborhood. There was the little corner store my mom used to send me to for milk, the familiar fire station, the Laundromat[2].

I cried like the sap[3] I never thought I'd be. I sat in the car, staring at my old house, tears welling up[4]. It had a fresh paint job, the gang graffiti[5] erased from the garage door. New curtains hung in the window.

I walked up and touched the doorknob[6] like it was the cheek of a lover just home from war. I noticed the darker paint where our old mezuzah[7] used to be. I sat on our scratchy brick stoop[8], dangling[9] my legs off the edge, feeling as rootless as I've ever felt.

You can't go home in a lot of ways, I discovered that night, when I met up with an ex-boyfriend.

1 cruise /kru:z/   vi. 巡游，到处逛
2 laundromat /ˈlɔːndrəmæt/ n. 自助洗衣店
3 sap /sæp/ n. 傻瓜
4 well up   涌出
5 gang graffiti /gæŋ/ /grəˈfiːti/   graffiti graffito的复数形式，涂鸦
6 doorknob /ˈdɔːnɒb/ n. 门把手
7 mezuzah /meˈzuːzə/ n. 门柱圣卷，一面记有《圣经》文字一面写着神的名字的羊皮纸卷
8 stoop /stuːp/ n. 门廊，门阶
9 dangle /ˈdæŋgl/ vt. 悬着

你过去就是这样的一个人。

一年之后，出于对家乡的想念，我回了趟旧金山。我的朋友们都因为过高的房租搬到市郊去住了。于是我订了间汽车旅馆，租了车开过去。

第二天我便到处走访那些老街坊——街道拐角的那家迷你便利店，过去妈妈常打发我到那儿去买牛奶，还有熟悉的消防站和洗衣店……

我从来没有想到，我会哭得像个傻瓜一样。我坐在车里，直直地盯着那栋老房子，泪如泉涌。此时的老屋被粉刷一新，车库门上的涂鸦被抹去，窗子上也挂起了新窗帘。

我走上前去摸着门把手，如同轻抚刚刚从战场归来的爱人的脸庞。我注意到一块颜色较暗的油漆正是我们过去贴门符的地方。我在不平整的砖面门阶上坐了下来，两腿悬荡着，一种前所未有的没有根的感觉涌上心头。

很多时候你是回不了家的，那天晚上我和前男友的碰面，使我明白了这一点。

"见到你真是太好了，"他说着，并给了我一个紧紧的拥抱。"不过我只有一小时的时间。"

"Great to see you," he said, giving me a tense hug. "The thing is, I only have an hour."

What am I, the LensCrafters[1] of social engagements?

As it happens, his new girlfriend wasn't too keen on[2] my homecoming. We had a quick drink and he dropped me back off at my motel where I scrounged[3] up my change to buy some Whoppers[4] from the vending machine[5] for dinner. I settled in for the evening to watch "Three to Tango" on HBO[6].

"You had to watch a movie with a Friends' cast member," said my brother, nodding empathetically[7]. "That's sad."

My brother and I met up at our old house, like homing pigeons. We walked down the street for some coffee and I filled him in on my trip. He convinced me to stay my last night at his new place in San Bruno, just outside the city. I'll gladly pay $98 a night just for the privilege of not inconveniencing anyone, but he actually seemed to want me.

"I love having guests," he insisted. So I went.

It's surprising how late in life you still get that "I can't believe I'm a grown-up feeling," like

1 LensCrafters　亮视点，一家眼睛连锁店
2 be keen on　喜欢
3 scrounge /skraʊndʒ/ vi. 凑
4 Whopper　n. 巨无霸，一种汉堡
5 vending machine　自动贩卖机
6 HBO, Home Box Office，美国最大的电影频道
7 empathetically /empəˈθetɪkəli/　adv. 动情地

他把我当成什么了？听起来像眼镜公司承诺的一小时快速配镜一样？

可想而知，他的新女友可不大喜欢我的到来。我们随便喝了点东西，然后他把我送回了旅馆。我凑了点零钱，在自动贩卖机上买了汉堡当做晚餐。晚上在旅馆里看了电影台播的《三人探戈》。

"你应该看一部由《老友记》那些演员演的片子，"我哥哥在电话里动情地劝道。"你看的那部太悲了。"

我和哥哥在老屋门口碰面，就像两只归家的鸽子。我们沿着街找了家咖啡店，我把这几天发生的事情原原本本地告诉了他。哥哥说服我最后一天去他的新家住，就在市郊不远的圣·布鲁诺。只要能不给别人带来不便，我倒乐意掏钱住每晚98美金的旅店，但他看起来真的很想让我过去住。

"我喜欢家里来客人，"他坚持道。所以我就去了。

当我看到哥哥——当年那个总强迫我观看重播的《傻子派尔》的家伙——如今已拥有了他自己的房子时，不由感叹"真不敢相信自己已经长大了"，在年岁渐长之时仍能产

when your big brother, the guy who used to force you to watch "Gomer[1] Pyle" reruns[2], owns his own place. It was small and sparse[3] and he had just moved in but it was his. The refrigerator had nothing but mustard[4], a few cheese slices and fourteen cans of Diet 7-Up.

We picked up some Taco[5] Bell, rented a movie, popped some popcorn and I fell asleep on his couch.

Insomniacs[6] rarely fall asleep on people's couches, I assure you. I don't know why I slept so well after agonizing[7] all weekend over the question of home, if I had one anymore, where it was. I only know that curled up under an old sleeping bag, the sound of some second-rate guy movie playing in the background, my brother in a chair next to me, I felt safe and comfortable and maybe that's part of what home is.

But it's not the whole story. As much as I'd like to buy the cliches[8] about home being where the heart is, or as Robert Frost[9] put it, "The place where when you have to go there, they have to take you in," a part of me thinks the truth is somewhere between the loftiness[10] of all those platitudes[11] and the

---

1 Gomer /ˈgəʊmə(r)/　爱尔兰语，傻子
2 rerun /ˈriːrʌn/　　n.　复映的影片
3 sparse /spɑːs/　　adj.　东西少的
4 mustard /ˈmʌstəd/　n.　芥菜
5 Taco Bell: 塔可钟，一家很有名的饭店，招牌菜叫做Taco
6 Insomniac /ɪnˈsɒmniæk/　n.　失眠症患者
7 agonize /ˈæɡənaɪz/　vi.　烦恼
8 cliche /ˈkliːʃeɪ/　n.　陈词滥调
9 Robert Frost: 罗卜特·弗罗斯特（1874—1963），美国诗人，主要诗集有《孩子的意愿》、《波士顿以北》等
10 loftiness /ˈlɒftɪnɪs/　n.　深邃
11 platitude /ˈplætɪtjuːd/　n.　陈词滥调

生这种感觉，真是难以料想。哥哥刚搬进来不久，地方不大，摆设也少，但这是他自己的家。冰箱里只有芥菜、几片芝士切片和十四罐无糖装七喜。

我们在塔可钟速食店弄了些食物，租了部电影，吃了点爆米花，之后我就在他的沙发上睡着了。

我向你保证，常失眠的人是很难在别人家的沙发上睡着的。不知道为什么这次我却睡得这么好，尽管整个周末我都在苦苦思考一个问题——如果我有家的话，那么它在哪儿呢？我只知道，我蜷缩在老旧的睡袋里，房间里回响的是某个二流演员主演电影的声音，哥哥就坐在我旁边的椅子上，我觉得既安全又舒适，或许从某种程度上说这就是家。

但这并不是全部内容，我可以相信诸如"家即心之所在"那样的老生常谈，或是像罗伯特·弗罗斯特说的那样，"家就是永远向游子敞开大门的地方。"我也同样坚信，真正的家既是那些陈词滥调的缥缈莫测，也是26街上的那扇木门的具体真实。

在以后的日子里，我可能还会不止一次回来探望老屋。

concreteness of that wooden door on 26th street.

I'll probably be casing that joint[1] from time to time for the rest of my life. I'll sit outside, like a child watching someone take away a favorite toy, and silently scream, "MINE!"

我会坐在屋子外面，像个孩子看到有人拿走了他心爱的玩具一样，在心底大喊："那是我的！"

---

1 case the joint: （俚语）窥探一处所（尤指于抢劫前）

含英咀华

在这篇文章中作者写了回到自己最初的家时的经历，开着租来的车，睡汽车旅馆，可回家的感觉万分亲切。看着老房子熟悉的景物，自认为并不多愁善感的作者却再也忍不住思念的泪水。文章虽然叙事朴实，但却真切动人，让人感受到了家与亲人给人带来的温馨。

旧地重游

Once More to the Lake
重游缅湖

Oxford Revisited
重游牛津

The Forest Path to the Spring
通往山泉的林间小径

Elwyn Brooks White
埃尔文·布鲁克斯·怀特

埃尔文·布鲁克斯·怀特（1899—1985），美国当代著名散文家、评论家，以散文名世，其文风冷峻清丽，辛辣幽默，自成一格。怀特在散文创作等方面取得了突出成绩，他在生前曾获得多项殊荣：1971年获美国"国家文学奖章"，1973年被选为美国文学艺术学院五十名永久院士之一，1978年获得普利策特别文艺奖，他还获得了美国七家大学及学院的名誉学位。除了他终生挚爱的随笔之外，他还为孩子们写了三本书：《精灵鼠小弟》（Stuart Little, 1945）、《夏洛特的网》（Charlotte's Web, 1952）与《吹小号的天鹅》（The Trumpet of the Swan, 1970）。这三本书同样成为儿童与成人共同喜爱的文学经典。

Once More to the Lake

重游缅湖

One summer, along about 1904, my father rented a camp on a lake in Maine[1] and took us all there for the month of August. We all got ringworm[2] from some kittens[3] and had to rub Pond's Extract[4] on our arms and legs night and morning, and my father rolled over in a canoe[5] with all his clothes on; but outside of that the vacation was a success and from then on none of us ever thought there was any place in the world like that lake in Maine. We returned summer after summer — always on August 1st for one month. I have since become a salt-water man, but sometimes in summer there are days when the restlessness of the tides and the fearful cold of the sea water and the incessant[6] wind which blows across the afternoon and into the evening make me wish for the placidity[7] of a lake in the woods. A few weeks ago this feeling got so strong I bought myself a couple of bass[8] hooks and a spinner[9] and returned to the lake where we used to go, for a week's fishing and to revisit old haunts.

I took along my son, who had never had any fresh water up his nose and who had

有一年夏天，大约在1904年吧，我父亲在缅因州的一个湖边租了一间木屋，他带着我们到那儿过八月。我们都因几只小猫传染上了金钱癣，不得不日日夜夜在胳膊和腿上涂抹庞氏浸膏；父亲则和衣睡在小划子里，但是除此之外，假期过得棒极了。从那时起，我们所有人都认为世上没有比缅因州那个湖更好的去处了。我们在那度过了一个又一个的夏天——常常从八月的第一天开始，在那整整待一个月。这么一来，我竟变成了一个逐海而居的人。夏季里有时候湖里也会兴风作浪，湖水冰凉，阵阵寒风从下午刮到黄昏，使我向往林间湖泊的静谧。几周前，这渴望愈发强烈，于是我买了两根鲈鱼钓竿，一个旋转诱鱼器，又回到我们以前常去的那个湖，预备在那儿垂钓一个星期，还再去看看那些梦魂萦绕的老地方。

我带着儿子，他从未亲近过齐颈深的淡水；睡莲的叶盖儿，他也只是从火车窗子

1 Maine /meɪn/ 缅因州，美国东北角的州
2 ringworm /ˈrɪŋwəːm/ n. （医）金钱癣
3 kitten /ˈkɪtn/ n. 小猫
4 Pond's Extract /ˈekstrækt/ 旁氏浸膏
5 canoe /kəˈnuː/ n. 小船，独木舟
6 incessant /ɪnˈsesnt/ adj. 持续不断的
7 placidity /pləˈsɪdəti/ n. 宁静
8 bass /beɪs/ n. 鲈鱼
9 spinner /ˈspɪnə(r)/ n. 旋转诱鱼器

seen lily pads only from train windows. On the journey over to the lake I began to wonder what it would be like. I wondered how time would have marred[1] this unique, this holy spot — the coves[2] and streams, the hills that the sun set behind, the camps and the paths behind the camps. I was sure that the tarred[3] road would have found it out and I wondered in what other ways it would be desolated[4]. It is strange how much you can remember about places like that once you allow your mind to return into the grooves[5] which lead back. You remember one thing, and that suddenly reminds you of another thing. I guess I remembered clearest of all the early mornings, when the lake was cool and motionless, remembered how the bedroom smelled of the lumber[6] it was made of and of the wet woods whose scent entered through the screen. The partitions[7] in the camp were thin and did not extend clear to the top of the rooms, and as I was always the first up I would dress softly so as not to wake the others, and sneak[8] out into the sweet outdoors and start out in the canoe, keeping close along the shore in the long shadows of the pines. I remembered being very careful never to rub

望过。在去湖的一路上，我都在猜想着这湖如今的模样儿，猜想着时光会怎样毁坏这个独特而神圣的地方——那一个个小海湾，那一条条溪河，还有那一座座落日依偎的山峰，林中那一间间木屋以及屋后的一条条小道。我肯定沥青路会通到了湖边，但还是想知道它会以别的什么方式荒凉着。奇怪的是，一旦你的思绪回到通向往昔的道路上时，你对它们的记忆竟是如此之多。你记起了一件事，很快地，那事会让你记起另一件事。我想，我对于那些清晨的记忆是最清晰的。彼时，湖水清凉，水波不兴。我记得，木屋的卧室可以闻得到圆木的香味，这味道和从纱窗透进来的湿木的潮味混在一起。屋里的隔板很薄，没有伸到屋顶。我总是最早起床，轻轻地穿好衣服，以免吵醒其他人，蹑手蹑脚地溜到芬芳馥郁的门外，把小木船划出去，紧紧地挨着岸边划，松树长长的

1 mar /mɑː(r)/ vt. 毁损
2 cove /kəʊv/ n. 小海湾
3 tarred /tɑːd/ adj. 涂了焦油的
4 desolate /'desələt/ vt. 使荒芜
5 groove /gruːv/ n. 车辙
6 lumber /'lʌmbə(r)/ n. 木材
7 partition /pɑː'tɪʃn/ n. 隔板
8 sneak out /sniːk/ 偷偷地走，溜

my paddle[1] against the gunwale[2] for fear of disturbing the stillness of the cathedral[3].

The lake had never been what you would call a wild lake. There were cottages sprinkled[4] around the shores, and it was in farming although the shores of the lake were quite heavily wooded. Some of the cottages were owned by nearby farmers, and you would live at the shore and eat your meals at the farmhouse. That's what our family did. But although it wasn't wild, it was a fairly large and undisturbed lake and there were places in it which, to a child at least, seemed infinitely remote and primeval[5].

I was right about the tar[6] it led to within half a mile of the shore. But when I got back there, with my boy, and we settled into a camp near a farmhouse and into the kind of summertime I had known, I could tell that it was going to be pretty much the same as it had been before — I knew it, lying in bed the first morning, smelling the bedroom, and hearing the boy sneak quietly out and go off along the shore in a boat. I began to sustain the illusion that he was I, and therefore, by simple transposition[7], that I was my father. This sensation persisted, kept cropping up[8] all the time we were there. It was not an entirely new feeling, but in this setting it grew much stronger.

1 paddle /ˈpædl/   n. 短而阔的桨
2 gunwale /ˈgʌnl/   n. 船缘
3 cathedral /kəˈθiːdrəl/   n. 大教堂
4 sprinkle /ˈsprɪŋkl/   vi. 散布
5 primeval /praɪˈmiːvl/   adj. 原始的
6 tar /tɑː(r)/   n. 柏油路
7 transposition /trænspəˈzɪʃn/   n. 调换，换位
8 crop up /krɒp/   突然出现

树荫投落在岸边。我记得，我总是小心翼翼地不让船桨擦到舷缘，唯恐打破那种教堂般的宁静。

那湖绝不是你认为的那种荒无人烟的湖。它坐落在耕种了的田野上，周围被蓊蓊郁郁的树林环抱。岸边星星点点地散布着小木屋。有些小木屋是邻近居民的，你可以住在湖边，去旁边的农庄就餐。我们家就是这样。然而，这湖虽然算不上荒芜，却也相当大，宁静至极。至少对一个孩子来说，有些地方是无限遥远和原始的。

关于那条沥青路我的猜测是正确的，它一直通到距湖畔半英里的地方。当我带着儿子回到那里，在农庄附近落下脚，沐浴着我熟悉的夏日时光时，我只能说，它与往日了无差异。第一个清晨，躺在床上，闻着房间里特殊的味道，听到儿子蹑手蹑脚地溜出屋子，划着小船沿岸远去，我开始产生一种幻觉：儿子就是我，而我，自然就成了我自己的父亲。我们在那儿的那几天里，这种感觉时时涌上心头，挥之不去。当然，这种感觉并不新鲜，但在这种场景里，它

I seemed to be living a dual existence. I would be in the middle of some simple act, I would be picking up a bait[1] box or laying down a table fork, or I would be saying something, and suddenly it would be not I but my father who was saying the words or making the gesture. It gave me a creepy[2] sensation.

　　We went fishing the first morning. I felt the same damp moss[3] covering the worms in the bait can, and saw the dragonfly alight on[4] the tip of my rod[5] as it hovered a few inches from the surface of the water. It was the arrival of this fly that convinced me beyond any doubt that everything was as it always had been, that the years were a mirage[6] and there had been no years. The small waves were the same, chucking the rowboat under the chin as we fished at anchor[7], and the boat was the same boat, the same color green and the ribs[8] broken in the same places, and under the floor-boards the same freshwater leavings and debris[9] — the dead hellgrammite[10], the wisps of moss, the rusty discarded fishhook, the dried blood from yesterday's catch. We stared silently at the tips of our rods, at the dragonflies that came and

1 bait /beɪt/　n.　鱼饵
2 creepy /'kriːpi/　adj.　毛骨悚然的
3 moss /mɒs/　n.　苔藓
4 alight on　飞落在
5 rod /rɒd/　n.　钓竿
6 mirage /'mɪraːʒ, mɪ'raːʒ/　n.　幻境
7 at anchor /'æŋkə(r)/　抛锚，停泊着
8 rib /rib/　n.　船肋
9 debris /'debriː, 'deɪbriː/　n.　残骸
10 hellgrammite /'helgrəmaɪt/　n.　翅虫蛹

愈发地强烈。我好像生活在两个并存的世界中。我也许正在做着某个普通的动作，正捡起一只鱼饵盒，或是放下一只餐叉，或是在说着什么，忽然间，我感觉那不是我，而是我的父亲在说那些话，在做那些事。这种感觉令我悚然而惊。

　　第一天上午我们就去钓鱼。我摸着鱼饵罐上的青苔，感觉依然是那种湿润。我观察着蜻蜓在湖面上低低地盘旋，落到钓竿头上，亮闪闪的。正是这只蜻蜓的光临让我坚定地相信：一切还像原来那样，岁月流转只是一种幻觉，根本不曾有过。我们把船泊在湖上垂钓，依旧是那微微的浪，拍打着船舷。船还是那条船，同样的绿色，破裂的船肋依旧。舱板下面昔日那些残留废弃之物仍然可见：死掉的翅虫蛹，一缕枯苔，生锈了的废鱼钩，旧日捕鱼留下的斑斑血迹。我们静静地凝视着钓竿头，凝视着飞来飞去的蜻蜓。我试探性地把钓竿梢缓缓浸入水中，希望能使蜻蜓离开我的钓竿。可它马上飞开两英尺远，在半空中稍作停留，然后又回落到钓竿头上稍稍远的地方。今天戏水的这只蜻蜓和我记忆之

went. I lowered the tip of mine into the water, tentatively[1], pensively[2] dislodging the fly, which darted two feet away, poised[3] darted two feet back, and came to rest again a little farther up the rod. There had been no years between the ducking[4] of this dragonfly and the other one — the one that was part of memory. I looked at the boy, who was silently watching his fly, and it was my hands that held his rod, my eyes watching. I felt dizzy and didn't know which rod I was at the end of.

We caught two bass, hauling them in briskly as though they were mackerel[5], pulling them over the side of the boat in a businesslike manner without any landing net, and stunning[6] them with a blow on the back of the head. When we got back for a swim before lunch, the lake was exactly where we had left it, the same number of inches from the dock[7], and there was only the merest suggestion of a breeze. This seemed an utterly enchanted[8] sea, this lake you could leave to its own devices[9] for a few hours and come back to, and find that it had not stirred, this constant and trustworthy body of water. In the shallows[10], the dark, water-soaked

中的那一只之间不见岁月的跌宕。我看着我的儿子，他正静静地注视着蜻蜓，就好像我的手在握着他的钓竿，我的眼睛在注视。我头晕目眩，分不清自己握着的究竟是哪根钓竿的末端。

我们钓到了两条鲈鱼，轻快地拽着它们，像是拽着鲭鱼一样。我们连抄网都没用就把它们稳稳实实地拖进舱里，把它们敲晕。当我们赶回来，想在午饭前游泳的时候，湖上的景致与我们离开前的一模一样。靠船的码头与这里隔着的还是那么远，只是这时湖面吹来一阵微风。这面湖水仿佛是一片被施了魔法的汪洋。你要是离开它，由着它去，几个小时后你再回来，它还是水波不兴，还是那么平静可靠。在水浅之处，被水浸透深色的枝枝丫丫，陈旧而光滑，在湖底清澈起伏的沙底上簇拥晃动，贻

1 tentatively /'tentətɪvli/ adv. 试探性地
2 pensively /'pensɪvli/ adv. 沉思地
3 poise /pɔɪz/ vi. 保持平衡，保持……姿势
4 ducking /'dʌkɪŋ/ n. 闪避
5 mackerel /'mækrəl/ n. 鲭鱼
6 stun /stʌn/ vt. 把……打晕
7 dock /dɒk/ n. 码头
8 enchanted /ɪn'tʃɑːntɪd/ adj. 被施魔法的
9 leave to one's own devices 任由……自己处置
10 shallow /'ʃæləʊ/ n. 水浅处

sticks[1] and twigs[2], smooth and old, were undulating[3] in clusters on the bottom against the clean ribbed sand, and the track of the mussel[4] was plain. A school of minnows[5] swam by, each minnow with its small, individual shadow, doubling the attendance, so clear and sharp in the sunlight. Some of the other campers were in swimming, along the shore, one of them with a cake of soap, and the water felt thin and clear and insubstantial[6]. Over the years there had been this person with the cake of soap, this cultist[7], and here he was. There had been no years.

贝爬过的痕迹清晰可见。一群小鱼游过，每一条都投下细小的瘦影，形影相随，在阳光的照耀下，那么清晰，明显。一些度假的人正沿着岸边游泳，其中一人拿着一块肥皂，水便变得模糊和不真实了。多少年了，总有这样的人拿着一块肥皂，这个有洁癖的人，现在就在眼前。今昔并没有悠悠的岁月之隔。

1 stick /stɪk/ n. 树枝
2 twig /twɪg/ n. 嫩枝
3 undulate /'ʌndjuleɪt/ vi. 波动，起伏
4 mussel /'mʌsl/ n. 贻贝
5 minnow /'mɪnəu/ n. 鲤科小鱼
6 insubstantial /,ɪnsəb'stænʃl/ adj. 不真实的
7 cultist /'kʌltɪst/ n. 有洁癖的人

含英咀华

　　《重游缅湖》是美国文学史上的散文名篇。其语言直白美丽、空灵缥缈却又大彻大悟，浪漫中不失睿智，婉约中不乏深邃，充满了作者对自然与生命、生存与死亡的哲学思考，反映出作者从生存终极意义上考察人性与自然的水乳交融。

James Anthony Froude
詹姆斯·安东尼·弗劳德

詹姆斯·安东尼·弗劳德（1818—1894），英国历史学家、小说家、传记作家、《弗雷泽杂志》(Fraser's Magazine)编辑。受英雄史观的影响，弗劳德强调个人在历史上的作用，著有两部《卡莱尔传》(Life of Carlyle, 1884)。主要著作为十二卷《从沃尔西沦陷到击败西班牙无敌舰队的英国史》(History of England from the Fall of Wolsey to the Defeat of the Spanish Armada, 1856-1870)。文学方面的建树主要在于散文。他早期追随牛津运动领袖纽曼(Venerable John Henry Newman, 1801-1890)，后因发表小说《信仰的报应》(The Nemesis of Faith, 1849)招致非议，辞去教职，以笔耕为生。他发表于杂志上的评论等大量作品都是令人称道的随笔。

Oxford Revisited

重游牛津

Many long years had passed since I visited Oxford, — some twenty-eight or more. I had friends among the resident members of that venerable[1] domicile[2] of learning. Pleasant had been the time that I had spent there, of which intervening[3] years had not diminished[4] the remembrance — perhaps heightened the tone of its coloring. On many accounts I regarded that beautiful city with affectionate veneration[5]. There were more than local attractions to render it interesting. There were the recollections of those who ceased in the interval to be denizens[6] of this world. These could not but breathe sadness over the noble edifices[7] that recalled men, conversations, and conviviality[8] which, however long departed, shadowed upon the mind its own inevitable destiny. Again were those venerable buildings before me in their architectural richness. There was tower, and roof, and gateway, in all their variety of outline, defined with the sharp light and shade peculiar to ecclesiastical[9] architecture. There were

自从我游学牛津以来，许多漫长的岁月已经流逝，——大约有二十八年或是更久了吧。在那所庄严肃穆的学府里，我和一些住校教师是朋友。我在那里度过了十分愉快的时光，时光荏苒并没有磨灭我的记忆，反而使得它颜色更加鲜明。我怀着眷恋、崇敬的心情注视着那座美丽的城市，这心情自有许多成因。它并不只因一方风土令人神往，这有许多对故人的追忆，而他们却已中场休息，不再是这个世界的居民。这些回忆让宏伟的建筑们散发出悲伤的气息，想起旧时友朋，谈天说地，觥筹交错，他们虽然早已远逝，却总在人心灵之上投下命中注定无可逃脱的阴影。我的眼前再次展现出那些风格多样的建筑，庄严、肃穆。塔楼、屋顶、门廊，轮廓各异，体现了宗教建筑独有的明暗对比鲜明的特色。一簇簇的小树林，为在此出没的求知者遮阳蔽日；还有古老的马格得林学院，它还像从前一样，在我们踏进这个城市时，那么赏心悦目地映入眼帘。我开始幻想自己并没有

1 venerable /ˈvenərəbl/ adj. 令人肃然起敬的，可尊敬的
2 domicile /ˈdɒmɪsaɪl/ n. 处所
3 intervening /ˌɪntəˈviːnɪŋ/ adj. 介于中间的，发生于其间的
4 diminish /dɪˈmɪnɪʃ/ vt. 减少，减小，缩减
5 veneration /ˌvenəˈreɪʃn/ n. 崇敬
6 denizen /ˈdenɪzn/ n. 居住者，居民
7 edifice /ˈedɪfɪs/ n. 大厦，雄伟的建筑物
8 conviviality /kənˌvɪviˈæləti/ n. 宴饮交际，欢乐，愉快
9 ecclesiastical /ɪˌkliːzɪˈæstɪkl/ adj. (基督)教会的，教士的

tufted groves[1] overshadowing the haunts of learning; and there, too, was old Magdalen, which used to greet our sight so pleasantly upon our approach to the city. I began to fancy I had leaped no gulf of time since, for the Cherwell ran on as of old. I felt that the happy allusion[2] of Quevedo[3] to the Tiber[4] was not out of place here, "The fugitive[5] is alone permanent." The same river ran on as it had run on before, but the cheerful faces that had been once reflected in its stream had passed away. I saw things once familiar as I saw them before; but "the fathers, where were they?" I was in this respect like one awaked from the slumber of an age, who found himself a stranger in his own land.

At length[6] I adjourned to the Star, somewhat moody, more than half wishing I had not entered the city. I ordered my solitary[7] meal, and began ruminating[8], as we all do, over the thousandth-time told tale of human destiny by generation after generation. I am not sure I did not greet with sullen[9] pleasure a heavy, dark, dense mass of cloud that at that moment canopied[10] the city. The mind finds all

跨越时间的沟壑，因为查维尔河还在一如当年地流淌。我认为，这里用到克维多在提到台伯河时的巧妙典故并无不当，"逃亡者永远孤单。"河流依然流淌如故，可曾经在溪水中映出的欢快面容如今俱已消逝。我看到了往昔熟悉的景物，但是"先辈们，他们在哪里呢？"我仿佛沉睡初醒，恍若隔世，身在故乡，却似异客。

最后我转去星楼，略带忧悒，真希望我没重返这牛津城。我点了份单人餐，开始思索世代代讲了千百遍的人类命运的故事。追忆故往，人人都会难免如此。那时浓密的云朵笼罩了城市上空，我心中百感交集。在这样的时刻，头脑中会有各种令人欣然的思绪。天空中开始飘落雨滴，继而下起了阵阵宜人细雨。我不能像原本打算的那样出去走走了。就坐在那儿抿酒，想着城邑兴

1 tufted groves /'tʌftɪd//grəʊvs/ 一簇簇的小树林
2 allusion /ə'luːʒn/ n. 典故
3 Quevedo: 佛朗西斯科·戈麦斯·德·克维多·伊·比列加斯 (Francisco Gomez de Quevedo y Villegas, 1580-1645)，西班牙散文家、诗人和小说家，有语言大师之称
4 Tiber n. 台伯河，位于意大利中部，流经罗马
5 fugitive /'fjuːdʒɪtɪv/ n. 逃亡者，逃犯，亡命者
6 at length 最后，最终
7 solitary /'sɒlətri/ adj. 单独的，单个的
8 ruminate /'ruːmɪneɪt/ vi. 沉思，反复思考
9 sullen /'sʌlən/ adj. 阿阿不乐的
10 canopy /'kænəpi/ vt. 遮盖，覆盖

kinds of congenialities[1] grateful at such moments. Some drops of rain fell; then a shower, tolerably heavy. I could not go out again as I intended doing. I sat and sipped my wine, thinking of the fate of cities, — of Nineveh[2] the renowned, of the marbles lately recovered from thence[3] with the mysterious arrow-headed characters[4]. I thought that some future Layard might exhume[5] the cornices[6] of the Oxford temples. The deaths of cities were as inevitable as those of men. I felt that my missing friends had only a priority in mortality, and that the law of the Supreme existed to be obeyed without man's questionings.

But a sunburst took place, the shower ceased, all became fresh and clear. I saw several gownsmen pass down the street, and I sallied forth[7] again. Several who were in front of me, so full was I of old imaginings; I thought might be old friends whom I should recognize. How idle! I strolled to the Isis[8]. It was all glitter and gaiety. The sun shone out warmly and covered the surface of the river with gold. Numerous skiffs[9] of the university-men were alive on the water, realizing the lines, —

Some lightly o'er the current swim,
Some show their gaily gilded trim
Quick glancing to the sun.

替，——想到闻名的尼尼微，想到新近在那里发现的上面刻有神秘楔形文字的大理石。我想往后不久也许会在莱亚德发掘出牛津殿堂的飞檐。城市的消亡如同人类的死亡一样无法避免。我想，我已逝的朋友们只不过是对死亡有了优先权，人类还是要毋庸置疑地服从上苍的法则。

但是雨过天晴，日光冲破云层洒向大地，一切变得清新明澈。我看到几位身着长袍的学者沿街行走，然后我也重又起身出发了。有几个人在我前面，我竟异想天开，认为他们会是我能认出的老朋友。多么悠闲啊！我漫步至泰晤士河。只见处处波光粼粼，欢快喜气。阳光温暖地照射下来，给河面染上了一层金色。莘莘学子泛舟河上，在水上热闹嬉戏，体会着诗情画意：

有人轻快愉悦顺流而游，
有人衣着艳丽光彩照人，
瞥一眼骄阳。

---

1 congeniality / kənˌdʒiːniˈæliti /   *n.*   相宜的意绪
2 Nineveh   尼尼微，古代亚述的首都
3 thence /ðens/   *adv.*   从那里
4 arrow-headed characters   楔形文字
5 exhume /eks'hjuːm, ig'zjuːm/   *vt.*   挖掘
6 cornice /'kɔːnɪs/   *n.*   飞檐
7 sally forth /'sæli/   出发，动身
8 the Isis   指泰晤士河
9 skiff /skɪf/   *n.*   轻舟，小船

Here was the repetition of an old performance, but the actors were new. I too had once floated over that glittering water, or lain up by the bank in conversation, or reciting verses, or, perhaps, in that silent, dreamy vacancy in which the mind ruminates or rests folded up within itself in the consciousness of its own immortality[1].

There seems of late years much less of that feeling for poetry than once existed; the same may be observed in respect to classical learning. Few now regard how perished nations lived and passed away, how men thought, acted, and were moved, for example, in the time of Pericles[2] or the Roman Augustus. What are they to us? What is blind Maeonides[3] to us, or that Roman who wrote odes so beautifully — who understood so well the philosophy of life and the poetry of life at the spring of Bandusia? In the past generation a part of the adolescent[4] being and of manhood extended a kindly feeling towards them. We hear no admiration of those immortal strains now. We must turn for them to our universities. People are getting shy of them, as rich men shirk[5] poor friends. Are we in the declining state, which of "mechanical arts and

这是旧戏重演，不过演员都是一色新人。我也曾荡漾在那波光粼粼的河面之上，或者是躺在岸上与人谈古论今，吟诵诗赋；抑或处于静静的、梦幻般的虚空状态之中，精神陷入沉思，或者是封闭起来，在其永恒的意识之中休憩。

近年来，往昔存在的诗赋情怀似乎大不如前；古典研究方面的情况也是如此。已经消亡的民族是怎样生活和消逝的，比如说在伯里克利统治下或是罗马的奥古斯塔斯时代，人们如何思维行事，如今关心这些问题的人寥寥无几。他们对我们来说意味着什么？失明的马奥尼德斯，或是写下如此美妙颂歌的那个罗马人——他在班都西亚泉水边领悟了生命的哲学和生命的诗歌，他们对我们来说意味着什么？我们的上一辈中间，有一部分青年人和成年男子对他们怀有一种亲善之情。现在我们则无从听到对那些不朽品质的称赞。我们必须把他们重新搬回我们的校园。人们如今对先贤存有戒心，不愿亲近，正犹如富人对穷朋友避之不及那样。我们正处于衰退的状态中吗？用培根勋爵的话说，处于"机械艺

---

1 immortality /ˌɪmɔːˈtæləti/ n. 不朽
2 Pericles: 伯里克利（约公元前495—前429），古雅典民主派政治家，出身贵族。公元前444年前后历任首席将军，成为雅典国家的实际统治者
3 Maeonides, 即荷马（约公元前8世纪），古希腊叙事诗人，一般认为是叙事诗《伊利亚特》（Iliad）、《奥德赛》（Odyssey）作者
4 adolescent /ˌædəˈlesnt/ n. 青少年
5 shirk /ʃɜːk/ vt. 逃避

merchandize" to use Lord Bacon's[1] phrase, and is our middle age of learning past? Even then, thank Heaven, we have our universities still, where we may, for a time at least, enter and converse with the spirits of the good, that "sit in the clouds and mock" the rest of the greedy world. They will last our time — glorious mementos[2] of the anxiety of our forefathers for the preservation of learning; hallowed[3] by grateful recollections, by time, renown, virtue, conquests over ignorance, imperishable gratitude, a proud roll of mighty names in their sons, and the prospect of continuing to be monuments of glory to unborn generations. Long may Oxford and Cambridge stand and brighten with years, though to some they may not, as they do to me, exhibit a title to the gratitude and admiration of Old England, to which it would be difficult to point out worthy rivals.

术和商业化"，我们学术界的盛年已逝？谢天谢地，尽管那样，我们仍旧拥有我们的学府，至少我们可以暂时进去和英才神交，"在云间调侃"世人的贪婪。我们的祖先心怀传承知识之热望而留下了辉煌灿烂的文化。他们在我们心怀感念的回望中变得神圣起来，同时，随着时光的流逝，他们的德誉日隆，愚昧无知被征服，人们对他们的恩惠没齿不忘，其子孙才俊辈出，并且他们还将永久成为后世子孙心中的丰碑，这也使他们得以获得尊崇。他们将因此而永垂不朽。牛津剑桥可能会经久不衰，因年岁久远而日益生辉。虽然在一些人看来，这两座学府不一定能够承当得起古英格兰的感激和崇敬，可在我看来，它们享此荣耀无可非议，要指出能与之相匹敌者绝非易事。

---

1 Lord Bacon, 即弗兰西斯·培根（1561—1626），英国哲学家、散文家、实验科学的先驱，著有《学术的进展》、《新工具》、《随笔集》和《新大西岛》等
2 memento /mɪˈmentəʊ/ n. 引起回忆的东西，纪念品，纪念物
3 hallow /ˈhæləʊ/ vt. 使……神圣

含英咀华

　　本文是在作者重回校园时写下的怀旧之作。作者今日看到的景色与往昔形成鲜明对比，对旧日欢乐时光的怀念悠然涌上心头，不禁生出物是人非的感叹。

Malcolm Lowry
马尔科姆·劳里

马尔科姆·劳里（1909—1957），英语诗人、小说家，生于英格兰，1940年之后定居温哥华，曾就读于剑桥大学圣·凯瑟琳学院。他最著名的小说是《火山下面》（*Under the Volcano*, 1947），这部作品的成功为他赢得了"本世纪加拿大最伟大的作家之一"的荣誉。劳里有许多未完成的手稿，其中大部分都是被他的遗孀汇编出版的，这其中有《在您居住的天国听我们说》（*Hear Us, O Lord from Heaven Thy Dwelling Place*, 1961）、《黑暗如我朋友的墓穴》（*Dark as the Grave Where in my Friend is Laid*, 1968）等。

The Forest Path to the Spring

通往山泉的林间小径

Our first little house we had rented from the good Scotsman passed into other hands on his death, though sometimes we used to go down the path by the spring and look at it, and it was only the other day that we did this again. Many years have passed.

Our hamlet[1] on the beach had scarcely changed. On the front of our first house where we had been so happy was a large wooden plaque[2] bearing a name that perhaps had no merit even according to the special categories of waggery[3] through which one was obliged to[4] perceive it: Wuzz-it-2-U? But otherwise it had been improved. The house now had a roof ladder, though my old ladder still did duty as steps. There was a new roof-jack[5] and a new chimney.

A tree we had planted in the back was now the height of the shack[6], a dogwood[7] clustered[8] like white stars, another wild cherry that had failed to blossom for us was a snow of blooms, while our own primroses[9] we had left for the Scotsman were in flower.

1 hamlet /'hæmlɪt/ n. 小村庄
2 plaque /plæk, plɑːk/ n. 匾，饰板
3 waggery /'weigəri/ n. 滑稽
4 be obliged to 不得不
5 roof-jack /ruːfdʒæk/ 梁柱。
6 shack /ʃæk/ n. 简陋的木屋
7 dogwood /'dɒgwʊd/ n. 山茱萸
8 cluster /'klʌstə(r)/ vi. 丛生，成串
9 primrose /'prɪmrəʊz/ n. 报春花

我们的第一间小屋租自一位好心肠的苏格兰人，在他去世之后，这座房子也随之转手易主。我们过去有一段时间总时不时地沿着泉边的那条小径去看望它，然而我们前几天的这次重访却已时隔多年。

海滩上的那片小村落几乎没有任何变化。我们曾在那间小屋里度过了一段快乐的时光，记得小屋的前边嵌有一块大大的木质匾额，上有"Wuzz-it-2-U?"字样，若需探得其含义，即使寻检专门的谐趣图书恐怕也无所裨益。但从其他方面来看，房屋已有所改观，新增了一架屋顶梯，虽然我的旧梯子仍担当着供人上下踩蹬的功用。梁柱是新的，烟囱也是新的。

当年我们在屋后种下的一棵树如今已与屋子比肩，一株山茱萸花团锦簇，如同满天星辰，另一株我们居于此处时尚未开花的野樱桃树正繁花满枝，恰如雪降，我们留给那个苏格兰人的那些报春花也正值花期。

There was a new stove, but the old table and two chairs where we ate in front of the window were still there. There was the bunk[1] where we had spent our honeymoon — and what a long honeymoon it had turned out to be — and desired each other and anguished[2] at the fear of losing each other and our hearts had been troubled, and we had seen the stars and moon rise, and listened to the roar of the surf on the wild stormy nights of our first winter, and the grandmother of the cat that accompanied us now had slept with us and pulled our hair in the morning to wake us up.

Yet who would think, to look at the place idly, with its ramshackle[3] air, its sense of impermanence, of improvisation[4], that such a beauty of existence, such happiness could be possible there, such dramas have taken place?

The path had scarcely changed; nor, here, had the forest. And the spring? Here it was. It still ran, down through the jack-in-the-pulpits[5]. It always carried with it a faint tang[6] of mushrooms, earth, dead leaves, pine needles, mud and snow, on its way down to the inlet and out to the Pacific. In the deeper reaches of the forest, in the somber[7] damp caves, where the dead

屋子里的炉灶是新的，但原来我们就餐时的那张桌子和两把椅子依然摆放在窗前。还有那张窄窄的床，在那张床上，我们度过了蜜月——我们后来才明白那是多么长的一个蜜月啊；在那张床上，我们彼此迷恋，同时又因害怕失去对方而痛苦，心境难以平息；在那张床上，我们观看过月升星现；在那张床上，我们倾听着海浪在狂风暴雨的冬夜里的咆哮，那是我们在一起的第一个冬天；在那张床上，还有一只猫与我们共眠一处，每到早上就会扯着我们的头发把我们弄醒，而如今与我们朝夕相处的这只猫已是它的孙辈了。

若是漫不经心地看着这个地方，它破败不堪的样子给人难以长久居留的感觉，然而谁能即刻想到这是一个如此美好如此幸福的所在，谁又能想到这里曾发生过如此令人激动不已的故事呢？

那条小径几乎还是原来的模样，这儿的树林也一如旧貌。那眼山泉呢？它还在。它仍然涌淌着，流过一丛丛的天南星。它总是带着一股淡淡而独特的味道，那里面混合着蘑菇的味道、土壤的味道、腐叶

---

1 bunk /bʌŋk/ n. 床
2 anguish /ˈæŋgwɪʃ/ vi. 感到痛苦
3 ramshackle /ˈræmʃækl/ adj. 摇摇欲坠的，破败不堪的
4 improvisation /ˌɪmprəvaɪˈzeɪʃn/ n. 即兴创作
5 jack-in-the-pulpit: 印度天南星，一种植物
6 tang /tæŋ/ n. 特殊气味
7 somber /ˈsɒmbə(r)/ adj. 阴森的，昏暗的

branches hang bowed down with moss[1], and the destroying angel[2] grow, it was haggard[3] and chill and tragic, unsure measurer of its path. Feeling its way underground it must have had its dark moments. But here, in springtime, on its last lap to the sea, it was as at its source a happy joyous little stream.

High above the pine trees swayed against the sky; out of the west came the seagulls with their angelic wings, coming home to rest. And I remembered how every evening I used to go down this path through the forest to get water from the spring at dusk… Looking over my wife's shoulder I could see a deer swimming toward the lighthouse.

Laughing we stooped down to the stream and drank.

1 **moss** /mɒs/　*n.*　苔藓
2 **destroying angel** /dɪˈstrɔɪŋ//ˈeɪndʒl/　一种有毒的蘑菇
3 **haggard** /ˈhæɡəd/　*adj.*　枯槁的

的味道、松针的味道、泥和雪的味道。带着这味道，它流入水湾，汇入太平洋。在流经森林的幽深地带时，在穿越阴暗潮湿的洞穴时，那里枯枝低垂，苔藓、毒菌层生其上，它就变得形容枯槁、不寒而栗、意恻情伤，难以测明其前路何在。想到它的地下之途，也一定是它的黑暗时刻。但是，此时此地，春光明媚，距离大海仅余最后一程，它又变成了一条如同在源头时幸福欢跃的小溪。

松树在天穹之下高高地摇摆着，自西方而来的海鸥鼓着它们天使般的翼翅欲归巢想息。我还记得那时，我每天总在薄暮时分沿着这条林间小径去那眼山泉取水……从我妻子的肩膀上看过去，一只鹿正向灯塔游去。

欢笑中，我们在溪流之旁俯下腰身，掬起清清的溪水，畅饮。

含英咀华

文中，作者与妻子重访多年以前在森林生活过的地方，人虽已老，但心依然年轻。我们最后一次去领略那条小路，那条通往供我们吃水的山泉小路，回忆起很多以前的事，以前用过的东西。我们幸福地蹲下身，去品尝我们舀的泉水。

风俗田园

Fog
雾

Sunday Before the War
战前星期天

The Toy Farm
玩具农场

George Slythe Street

乔治·斯莱思·斯特里特

乔治·斯莱思·斯特里特（1867—1936），英国评论家、记者、小说家。其作品文字简俊有力，精当老练，又不乏洒脱俏皮；意义的表达含蓄曲折，句与句间的衔接灵活，跳跃性大；攻击对象一般为社会各阶层的势力、伪善、粗俗以及美学家和上层社会的自命不凡。正因为他谴责逐步侵占人们生活的喧嚣、粗糙和他所处时代的平庸，所以在他的散文中，他将过去的时代理想化，尤其以十八世纪为最。其代表作为《一个男孩的自传》（The Autobiography of a Boy, 1894）。他的散文以口语化的表达为基础，具有浓厚的英国味。

Fog

An acquaintance has kindly informed me that there is in these scribblings of mine too much introspection[1], meditation[2], reflection. "Go out," quoth[3] he, "into the beautiful world, and write down what you see there." I think he is wrong. There is far too much description done as it is. It is easy to go to a place and easy to write a sort of cataloguing[4] description when one goes. Fitly to describe any visible thing whatever is the work of an artist, I question not. But artists are few and easy work is tempting: it seems well to me that some of us scribblers[5] should sit at home and think. The result may not be magnificent, but there is sufficient rarity[6] in the exercise to give it a sort of an odd flavour which may not be so dull to everybody as to my acquaintance. I always follow advice, however, and so, having received this, I took my hat and went out into the beautiful world, with the intention — but it really is a base intention — of writing down what I saw there.

Unfortunately there was a thick fog. Now the cultivated reader is assured, of course, that

---

1 introspection /ˌɪntrəˈspekʃn/   n.   内省
2 meditation /ˌmedɪˈteɪʃn/   n.   冥想
3 quoth /kwəʊθ/   vi.   （古）说
4 cataloguing /ˈkætəlɒɡɪŋ/   adj.   流水账似的
5 scribbler /ˈskrɪblə(r)/   n.   三流作家
6 rarity /ˈreərəti/   n.   稀有

雾

一位熟人曾经友好地向我指出，我那些随意乱涂的文字中内省、冥想、反思的东西太多。"走出去，"他说，"到那美好的世界里去，然后写下你在那儿的见闻。"我认为他错了。现在这类描述性的文章才是过于繁多。去一个地方，并在游历时写下流水账似的记述，这有何难。我毫不怀疑，准确地描述一件有形之物是艺术家的天职。但艺术家为数不多，而人们又倾向于做简单的工作。在我看来，我们当中的一些三流作家完全应该坐在家里沉思一番。成效也许并不显著，但是这种并不常见的做法会给其作品佐以某种特别的风味，以使其不至于人人读来都觉无聊，像我那位熟人感觉到的那样。然而，我经常会采纳别人的建议，于是闻听此建议后，我就戴上帽子，走进了美妙的世界，而目的——虽然目的并不高尚——就是记录下我的见闻。

但不幸的是空中弥漫着浓雾。如今有教养的读者当然会

a London fog is a beautiful thing. But the only writing Londoner[1] who has never described one may as well cling to this negative distinction. Besides, I doubt my esthetic quality[2] is old-fashioned. Curious, weird[3], interesting, I perceive a London fog to be: its beauty something eludes[4] my gross vision. A mist, or a light fog, when one can see forty yards about one, has a fugitive[5] fantastic charm, but so has not a dense and isolating vapour[6]. I could write, with feeling and gratitude at least, of the beauty I saw at dusk, all last week, in the trees and distances of Hyde Park[7] and Kensington Gardens. The lonely grace of the winter trees, their bare tracery[8], unspeakable delicate, clear against a purple or violet haze[9] in the sky, and the pretty fairyland[10] where the yellow lamps made spots of colour — all this was beauty wonderful and magical, and I blessed my lot[11] for once that I could go and gaze on it day by day. Immediately thereafter to perceive that masses of dirty vapour had their beauty also was too swift a turn for my senses. So I will let the description alone. After all, it has been claimed for a fog that it is a blessing to

1 the only writing Londoner   此处指作者自己
2 esthetic quality /iːsˈθetɪk, es-/ /ˈkwɒlɪti/ 审美观点
3 weird /wɪəd/   adj. 神秘的
4 elude /ɪˈluːd/   vt. 逃避，躲避
5 fugitive /ˈfjuːdʒɪtɪv/   adj. 即隐即现的
6 vapour /ˈveɪpə(r)/   n. 水汽
7 Hyde Park: 伦敦的海德公园，因常被用作政治性集会场所而著称
8 tracery /ˈtreɪsəri/   n. 枝干
9 haze /heɪz/   n. 暮霭
10 fairyland /ˈfeərilænd/   n. 仙境
11 lot /lɒt/   n. 命运

肯定伦敦的雾是十分美妙的事物。但是这位唯一没有描写过雾的伦敦文人，还是保持着他未写的名声。此外，我对自己的审美观点是否过时也全无把握。稀奇古怪、神秘莫测、富有趣味是我对伦敦雾的看法，而它的美却逃逸出了我粗俗的视野。一层薄雾或一阵轻雾，这时我们可以看到大约四十码远，它还有一种变幻莫测、迷离奇异的魅力，而一场浓密障翳的迷雾则全非如此了。至少整整上个礼拜我可以带着感知心怀热情地去写我于黄昏时分在海德公园与肯星顿公园所见的树木与远景之美。冬季树木孤寂的优雅，它们光秃错综的枝杈，无法言表的秀美，在天际一片溟蒙的紫色雾霭的映衬下显得格外清晰。昏黄的灯光星星点点，使这美如仙境——这一切都有着奇幻与魔法般的美，我也庆幸自己的好运，可以有机会连日来这里观赏。其后突然就要去感知一团污浊的雾气也大有美丽可言，我的感官一时间无法适应。于是我把这番描述搁置一边。毕竟，雾被认作是对文人的恩赐，因为它迫使他们做一些自省，而这场雾也让我再度陷入反思，因

men of letters, because it forces them in upon themselves, and this fog drove me once more to reflection, since it is fated I should disappoint my acquaintance.

Beauty or none, there is much to be said for a London fog. It gives us all that "change" which we always need. When our world is all but invisible, and growing visible bit by bit looks utterly different from its accustomed self, the stupidest of us all can hardly fail to observe a change for our eyes at least as great as there would have been in going to Glasgow[1]. When, arriving at one's house or one's club, that monotonous[2] diurnal[3] incident seems an almost incredible feat, accomplished with profound relief and gratitude for a safe deliverance, one has at least an unaccustomed sensation. One is not a man going into his club, but a mariner[4] saved from shipwreck[5] at the last gasp[6], to be greeted with emotion by erst[7] indifferent waiters. Yes, a fog gives Londoners a more thorough change than going to the Riviera[8] to avoid it. Then it brings out the kindness and cheerfulness, which are their prime claim to honour, into strong relief. True, it also throws into relief the incomparable egoism[9] of the prosperous among

1 Glasgow /ˈglæzgəʊ, ˈglɑːz-/ 格拉斯哥，英国城市
2 monotonous /məˈnɒtənəs/ adj. 平常单调的
3 diurnal /daɪˈɜːnl/ adj. 日常的
4 mariner /ˈmærɪnə(r)/ n. 水手
5 shipwreck /ˈʃɪprek/ n. 海难
6 at the last gasp /gɑːsp/ 奄奄一息
7 erst /ɜːst/ adj. （古）之前的
8 Riviera: 里维埃拉，南欧沿地中海一地区，是欧洲人的避寒胜地
9 egoism /ˈegəʊɪzəm, ˈiːg-/ n. 自私自利

为天意注定我是要让我那位熟人失望的。

无论是美与否，对于伦敦的雾还是大有文章可作的。它能给我们带来我们一直需要的"变化"的全部。当我们的世界变得不可辨识，而又逐渐变得清晰可见时，它看上去与其常态大相径庭，即使我们当中最愚蠢的人也能看出我们眼前的变化之大，不亚于他们去了趟格拉斯哥。有时候，回到家里或是去俱乐部，这类平凡单调的日常琐事似乎变成了不可置信的壮举，功成之后不免深深地松一口气，庆幸自己的安全抵达，人们至少获得了一种不寻常的新鲜感。这时你已不是那个去俱乐部玩乐的人，而是海难中，在奄奄一息的时刻获救的水手，并受到此前十分冷漠的侍者热情万分的欢迎。的确，较之去里维埃拉避雾，一场雾给伦敦人带来了更彻底的变化。其次，雾还能把最足以为人们博得荣誉的宽厚仁爱、欢欣愉悦等美德充分发挥出来。当然，它也会揭露出富人们极度的自私自利。世界上那些无忧无虑的人们，当然会不满并责骂这种无关紧要的不便。但是辛勤劳作、艰苦奋

them. People with no serious cares or worries in the world of course bemoan[1] and upbraid[2] this trifling inconvenience. But the working, struggling Londoners, cabmen[3] and busmen[4], you and I, display our indomitable[5] good-humour to advantage. I stayed on top of a bus for half an hour in the block on Monday at Hyde Park Corner and talked with the driver. People are often disappointed in a bus-driver because they expect a wit and a pretty swearer. They find neither, but they find an overworked man of extraordinary cheerfulness responsive, ready to laugh. He is master of his business — a fact emphasized by the fog — to a degree refreshing to one whose experience of men professing some practical calling[6] is that the great majority, some from mere stupidity, some from over-hasty[7] enthusiasm, are quite incompetent. When finally I left him, his mate[8] piloted me through wheels and horses to the pavement, and I felt I had been among folk who deserve to live. On Sunday night I walked a mile to my abode[9], and made a point of asking my whereabouts of every one I met. Not one churlish[10] or even hurried answer: politeness, jokes, reminiscences, laughter. We are

1 bemoan /bɪˈməʊn/   vt.   不满于
2 upbraid /ʌpˈbreɪd/   vt.   责骂
3 cabmen /ˈkæbmən/   n.   马车夫
4 busmen /ˈbʌsmən/   n.   公车司机
5 indomitable /ɪnˈdɒmɪtbl/   adj.   百折不回的
6 men professing some practical calling: 从事某种手艺活或服务的人
7 over-hasty /əʊvəˈheɪsti/   adj.   冒失的
8 mate /meɪt/   n.   副手
9 abode /əˈbəʊd/   n.   住处
10 churlish /ˈtʃɜːlɪʃ/   adj.   粗鲁的

斗的伦敦人，马车夫和公车司机，你和我，却会把我们那种百折不回的欢快幽默发扬光大。星期一，我在海德角附近的街会乘了半小时电车，并一路与司机交谈。人们常常对公车司机感到失望，因为人们期望他是个聪明的家伙，说着满嘴脏话。事实却恰恰相反。但是，他却是个虽过度辛劳可勤快周到，笑口常开的人。对于自己的工作，他可是个行家——这点在雾天更为突出——一些人根据经验总以为从事实际行业的人往往不是愚蠢就是冒失，因而就其绝大多数都不称职，对于那种人来说，这位司机的业务熟练程度之高，足以让他们感到耳目一新。但我最后离开他的时候，他的副手带我避过车轮马蹄直到人行道上，我觉得我的身边都是好人。上周日晚上，我步行一英里路回我的住处，每遇到一个人我就向他问路。没有一个人粗鲁甚至匆忙地回答我，他们都彬彬有礼、俏皮风趣、话古论今、笑声连连。我们的民族确实是一个友善的民族，能体会这一点，即使是通过一场雾也是值得的。雾的另一种乐趣，类似我们听说某

a kindly people, and it is worth a fog to know it. Another pleasure of a fog is a mild but extended form of the pleasure we feel when we hear that a millionaire has broken his leg. The too fortunate are suffering a discontent health cannot remove. There was in that block a fat brougham[1] containing an important-looking old man who foamed at the mouth, and one reflected that there was a temporary equality of fortunes.

Such are the pleasures we may take in a London fog.

个百万富翁摔断了腿时候的感觉，但是要更加温和、淡然。那种命运太好的人往往并不快乐，即使躯体康泰也不能使他们摆脱这种折磨。那边街区一辆宽敞的老爷车上，一位派头十足的老人，口吐白沫，大发雷霆，看到此情此景，这时人们会感到一种命运的短暂的平等。

这就是我们会在一场伦敦的雾中可能体会到的乐趣。

---

1 brougham /ˈbruː(ə)m/ n. 老爷车

含英咀华

在该篇文章中，作者通过切身的体验，描述了他对世界闻名的雾都伦敦的感受。伦敦因雾而变得美如仙境，雾带给人们对于这个世界的重新认识，更重要的是雾把这个民族的友善宽厚、欢欣愉悦等美德尽形展现。作者文笔典雅优美，幽默风趣，而又机锋暗含。

Arthur Clutton-Brock
阿瑟·克拉顿-布洛克

阿瑟·克拉顿-布洛克 (1868—1924)，英国散文家、文艺评论家，曾就读于伊顿公学和牛津大学，早期从事律师职业。1904年起，他开始为《泰晤士报文学副刊》（Times Literary Supplement）撰稿，并任伦敦一刊物的文学编辑。此后成为《论坛报》（The Tribune）等报刊的艺术评论家。其代表作有《雪莱——其人其诗》（Shelley, the Man and the Poet，1909）、《威廉·莫里斯》（William Morris，1914）等。

Sunday Before the War

On Sunday, in a remote valley in the West of England, where the people are few and scattered and placid[1], there was no more sign among them than among the quiet hills of the anxiety that holds the world. They had no news and seemed to want none. The postmaster[2] had been ordered to stay all day in his little post-office, and that was something unusual that interested them, but only because it affected the postmaster.

It rained in the morning, but the afternoon was clear and glorious and shining, with all the distances revealed far into the heart of Wales and to the high ridges[3] of the Welsh mountains. The cottages of that valley are not gathered into villages, but two or three together or lonely among their fruit-trees on the hillside; and the cottagers who are always courteous and friendly, said a word or two as one went by, but just what they would have said on any other day and without any question about the war. Indeed, they seemed to know, or to wish to know, as little about that as the earth itself, which, beautiful there at any time, seemed that afternoon to wear an extreme and pathetic[4] beauty. The

---

1 placid /ˈplæsɪd/ *adj.* 平静的
2 postmaster /ˈpəʊstmɑːstə(r)/ *n.* 邮差
3 ridge /rɪdʒ/ *n.* 山脊
4 pathetic /pəˈθetɪk/ *adj.* 凄婉的

战前星期天

星期天，忧虑笼罩着世界，而英格兰西部一个人烟稀少、宁静偏僻的山谷却一如静静的群山，毫无不安之兆。当地人没有外部世界的消息，似乎也不想去打听。邮差接到通知，要他整天待在自己小小的邮局里，这件不寻常的事引起了大家的注意，但这也仅是因为事关邮差而已。

早上下过雨，但是午后天气放晴，阳光明媚，呈现在眼前的是透迤延伸到远处的威尔士腹地和威尔士群山的巍峨山峰。山谷里的农舍没有聚成村落，而是三三两两或孤零零地坐落在山坡上的果树丛中。农舍的居民向来谦和友好，有人经过时便搭讪两句，却只是些平日里的家常话，绝不问打仗的事。看来，他们对于战事知之甚少，也不想了解更多，漠不关心如同脚下的土地。这片大地美丽常驻，而那天下午却蒙上了一层哀伤，仿佛美到了极致。这里比英格兰的任何其他乡野，更谙知和平的奥秘。

country, more than any other in England, has the secret of peace. It is not wild, though it looks into the wildness of Wales; but all its cultivation, its orchards and hopyards[1] and fields of golden wheat, seem to have the beauty of time upon them, as if men there had long lived happily upon the earth with no desire for change or fear of decay[2]. It is not the sad beauty of a past cut off from the present, but a mellowness[3] that the present inherits from the past; and in the mellowness all the hillside seems a garden to the spacious farmhouses and little cottages; each led up to by its own narrow, flowery lane. There the meadows[4] are all lawns with the lustrous[5] green of spring even in August, and often over-shadowed by old, fruit-trees — cherry, or apple, or pear; and on Sunday after the rain there was an April glory and freshness added to the quiet of the later summer.

Nowhere and never in the world can there have been a deeper peace; and the bells from the little red church down by the river seemed to be the music of it, as the song of birds is the music of spring. There one saw how beautiful the life of man can be, and how men by the innocent[6] labours of many generations can give to the earth a beauty it has never known in its wildness.

虽说面向威尔士荒原，但这里并不荒芜；倒是它的耕作，它的果园和啤酒花藤种植场还有金黄色的麦田，似乎还保有历时久远之美，仿佛这儿的人长久以来一直在这土地上幸福度日，既不期盼改变，也不惧怕衰亡。这不是与现今隔绝的往昔的凄美，而是现今继承自往昔的芳醇。就在这片芳醇之中，四周的山腹就好似宽敞农宅和玲珑家舍的园子，每座门前都有花色烂漫的窄径。这儿的牧场全是草地，即使到了八月份也仍然青葱翠绿，并且很多都掩映在经年的果树中——樱桃、苹果或是梨子树；在雨后的星期天，除去残夏的宁静，这还有着四月的灿烂与清新。

世上任何地方任何时候都不会领略比这更深沉的宁静。从山下河畔那座红色小教堂里传来的钟声就像这和平的音乐，正如鸟儿们的鸣唱是春天的音乐一样。在这儿，你看到了人类的生活可有多么美好，

---

1 **hopyard** /ˈhɔpjaːd/　*n.*　啤酒花藤种植场
2 **decay** /dɪˈkeɪ/　*n.*　衰亡
3 **mellowness** /ˈmeləunɪs/　*n.*　芳醇
4 **meadow** /ˈmedəu/　*n.*　牧场
5 **lustrous** /ˈlʌstrəs/　*adj.*　葱郁的
6 **innocent** /ˈinəsnt/　*adj.*　单纯的

And all this peace, one knew, was threatened; and the threat came into one's mind as if it were a soundless message from over the great eastward plain; and with it the beauty seemed unsubstantial[1] and strange, as if it were sinking away into the past, as if it were only a memory of childhood.

So it is always when the mind is troubled among happy things, and then one almost wishes they could share one's troubles and become more real with it. It seemed on that Sunday that a golden age had lasted till yesterday, and that the earth had still to learn the news of its ending. And this change had come, not by the will of God, not even by the will of man, but because some few men far away were afraid to be open and generous with each other. There was a power in their hands so great that it frightened them. There was a spring[2] that they knew they must not touch, and, like mischievous[3] and nervous children, they had touched it at last, and now all the world was to suffer for their mischief.

So the next morning one saw a reservist[4] in his uniform saying goodbye to his wife and children at his cottage-gate and then walking up the hill that leads out of the valley with a cheerful smile still on his face. There was the first open sign of trouble, a very little one, and

人类又是如何通过世世代代纯朴的劳作，给大地带来荒蛮时代不曾有过的美。然而你也察觉到，这儿的一切和平都受到了威胁。这威胁进入人的头脑，就像是穿越向东延伸的大平原传来的无声信息。随之，这片土地的美变得虚幻而陌生，仿佛正退回往昔，仿佛只是儿时的回忆。

每当人身在乐土而心怀忧虑时，他总会希望原本的快乐可以分担烦扰，并以此使其变得更加真实。在那个星期天，仿佛一个黄金时代已在昨天宣告结束，而大地对它的结束仍浑然不知。这场改变的发生，不是因为上帝的旨意，甚至也非人类的意愿，只不过因为远在别处的少数几个人怯于开诚布公地相互对待。他们手中握有足以让他们战栗的大权。明知有个弹簧无论如何不能触碰，却像顽劣而又胆怯的孩童一样，最终还是碰了，如今全世界都要为他们的淘气而遭罪了。

于是第二天一早，人们看见一个预备役士兵穿着制服，在农舍门口与妻儿告别，然后

---

1 unsubstantial /ˌʌnsəbˈstænʃl/ *adj.* 虚幻的
2 spring /sprɪŋ/ *n.* 弹簧
3 mischievous /ˈmɪstʃɪvəs/ *adj.* 调皮的
4 reservist /rɪˈzɜːvɪst/ *n.* 预备役士兵

he made the least of it; and, after all, this valley is very far from any possible war, and its harvest and its vintage[1] of perry[2] and cider[3] will surely be gathered in peace.

But what happiness can there be in that peace, or what security in the mind of man, when the madness of war is let loose in so many other valleys? Here there is a beauty inherited from the past, and added to the earth by man's will; but the men here are of the same nature and subject to the same madness as those who are gathering to fight on the frontiers. We are all men with the same power of making and destroying, with the same divine[4] foresight mocked by the same animal blindness. We ourselves may not be in fault to-day, but it is human beings in no way different from us who are doing what we abhor[5] and they abhor even while they do it. There is a fate, coming from the beast in our own past, that the present man in us has not yet mastered, and for the moment that fate seems a malignity[6] in the nature of the universe that mocks us even in the beauty of these lonely hills. But it is not so, for we are not separate and indifferent like the beasts; and if one nation for the moment forgets our common humanity and its future, then another must take over that sacred[7] charge and

1 vintage /ˈvɪntɪdʒ/   n.   酿酒
2 perry /ˈperi/   n.   梨酒
3 cider /ˈsaɪdə(r)/   n.   苹果酒
4 divine /dɪˈvaɪn/   adj.   如神一般的
5 abhor /əbˈhɔː(r)/   vt.   憎恨
6 malignity /məˈlɪɡnɪti/   n.   邪恶
7 sacred /ˈseɪkrɪd/   adj.   神圣的

爬山出谷了，脸上还带着愉快的笑容。这是麻烦的第一个征兆，不过只是蛛丝马迹，那士兵也尽量没有声张。毕竟，这片山谷远离任何可能的战事，用于酿酒的梨子和苹果也当然会在和平的环境中收获和采摘。

但是，当战争的疯狂在其他许多山谷肆意放纵之际，在那样的和平中有什么幸福可言，抑或说，人的心态怎能平和释然？这里有一种继承自往昔的美，它因人的意志被赋予这片土地；可这儿的居民和那些奔赴边疆投入战斗的士兵有着同样的天性，并为同样的疯狂所驱使。我们都是人，同样能创造也能破坏，同样能料事如神，却又被同样如兽般的蒙昧所戏弄。也许我们自己今天并未做错事，但是正在做着我们憎恨之事的却恰恰是与我们毫无区别的人类，他们甚至也憎恶自己的所作所为。人类曾经是野兽，至今人性也未能驯服兽性，人的宿命即根源于此。而眼下，宿命似乎成了宇宙本性中的邪恶，纵然在美轮美奂的幽僻山谷中，这邪恶也要嘲弄我们。但是，事情并非如此，因为我们不是孤立分散

guard it without hatred or fear until the madness is passed. May that be our task now, so that we may wage[1] war only for the future peace of the world and with the lasting courage that needs no stimulant[2] of hate.

又无动于衷的兽类。如果一个民族暂时忘却了我们共同的人性，忘却了人性的未来，那么另一个民族必须要接过这神圣的使命，不怀仇恨、无所畏惧地捍卫它，直至疯狂平息。希望这成为我们眼下的职责，以使我们只为世界和平而战，怀着无尽的勇气而战，而这勇气是不需要仇恨来刺激的。

---

1 **wage** /weɪdʒ/ *vt.* 发动
2 **stimulant** /ˈstimjələnt/ *n.* 刺激

含英咀华

在这篇文章中，作者将视线落在宁静美丽的边远山谷，那里的居民因战争的爆发而失去旧日生活的祥和宁静，作者从他们乡土生活的骤变来反映一次大战风云席卷而来的情景。虽然文章最后的落脚点为战争与和平，可是，从字里行间不难读出，作者对保留着往昔田园风光的恬然山谷的追忆与赞颂之情。本文笔触细腻，写景与议论巧妙结合，通过对比衬托等手法使文章主题凸显。

John Boynton Priestley
约翰·博因顿·普里斯特利

约翰·博因顿·普里斯特利（1894—1984），英国作家，20世纪上半叶英国最成功的小说家。普里斯特利的作品具有温文尔雅的讽刺性特征，并在作品中表达其自由的政治观点，这在小说《好伙伴》（The Good Companions, 1929）中表现得最为突出。《好伙伴》与现实主义小说《天使人行道》（Angel Pavement, 1930）奠定了他作为小说家的地位。他写过大量的戏剧作品，其中《危险的角落》（Dangerous Corner, 1932）奠定了他在戏剧界的地位。此外，他还写过游记、文学散文、社会评论以及传记。

The Toy Farm

Angela, at the house where I am staying, has just celebrated a birthday, her seventh, and is now the breathless mistress of a toy farm. You never saw such a farm. It has barns, haystacks[1], sties[2], hurdles[3], gates, trees, and a yellow tumbrel[4] with scarlet wheels. There are fat brown horses, cows that stand up and cows that sit down, black pigs and pink pigs, sheep with their lambs, a goat, two dogs, and a coloured host of[5] turkeys, ducks, hens and chicks. There are even people on this farm, five of them, and very fine people they are too. A man in his shirt-sleeves perpetually pushes a crimson[6] wheelbarrow[7]; and two carters, wearing white smocks[8], brown gaiters[9], red scarves, and little round hats, for ever stride forward, whips in hand, whistling tunes that we shall never catch. Then there is the farmer himself, bluff[10], whiskered, in all his bravery of scarlet waistcoat, white cravat[11], and green breeches[12], who grasps his stout stick and stares

1 haystack /'heɪstæk/　*n.*　干草堆
2 sty /staɪ/　*n.*　猪圈
3 hurdle /'hɜːdl/　*n.*　篱笆
4 tumbrel /'tʌmbrəl, -brɪl/　*n.*　翻卸式肥料运送车
5 host of　许多，一大群
6 crimson /'krɪmzn/　*adj.*　深红色的
7 wheelbarrow /'wiːlbærəʊ/　*n.*　手推车，独轮车
8 smock /smɒk/　*n.*　工作服
9 gaiter /'geɪtə(r)/　*n.*　绑腿
10 bluff /blʌf/　*adj.*　粗犷的
11 cravat /krə'væt/　*n.*　领结
12 breeches /'brɪtʃɪz/　*n.*　马裤

玩具农场

安吉拉在我暂住的这座房子里刚刚过完生日，她七岁了，现在她是一座玩具农场的女主人，兴奋得气也喘不过来。你绝未见过这样一个农场，有谷仓、干草堆、猪圈、篱笆、大门、树和一辆轮子鲜红的黄色施肥车。有健壮的棕马，或站或坐的奶牛，黑猪和粉猪，绵羊和羊羔，一只山羊，两条狗，还有一群群五颜六色的火鸡、鸭子、母鸡和小鸡。这农场上还有人呢，一共五个，也都精致。一个穿衬衫的男子永远推着辆深红色独轮车；两个马车夫，身穿白色工作服，打着棕色绑腿，系红围巾，带小圆帽子，永不停歇地大步前进，手握鞭子，嘴里哼着我们听不见的曲子。然后是农场主本人，粗犷，蓄络腮胡，穿着鲜红马甲显得十分英勇，白领结，绿马裤，挂一根粗手杖，从他那顶坚硬的棕色帽子下向外凝望。他的妻子体态匀称丰满，戴一顶蓝色女帽，穿一件粉色长衫，系雪白围裙，一手提篮，一手打一

at things from under his hard brown hat. His wife, neat and buxom[1] in a blue bonnet[2], a pink gown, and snowy apron, with a basket in one hand and a large green umbrella in the other, is setting out[3] upon some never-to-be-accomplished errand[4]. All these people, labourers, master, mistress, though not more than two inches high and only made of painted tin, stand there for ever confident, ruddy[5], smiling in perpetual sunshine: they seem to stare at us out of a lost Arcadia[6].

Perhaps that is why poor Angela has not so far had that farm to herself, being compelled to share it with a number of shameless adults. It is, of course, an engaging toy, and there is not one of us here, I am thankful to say, so old and wicked, so desiccated[7], as to have lost all delight in toys, particularly those that present something huge and elaborate, such as a fort crammed with soldiers, a battleship, a railway station, a farm, on a tiny scale and in brighter hues[8] that Nature ever knew. These toys transform you at a stroke into a god, and a happier god than any who look down upon our sad muddle. It is, of course, the more poetical of our activities that are

1 buxom /'bʌksəm/ *adj.* 体态丰满的
2 bonnet /'bɒnɪt/ *n.* 无边女帽
3 set out 启程
4 errand /'erənd/ *n.* 差事
5 ruddy /'rʌdi/ *adj.* 脸色红润的
6 Arcadia /ɑːˈkeɪdɪə/ 阿卡迪亚，古希腊一山区，以其居民过田园牧歌式纯朴生活著称，泛指世外桃源或乐园
7 desiccated /'desɪkeɪtɪd/ *adj.* 干燥的，分状的，引申为没有情趣的
8 hue /hjuː/ *n.* 色调

柄大绿伞，正要出门办一件永远无法完成的差事。所有这些人，卖力气的，男女主人，虽然身高不过两英寸，也仅仅是由上了漆的锡铁做成，却永远自信地站在那，脸色红润，在永恒的阳光下微笑：他们似乎是从一个失去的世外桃源里凝望我们。

也许这就是可怜的安吉拉直到现在还不能独自拥有这座农场的原因：她不得不和一些无视体面的大人们分享它。这当然是一件可爱的玩具，我们当中谁也没有，我要心存感激地说，我们这些人，年岁渐长，圆滑世故，了无情趣，似乎对玩具失去了所有的兴趣，尤其是展现那些体积庞大并且结构复杂的物体的玩具，比如重兵把守的堡垒、战舰、火车站、农场，不仅比例很小，而且色彩绚丽，巧夺天工。但这些玩具能一下子就把你变成一个高尚的神，并且比任何对我们可悲的混乱世界不屑一顾的神都快活。当然，这是因为像育儿室这些欢快明亮的玩具的主题都是选自我们日常活动中饱含诗意的事物，然而这些玩具本身所包含的诗意就如许之多，即使它们将生活中极为平

chosen as subjects for these bright miniatures[1] of the nursery, yet there is so much poetry in the toys themselves that even if they mirrored in little even the most prosaic[2] things, they would still be satisfying. I remember that when I was a child, the boy next door was given a tiny printing machine, a gasping, wheezing affair that would print nothing but the blurred image of three ducks. He and I, however, collecting all the paper we could lay our hands on, would spend hours, hours full to the brim[3] printing ducks, thousands and thousands of ducks, and while we were engaged in producing this monotonous[4] sequence of dim fowls we asked nothing more from life beyond the promise of suety[5] meals at odd intervals.

It may be, though, that there are special reasons why we should all be finding the toy farm so enchanting. Its little people, as I have said, seem to stare at us out of a lost Arcadia. Behind them, and their bright paraphernalia[6] of beasts and belongings, is the Idea, dominating the imagination. This farmer and his wife are the happy epitome[7] of all farmers and their wives, but they are unmistakably idealized. These whitesmocked carters, for ever soundlessly whistling among the clover[8], are not the

凡无奇的事物能够有略微呈现，它们也会让人称心如意。我记得小时候，有人给了邻居家的男孩一台微型印刷机，这是一个让你吭哧吭哧半天除了能印出一个模糊的三个蓝色鸭子图片外什么也印不了的玩意儿，可是，我和他却找来所有我们能找到的纸，花上几个小时，把那些纸满满当当地印上鸭子，成千上万只的鸭子。我们重复往返忙着一个接一个印那些模糊的鸭子图案时，对生活没有别的要求，只希望能偶尔吃上一顿板油饭。

然而，我们之所以觉得玩具农场如此迷人可能还存在其他特殊原因。我说过，那些小人似乎是从一个失去的世外桃源里凝望我们。在他们和他们的那些明快怡人的牲畜和财物背后，是主宰着想象的理想。这位农场主和他的妻子是所有农场主和他们妻子快乐的化身，但是他们无疑被理想化了。这两个身着白色工作服、永远在三叶草中吹着我们听不出是何曲调的口哨的马车夫，不是我们所知的乡下人的缩影，而是乡村旧梦中的形象。看着这些树木，我们也许会和济慈一起高呼：

---

1 miniature /ˈmɪnətʃə(r)/　*n.*　模型
2 prosaic /prəˈzeɪɪk/　*adj.*　平凡的
3 brim /brɪm/　*n.*　边
4 monotonous /məˈnɒtənəs/　*adj.*　单调的，千篇一律的
5 suety /ˈsuːɪti/　*adj.*　板油的
6 paraphernalia /ˌpærəfəˈneɪliə/　*n.*　随身用具
7 epitome /ɪˈpɪtəmi/　*n.*　缩影
8 clover /ˈkləʊvə(r)/　*n.*　三叶草，一种植物

countrymen we know in miniature, but are images from an old dream of the countryside. Looking at these trees, we might cry with Keats[1]:

Ah, happy, happy boughs! That cannot shed Your leaves, nor ever bid the Spring adieu.

Here is the bright epitome, not of the country we can find where the tram-lines come to an end and the street lamps fade out, but of the country that has always existed in our imagination, so clean, trim, lavishly coloured. None of us here, I venture to say, has any passion for agriculture as a pursuit, for real farms, with their actual lumbering[2] beasts, their mud and manure[3], their clumsy and endless obstetrics[4], their mortgages and loans and market prices, their long days of wet fields and dirty straw. We may regard the farmer as an excellent solid fellow or as a grasping ruffian[5], but certainly he never seems to us a poetical figure whose existence is passed in a golden atmosphere. Yet there is such a farmer somewhere at the back of our minds, a farmer in a picture-book, and this piece of painted, moulded tin is his portrait. If we could only find him in this actual life, not all the pleasures of the town would keep us from living in his shadow all the rest of our days, for we know that his world is one long dreamed of, that

1 Keats: 济慈（1795—1821），英国诗人
2 lumbering /ˈlʌmbərɪŋ/ adj. 笨拙的
3 manure /məˈnjʊə(r)/ n. 肥料
4 obstetrics /əbˈstetrɪks/ n. 分娩
5 ruffian /ˈrʌfiən/ n. 恶棍，无赖

呵，欢愉的树木！你的枝叶

不会凋落，也永不会与春光作别

这种美丽的化身，并不属于我们见到的那些不通电车、没有路灯的乡村，而是属于我们魂牵梦绕的乡村——如此洁净、整齐、色彩绚丽。我敢说，我们这些人中没有哪一个会满怀激情地以农活为职业，因为在现实生活中的农场上，牲畜动作迟缓，泥污和粪便随处可见，那些牲畜还笨拙不雅、生育不断，还要考虑抵押、贷款和市场价格诸问题，很多日子里田地是湿的，稻草是脏的。此种情境之中，我们可能会把农民看做是身体特别结实的家伙或是贪婪的恶棍，但他似乎永远不会是一个在黄金般的氛围中度过光阴的富有诗意的形象。然而，在我们脑海深处的某个地方确实有这样一个农夫，一个图画书上的农夫，这件着了色的锡铁模型就是他的肖像。如果我们真能在现实生活中找到这样一位农夫，即使城市有万千乐趣也不能阻止我们去追随他在他的庇护下度过余生。因为我们知道他的世界是我们长时间以来梦

countryside where there are no ugly downpours[1], no sodden fields, and lanes choked with[2] mud, where only the gentlest shower of rain breaks through the sunshine, where everything is as clean as a new pin and fresh from the paint-box, where men and women are innocent and gay and the very beasts are old friends, where sin and suffering and death are not even a distant rumour. Is not this the Arcadia that men lost long ago and have never found again?

How long this dream has lasted no man can say. It shines through all literature, from the poets and novelists of yesterday to Virgil[3] and Theocritus[4]. It is the burden of more than one half of our old songs, with all their "Hawthorn[5] buds, and sweet Eglantine[6], and girlonds[7] of roses", their Corydons[8] and neat-handed Phyllises[9], their haymakers, rakers[10], reapers[11], and mowers waiting on their Summer Queen, their hey-down-derry[12] or shepherd[13] lovers in the shade. And always this lovely time

寐以求的, 在那样的乡村里, 没有可恶的倾盆大雨, 没有潮湿泥泞的田地和尽是泥浆的巷子, 那里有的是阵阵冲破阳光的温柔细雨, 一切事物都像从颜料盒里拿出来的新别针那样干净, 男男女女都纯真快乐, 那些牲畜都是老朋友, 罪恶、苦难和死亡更如一个遥远的传言。这不正是那个人类失去已久, 再也没有找回的世外桃源吗?

没有人能说清楚这梦做了多久。这个梦在所有的文学作品中一再出现, 从过去的诗人、小说家到维吉尔和斯奥克里帝斯。它充斥着我们半数以上的古老歌谣, 歌唱 "山楂的花蕾, 芬芳的蔷薇, 玫瑰的花环", 歌唱牧童和巧手姑娘, 歌唱服侍夏日女皇的晒干草的、耙草的和割草的农夫, 歌唱民谣或是树荫下相恋的牧羊人。并且这些美好的时光

---

1 downpour /'daʊnpɔː(r)/ n. 倾盆大雨
2 choked with /tʃəʊkdwɪð/ 阻塞
3 Virgil: 维吉尔（公元前70—公元前19）, 古罗马诗人
4 Theocritus /θɪˈɒkrɪtəs/ 斯奥克里帝斯, 古希腊诗人, 始创田园诗
5 hawthorn /'hɔːθɔːn/ n. 山楂
6 eglantine /'egləntaɪn/ n. 野蔷薇的一种
7 girlond /'gɔːlɒnd / n. 花环
8 Corydon 田园诗中的牧童
9 Phyllis n. 乡村姑娘
10 raker /reɪkə(r)/ n. 耙草的人
11 reaper /'riːpə(r)/ n. 收割的人
12 derry /'deri/ n. 民谣
13 shepherd /'ʃepəd/ n. 牧羊人

When Tom came home from labour,
Or Cis to milking rose,
Then merrily went their tabor,
And nimbly went their toes

had just passed away. Nobody ever saw this countryside, but it was always somewhere round the corner; a turn at the end of a long road, a descent[1] from some strange hill, and there it might be, shining in the sun. It is not the perfervid[2] vision of townsmen, longing for the fields in their wilderness of bricks and mortar, a revolt[3] against the ugly mechanical things of today, but a dream that would appear to be as old as civilized man himself, touching men's imagination when towns were little more than specks[4] in the green countryside. Poets who lived in the country, who passed all their days among real shepherds and dairymaids[5], could sing of this other country where there was nothing ugly nor any pain and sorrow, knowing full well that this was not the land that stretched itself beyond their gates but a land they had never seen. It is one of the more homely manifestations[6] of that ideal of unchanging beauty which haunts the mind of man everywhere and in every age, and from which there is no escape except into brutishness[7]. Its shadow can fall even upon a number of little pieces of painted tin newly come from the toyshop.

1 descent /dɪˈsent/ n. 下山道
2 perfervid /pəˈfɜːvɪd/ adj. 热切的
3 revolt /rɪˈvəʊlt/ n. 厌恶，反感
4 speck /spek/ n. 微粒，小点儿
5 dairymaid /ˈdeərɪmeɪd/ n. 农场女工
6 manifestation /ˌmænɪfeˈsteɪʃn/ n. 展现
7 brutishness /ˈbruːtɪʃnɪs/ n. 野蛮，荒蛮

汤姆收工回家，
或是茜斯挤好奶，
欢快地敲起手鼓，
灵巧地跳着舞步。

总是刚刚过去。谁也没有见过这样的乡村，但它总是在我们周遭的某个地方，在一条长路尽头的转弯处，在某个陌生山上的下山道，可能它就在那儿，在阳光下熠熠闪耀，它不是城里人在他们砖块和灰浆的荒漠中对田野的渴望，也不是对今天丑陋的机械事物的反抗，而是一个似乎和人类自身文明同样古老的梦想，当城市无异于绿色乡村的星点微粒时就触动了人类的想象。那些住在乡村，一辈子同真正牧羊人和农场女工生活在一起的诗人们，可以唱诵那个既无丑陋也无痛苦哀伤的乡村，但他们心里十分清楚，乡村不是从他们家门前延伸出的那片土地，而是他们从未见过的地方。那是无时无刻不萦绕于人类头脑之中的那种永世不变之美这一理想更为朴实的表现，它是人类的退避之所，没有它，人类只能重归蛮荒。甚至从那些刚从玩具店买回的许多小巧艳丽的锡铁玩具上都可以找到它投射下来的影子。

含英咀华

　　本文从一个小女孩的生日礼物说起，由浅入深，谈到不仅小孩爱这玩具，就是大人也爱。其中的原因在于它代表着人们无限怀念的早已失去的乐园，以及那种纯朴恬静的理想生活方式。文章笔墨饱满，描写细腻入微，绚丽华美。

童年纪事

The Boys' Ambition
孩子的志愿

On Recollections of Childhood
童年回忆

Remembrance of Childhood
童年的记忆

The Most Important Day in My Life
我生命中最重要的那一天

My Mother's Gift
母亲的礼物

Memories of Christmas
圣诞回忆

Mark Twain

马克·吐温

马克·吐温（简介见《我童年时代的家》），成长于密西西比河岸，浪漫粗犷的河上生活及天真无邪的童年给他留下深刻印象。

The Boys' Ambition

孩子的志愿

When I was a boy, there was but one permanent ambition among my comrades[1] in our village on the west bank of the Mississippi River. That was, to be a steamboatman. We had transient[2] ambitions of other sorts, but they were only transient. When a circus came and went, it left us all burning to become clowns; now and then we had a hope that if we lived and were good, God would permit us to be pirates. These ambitions faded out, each in its turn; but the ambition to be a steamboatman always remained.

Once a day a cheap gaudy[3] packet arrived upward from St. Louis, and another downward from Keokuk. Before these events, the day was glorious with expectancy; after them, the day was a dead and empty thing. Not only the boys, but the whole village, felt this. After all these years I can picture that old time to myself now, just as it was then: the white town drowsing[4] in the sunshine of a summer's morning; the streets empty, or pretty nearly so; one or two clerks sitting in front of the Water Street stores, with

小时候，在我们那位于密西西比河西岸的村庄里，伙伴们持久不变的志愿只有一个，那就是成为一名轮船上的水手。我们有过其他短暂的愿望，但它们不过是心血来潮。村子里来过马戏团后，我们都激动着想要成为小丑；偶尔我们也希望，如果我们循规蹈矩，上帝会准许我们做海盗。渐渐地，那些愿望都一个接一个被淡忘了，但想成为水手的志愿依然如故。

每天一次，一艘廉价但外表华丽的邮轮从圣路易斯开到上游去，另一艘从科奥库克来的船则往下游开。它们到达之前，日子是美好和让人期待的；它们开走了以后，日子变得死气呆板、空洞乏味。并不只是孩子们，整个村子都有这种感觉。这么多年过去以后，至今我仍能想象出当日的情景，仿佛身临其境一般：夏日的晨光下，安逸的小镇在打着瞌睡；街上空空如也，或近乎于此；一两个店员在水街的商

---

1 comrade /'kɒmreɪd/   n. 伙伴，同伴
2 transient /'trænzɪənt/   adj. 短暂的，一时的，瞬间的
3 gaudy /'gɔːdi/   adj. 华丽而俗气的
4 drowse /draʊz/   v. 打瞌睡

their splint[1]-bottomed chairs tilted[2] back against the wall, chins on breasts, asleep; a sow[3] and a litter of pigs loafing[4] along the sidewalk, doing a good business in watermelon rinds[5] and seeds; two or three lonely little freight[6] piles scattered about the "levee"; the great Mississippi rolling its mile-wide tide along, shining in the sun; the dense forest away on the other side.

Presently a film of dark smoke appears, instantly a negro drayman[7], famous for his quick eye and prodigious[8] voice, lifts up the cry, "S-t-e-a-m-boat a-comin!" and the scene changes! The town drunkard stirs, the clerks wake up, a furious clatter of drays follows, and all in a twinkling the dead town is alive and moving. Drays, carts, men, boys, all go hurrying from many quarters to a common center, the wharf[9]. Assembled there, the people fasten their eyes upon the coming boat as upon a wonder they are seeing for the first time.

And the boat is rather a handsome sight, too. She is long and sharp and trim and pretty; she has two tall, fancy-topped chimneys; a fanciful pilot-house; the paddle-boxes[10] are

1 splint /splɪnt/　n.　薄木条，藤条
2 tilt /tɪlt/　vt.　使偏斜
3 sow /səʊ/　n.　母猪
4 loaf /ləʊf/　vi.　游荡，闲逛
5 rind /raɪnd/　n.　（瓜、果等的）皮，外皮
6 freight /freɪt/　n.　货船
7 drayman /'dreɪmən/　n.　运货马车车夫
8 prodigious /prə'dɪdʒəs/　adj.　巨大的
9 wharf /wɔːf/　n.　码头
10 paddle-box /'pædl bɒks/　（船）明轮外壳

店门前坐着，藤条椅子向后斜靠在墙上，下巴耷拉在胸前，呼呼大睡；一头大母猪带着几只小猪在人行道上游荡，寻找西瓜皮和西瓜子好美美地吃上一顿；两三尾形单影只的小货船零星停靠在码头边，壮丽的密西西比河向前推起一英里宽的潮浪，在太阳下闪耀着波光。河的彼岸是一片茂密的森林。

过不多久，就会看到一股黑烟，立刻，一个以眼疾声大而著称的黑人车夫，吊起嗓子喊开来，"汽——船——来——啦！"接着场景就变了！镇上的醉鬼会一下清醒过来，店员醒了，一阵热烈喧闹的马车声随之而来，顷刻间死气沉沉的小镇变得鲜活生动了。运货马车、手推车、大人、孩子，都急急忙忙地从各处的角落去一个共同的目的地——码头。人们聚集在那儿，眼睛紧紧盯着正在驶来的船，就好像看着一个他们头次见到的奇观一样。

话说回来，那船也真是美观的景致啊。她修长、惹眼、整洁、标致；她有两个高大、顶部异样的烟囱；一个新奇的领航室；镀金的船名上闪

gorgeous with gilded rays above the boat's name; there is a flag gallantly[1] flying from the jack-staff[2]; the furnace[3] doors are open and the fires glaring bravely; the upper decks are black with passengers; the captain stands by the big bell, calm, imposing, the envy of all; great volumes of the blackest smoke are rolling and tumbling out of the chimneys — a husbanded grandeur created with a bit of pitch pine[4] just before arriving at a town; the crew are grouped on the forecastle[5]; the pent steam is screaming through the gauge-cocks[6], the captain lifts his hand, a bell rings, the wheels stop. Then such a scramble as there is to get aboard, and to get ashore, and to take in freight and to discharge freight, all at one and the same time! Ten minutes later the steamer is under way again, with no flag on the jack-staff and no black smoke issuing from the chimneys. After ten more minutes the town is dead again.

My father was a justice of the peace[7], and I supposed he possessed the power of life and death over all men and could hang anybody that offended him. This was distinction enough for me as a general thing; but the desire to be a steamboatman kept intruding, nevertheless. I first wanted to be a cabin-boy[8], so that I could come

1 gallantly /ˈɡæləntli/ adv. 勇敢地，豪侠地
2 jack-staff 船首旗杆
3 furnace /ˈfɜːnɪs/ n. （建筑物内的）暖气炉
4 pitch pine /pɪtʃ /paɪn/ 北美脂松
5 forecastle /ˈfəʊksl/ n. 前甲板
6 gauge-cock /ˈɡeɪdʒˈkɒk/ 汽笛
7 justice of the peace 治安法官
8 cabin-boy /ˈkæbɪnbɔɪ/ 船上侍者

烁着太阳的光辉，在它的点缀下船体显得华丽绚烂；船首旗杆上的旗子迎风飘扬，气派非凡；煤炉的门没有关，火光熊熊，蔚然可观；上层甲板上黑压压的都是乘客；船长站在大钟旁，沉着冷静，气宇非凡，他是所有人钦慕的对象；大量最黑的滚滚浓烟，从烟囱中转动、翻腾而出——这壮观景象是在马上要到达村镇前，在火里加点松脂制造出来的；船员们在前甲板上集合；蒸汽从被关闭了的蒸汽机中跑出来，穿过汽笛发出响亮的鸣叫，船长举起手，钟声响起，轮船停了下来。紧随其后的是一阵杂乱，大伙忙着上船、登岸、提取行李、卸下货物，这一切都是同时进行的。十分钟以后，汽船又重新启程了，旗杆上已经没有旗子了，烟囱也没有了黑烟。再过十分钟以后，小镇重又变得死气沉沉了。

我父亲是名治安法官，我认为他掌控着对每个人生杀予夺的大权，可以吊死每个得罪他的人。大体上来说，这让我足够风光了，不过当水手的愿望还是在我脑中挥之不去。我先是想做个小伙计，这样的话，我就可以系一条白围裙走

out with a white apron on and shake a tablecloth over the side, where all my old comrades could see me; later I thought I would rather be the deckhand[1] who stood on the end of the stage-plank with the coil of rope in his hand, because he was particularly conspicuous. But these were only day-dreams, — they were too heavenly to be contemplated as real possibilities.

By and by[2] one of our boys went away. He was not heard of for a long time. At last he turned up as apprentice engineer or "striker" on a steamboat. This thing shook the bottom out of all my Sunday-school[3] teachings. That boy had been notoriously[4] worldly, and I just the reverse; yet he was exalted[5] to this eminence[6], and I left in obscurity[7] and misery. He would always manage to have a rusty bolt[8] to scrub[9] while his boat tarried[10] at our town, and he would sit on the inside guard and scrub it, where we could all see him and envy him and loathe[11] him. And whenever his boat was laid up he would come home and swell around the town in his blackest and greasiest[12] clothes, so that nobody could help remembering that he was a steamboatman;

1 deckhand /'dekhænd/ n. 甲板水手，普通水手
2 by and by 不久
3 Sunday-school: 主日学校，基督教教会为了向儿童灌输宗教
　　思想，在星期天开办的儿童班
4 notoriously /nəʊˈtɔːrɪəsli/ adv. 声名狼藉地
5 exalted /ɪgˈzɔːltɪd/ adj. 情绪高昂的，意气风发的
6 eminence /'emɪnəns/ n. 显赫，出众
7 obscurity /əbˈskjʊərəti/ n. 身份低微
8 bolt /bəʊlt/ n. 螺钉
9 scrub /skrʌb/ vi. 擦，蹭
10 tarry /'tæri/ vi. 停留
11 loathe /ləʊð/ vt. 憎恶
12 greasy /'griːsi/ adj. 沾有油的

出船来，在船边抖一抖桌布，我的老朋友就都能看见我了；之后我想，我宁愿做水手，手里拿一盘绳索站在甲板最后，因为他尤其引人注目。但是这些都只能是白日梦——这些梦太美好了，让人不敢奢望能成为现实。

不久以后，我们中的一个男孩离开了镇上。大家好长时间都没有他的消息。最后，他突然以见习机械师或者说成"锤手"的身份出现在一艘轮船上。这件事彻底颠覆了我在主日学校学到的一切。那小子曾臭名昭著于全世界，而我恰恰相反；然而他在因自己一下子的出人头地而意气风发，而我却仍默默无闻，痛苦哀伤。每当他的船在我们小镇上靠岸后，他总是能找到一块生了锈的螺栓来擦，并且他总是坐在护栏的里侧擦啊擦，这样我们都能看见他，这让人又羡慕又憎恨。每逢他那艘船停得久一些，他就会回家，穿着他那件油迹斑斑、黑得要命的外套满镇上招摇，好让人没忘了他是个汽船上的水手。他说起话来满是各种汽船术语，就好像他已经对它们如此熟悉，以至于忘记了一般人根本听不

and he used all sorts of steamboat technicalities in his talk, as if he were so used to them that he forgot common people could not understand them. This fellow had money, too, and hair oil. He wore a leather belt and used no suspenders. If ever a youth was cordially[1] admired and hated by his comrades, this one was. No girl could withstand his charms. He "cut out[2]" every boy in the village.

This creature's career could produce but one result, and it speedily followed. Boy after boy managed to get on the river. The minister's son became an engineer; the wholesale liquor dealer's son became a barkeeper on a boat; four sons of the chief merchant, and two sons of the county judge, became pilots. Pilot was the grandest position of all. The pilot, even in those days of trivial wages, had a princely salary. Two months of his wages would pay a preacher's salary for a year. Now some of us were left disconsolate[3]. We could not get on the river — at least our parents would not let us.

懂似的。这家伙也有钱，还有发油。他用的是一条皮裤带，不用背带。如果有哪个年轻人能让他的同伴既真心羡慕，又恨之入骨，那就是他没错了。没有女孩能抵挡他的魅力。他"盖过"了镇上所有的男孩。

这家伙的经历只能带来一个结果，并且它的影响迅速蔓延开了。一个又一个男孩设法去了河上工作。部长的儿子成了技师；酒品批发商的儿子成了一只小船上的酒吧招待员；商人首领的四个儿子和县法官的两个儿子成了领航员。领航员是当中最了不起的职位。即使在那些工资微薄的日子里，领航员也有可观的薪水。他两个月的薪水就够传教士赚上一年了。现在，我们几个仍留在这儿的都闷闷不乐。我们没法去河上工作——至少我们的家长不让我们去。

---

1 cordially /ˈkɔːdɪəli/ *adv.* 真诚地
2 cut out （口语）打败，超过
3 disconsolate /dɪsˈkɒnsələt/ *adj.* 闷闷不乐的

含英咀华

　　本文节选自马克·吐温的《密西西比河》，文章描写了文中的"我"年幼时一心想当水手的强烈愿望。作者通过对小镇上汽船来前走后景象描写的强烈对比和最早去水上工作那个"家伙"的深度刻画，流露出作者小时候对成为船员这一志愿的强烈渴望。

Richard Steele

理查德·斯蒂尔

理查德·斯蒂尔（1672—1729），英国散文家、剧作家，出生于都柏林，大学期间弃学从戎，和约瑟夫·艾迪生(Joseph Addison, 1672—1719)两人先后合办散文刊物《闲话者》(The Tatler, 1709—1711)、《旁观者》(The Spectator, 1711—1714)，并著称于世。他常出没于咖啡馆和俱乐部，这也是构成了他的生活乐趣。在许多随笔中他记载了自己的所见所闻，从政治风云到家庭生活、从道德伦理到个人品行，笔触无所不及；对文明生活的各个方面发表观感，寓教于乐，笔调诙谐。他的主要剧作有《葬礼》(The Funeral, 1701)、《说谎的情人》(The Lying Lover, 1703)、《有心的情侣》(The Tender Husband, 1705)等，代表了当时的伤感主义精神。

On Recollections of Childhood

There are those among mankind, who can enjoy no relish[1] of their being, except the world is made acquainted with[2] all that relates to them, and think every thing lost that passes unobserved; but others find a solid delight in stealing by the crowd, and modeling their life after such a manner, as is as much above the approbation[3] as the practice of the vulgar[4]. Life being too short to give instances great enough of true friendship or good will, some sages[5] have thought it pious[6] to preserve a certain reverence for the manes[7] of their deceased friends; and have withdrawn themselves from the rest of the world at certain seasons, to commemorate in their own thoughts such of their acquaintance who have gone before them out of this life. And indeed, when we are advanced in years, there is not a more pleasing entertainment, than to recollect in a gloomy moment the many we have parted with[8], that have been dear and agreeable to us, and to cast a melancholy[9] thought or

童年回忆

有那么一些人，除非所有与之相关的事情都为世人所知晓，否则他们就无法享受人生的乐趣；只要他们所做的事情有一件不为人知，他们即认为是枉费了心机。相反，另外一些人则认为默默无闻并以超越于世俗所认可的方式来生活是人生之至乐。生命如此短暂，不足以充分说明友情之真挚和意愿之良善，因此一些贤哲认为对亡友灵魂保持一定敬意是一种虔诚并在某些时候抽身世务，以冥思缅怀先他们而去的故旧。诚然，年齿渐增之后，在情绪低落的时刻回忆那些已逝的挚亲知交，或对那些曾与我们一起欢谑终宵的朋友们偶兴愁绪，赏心愉悦之情莫过于此。昨晚怀着这样的心情，我走进了自己的密室，下定决心

---

1 relish /'relɪʃ/ n. 乐趣
2 make acquainted with 通晓，熟悉
3 approbation /ˌæprə'beɪʃn/ n. 认可
4 vulgar /'vʌlgə(r)/ n. 平民，百姓
5 sage /seɪdʒ/ n. 圣贤
6 pious /'paɪəs/ adj. 虔诚的
7 manes /'mɑːneɪz, 'meɪniːz/ n. 灵，灵魂
8 part with 跟……分手，离开
9 melancholy /'melənkəli/ adj. 犹豫的

two after those, with whom, perhaps, we have indulged ourselves in whole nights of mirth[1] and jollity[2]. With such inclinations[3] in my heart I went to my closet yesterday in the evening, and resolved to be sorrowful; upon which occasion I could not but look with disdain[4] upon myself, that though all the reasons which I had to lament the loss of many of my friends are now as forcible as at the moment of their departure, yet did not my heart swell with the same sorrow which I felt at the time; but I could, without tears, reflect upon many pleasing adventures I have had with some, who have long been blended with[5] common earth. Though it is by the benefit of nature, that length of time thus blots out[6] the violence of afflictions; yet, with tempers too much given to pleasure, it is almost necessary to revive the old places of grief in our memory; and ponder step by step on past life, to lead the mind into that sobriety[7] of thought which poises[8] the heart, and makes it beat with due time, without being quickened with desire, or retarded with despair, form its proper and equal motion.

The first sense of sorrow I ever knew was upon the death of my father, at which time I was not quite five years of age; but was rather

要伤感一番。虽然情理之中，我该像我的好友辞世时那样哀痛，但是我的心里却没有充溢那样的悲伤，这让我不由地鄙视自己；可我却能够抛却泪水，回想起那些早已化为尘埃的朋友和我共同经历过的诸多美好往事。虽然拜自然所赐，漫长的时间磨灭了强烈的痛苦，但性情一直耽于逸乐，甚有必要重温记忆中悲伤之境；通过对旧日生活逐渐地回想沉思，以达到头脑清醒，获得内心的平衡，使其跳动适时，不因欲望而加快，也不因绝望而变得迟缓，运行精确无误。

父亲的去世使我第一次感受到悲伤。那时我还不满五岁，我惊异的是家里的变故，而不是真正懂得了没人愿意陪我玩的缘故。记得我走进停放父亲尸体的房间，母亲就坐在尸体旁边独自啜泣。我手里拿着羽毛球拍，边在棺材上敲打边叫喊爸爸，因为我不知怎么隐约觉得他被锁在里面了。母

---

1 mirth /mɜːθ/　n. 欢笑，高兴
2 jollity /ˈdʒɒlɪti/　n. 酒宴
3 inclination /ɪnklɪˈneɪʃn/　n. 意向
4 disdain /dɪsˈdeɪn, -z-/　n. 轻蔑
5 blend with /blend/　混合
6 blot out /blɒt/　抹去，遮盖
7 sobriety /səˈbraɪəti/　n. 清醒
8 poise /pɔɪz/　vt. 使……平衡

amazed at what all the house meant, than possessed with a real understanding why nobody was willing to play with me. I remember I went into the room where his body lay, and my mother sat weeping alone by it. I had my battledore[1] in my hand, and fell a beating the coffin, and calling Papa; for, I know not how, I had some slight idea that he was locked up there. My mother caught me in her arms, and, transported beyond all patience of the silent grief she was before in, she almost smothered[2] me in her embraces; and told me in a flood of tears, 'Papa could not hear me, and would play with me no more, for they were going to put him under ground, whence[3] he could never come to us again.' She was a very beautiful woman, of a noble spirit, and there was a dignity in her grief amidst all the wildness of her transport; which, methought, struck me with an instinct of sorrow, that, before I was sensible of what it was to grieve, seized my very soul, and has made pity the weakness of my heart ever since. The mind in infancy is, methinks, like the body in embryo[4]; and receives impressions so forcible, that they are as hard to be removed by reason, as any mark with which a child is born is to be taken away by any future application. Hence it is, that good-nature in me is no merit; but having been so frequently overwhelmed

亲把我搂进怀里，她本来一直在默默忍受着所有的悲哀，闻听我的叫喊，情绪一下子迸发出来，她将我搂得差点透不过气来，并泪如泉涌，告诉我说："爸爸听不到你，再也不能陪你玩了，他们就要把他放入土里，他再也不会回到我们身边了。"她是个美丽的妇女，有着高贵的心灵，即使陷入悲痛欲绝的处境中也不失尊严。我想，正是这打动了我悲伤的本能，在我还没感觉到有什么可悲痛之前，这种本能就占据了我的心灵，自此它就使怜悯成了我内心的弱点。我想，幼年时的头脑恰如身体处于胚胎时期一样，它对事物的印象如此根深蒂固，以至于理智也难以将其消除，正如婴儿出生时带有的胎记，日后无论用什么方法也无法除掉。因此，我身上的好品性并非什么优点。母亲的眼泪往往使我尚未明白痛苦之缘由或自我判断中作出对痛苦的防范即悲从中来，我汲取了怜悯、懊悔和怯懦的和善，日后这些情感使我

---

1 **battledore** /ˈbætldɔ:/   *n.* 羽毛球拍
2 **smother** /ˈsmʌðə(r)/   *vt.* 使窒息，令……透不过气
3 **whence** /wens/   *adv.* 从何处，从哪里
4 **embryo** /ˈembrɪəʊ/   *n.* 胚胎

with her tears before I knew the cause of any affliction, or could draw defences from my own judgment, I imbibed[1] commiseration[2], remorse, and an unmanly gentleness of mind, which has since insnared[3] me into ten thousand calamities[4]; and from whence I can reap no advantage, except it be, that, in such a humour as I am now in, I can the better indulge myself in the softness of humanity, and enjoy that sweet anxiety which arises from the memory of past afflictions.

We, that are very old, are better able to remember things which befell[5] us in our distant youth, than the passages of later days. For this reason it is, that the companions of my strong and vigorous years present themselves more immediately to me in this office of sorrow. Untimely and unhappy deaths are what we are most apt to[6] lament; so little are we able to make it indifferent when a thing happens, though we know it must happen. Thus we groan under[7] life, and bewail[8] those who are relieved from it. Every object that returns to our imagination raises different passions, according to the circumstance of their departure. Who can have lived in an army, and in a serious hour reflect upon the many gay and agreeable men that might long

陷入了重重苦难。从中我难有得益，除了像处于我此刻的心境之中，我可以更好地沉湎于人性的柔和之中，体味回忆过去的痛苦时产生的甜蜜和忧虑。

我们上了年纪的人，更容易记起远在年轻时发生在我们身上的事，而难以记起青年之后的事情。鉴于这一原因，在这种悲伤的场合，我那些年富力强时的同伴的音容笑貌就会最先闪现在我的脑海里。我们最易于哀悼英年早逝者和不幸身亡者，虽然我们明知事情会发生，可当它发生了我们就无法做到对它漠然置之。因此我们在生活的磨难中呻吟，同时哀悼那些从中解脱了的人。每一个重现于我们记忆中的事物因其与我们作别情况不同而引发我们不同的情感。有过戎马生涯的人，有谁能够在庄严肃穆的场合回想起那些喋血疆场的快乐易处的军人？他们本可以在和平事业中大有作为，而

---

1 imbibe /ɪmˈbaɪb/ *vt.* 吸收（知识、思想等）
2 commiseration /kəˌmɪzəˈreɪʃn/ *n.* 同情
3 insnare /ɪnˈsneə(r)/ *v.* 落入陷阱，诱入圈套
4 calamity /kəˈlæmɪti/ *n.* 不幸，灾难
5 befall /bɪˈfɔːl/ *v.* 降临，发生
6 apt to /æpt/ 倾向于
7 groan under /ɡrəʊn/ 受虐待，受压迫
8 bewail /bɪˈweɪl/ *vt.* 哀悼

have flourished in the arts of peace, and not join with the imprecations[1] of the fatherless and widow on the tyrant[2] to whose ambition they fell sacrifices? But gallant[3] men, who are cut off by the sword, move rather our veneration[4] than our pity; and we gather relief enough from their own contempt of death, to make that no evil, which was approached with so much cheerfulness, and attended with so much honour. But when we turn our thoughts from the great parts of life on such occasions, and instead of lamenting those who stood ready to give death to those from whom they had the fortune to receive it; I say, when we let out thoughts wander from such noble objects, and consider the havoc[5] which is made among the tender and the innocent, pity enters with an unmixed softness, and possesses all out souls at once.

不必成为暴君野心的牺牲品，使孤儿寡母为此诅咒不已。但是那些丧命于刀剑之下的勇士更能引起我们的崇敬，而非怜悯。我们从他们自己对死亡的蔑视中得到了足够的宽慰，他们欣然向死并死得其所，这绝非邪恶。但是在这样的场合，当我们不去想人生的重大职责，不去哀悼那些准备迎接死亡的人，而是想想那些有幸面对死亡的人，我是说，当我们不从这些崇高的角度想问题，而是考虑战争给弱小无辜者带来的浩劫，纯粹温柔的怜悯之情便会瞬间占据我们的心灵。

---

1 imprecation /ɪmprɪ'keɪʃn/ n. 诅咒
2 tyrant /'taɪrənt/ n. 暴君
3 gallant /'gælənt/ adj. 英勇的，豪侠的
4 veneration /venə'reɪʃn/ n. 尊敬
5 havoc /'hævək/ n. 浩劫

含英咀华

这篇怀旧随笔追溯了作者儿时的亲身经历，感慨系之，真诚而深沉，令人动容，是英国文学史上历来传诵的名篇。作者将近不惑之年，在作文的前夜闭门思亲人，念故旧。扪心自问之余，感到羞愧的是哀伤之情不如当年那么深切。于是他把昔日的悲痛和哀思形诸笔墨，这就是本文的缘起。

Charlotte Brontë
夏洛蒂·勃朗特

夏洛蒂·勃朗特（1816—1855），英国女作家，出生在英格兰北部约克郡一个与世隔绝的村子里，父亲是个穷牧师，她曾和其他几个姐妹一起被送进一家生活条件恶劣、教规严厉的寄宿学校读书。夏洛蒂当过教师和家庭教师，也曾与妹妹艾米莉一起于1842年去比利时布鲁塞尔学习法语和古典文学。夏洛蒂的作品主要描写贫苦的小资产者的孤独、反抗和奋斗，属于被马克思称为以狄更斯为首的"出色的一派"。《简·爱》(Jane Eyre, 1847)是她的处女作，也是代表作，至今仍受到广大读者的欢迎。夏洛蒂还出版过诗集，她的其他小说有《雪莉》(Shirley,1849)、《维莱特》(Villette, 1853)和《教师》(The Professor, 1857)。她的最后一部重要作品是自传体小说《维莱特》。

Remembrance of Childhood

童年的记忆

It was in the cold weather which follows the shortest day that we first came to England. I was a little child at the time — perhaps four years old, or between that and five. The sea voyage is well remembered by me; the milky greenness of the waves, the curl of the foam, the dark meeting of December sea and sky, the glinting[1] seabirds and passing ships, made each an imprint[2] on my vision which I yet retain — worn but not obliterated[3].

Whence did we come? Where had we lived? What occasioned[4] this voyage? Memory puzzles herself to reply to these questions. She reflects with finger raised to her lips and eyes bent on the pavement. She turns to her chronicle[5] and searches its faded pages where the records are so pale, brief, and broken: this is all she reads — we came from a place where the buildings were numerous and stately[6], where before white house-fronts there rose here and there trees straight as spires[7], where there was one walk broad and

紧挨着最短的白昼，到来的是寒冷的天气，这时我们初次来到了英格兰。当时我还是个小孩子——大概只有四岁，或者是在四岁至五岁之间。那次航海的经历让我记忆犹新：那葱白色的海浪，翻滚的泡沫，阴沉沉的十二月的海色与天光的交融，一闪而过的海鸟和来往的船只，给我留下了深刻的印象——虽经岁月的磨损，但依然历历在目。

我们从哪里来？住在哪里？什么事促成了这次远航？记忆本身混混沌沌，回答不了这些问题。她把手指抬到唇边，眼睛盯着人行道，思索着。她翻开她的编年史，在发黄的纸页中查阅那苍白、简洁、支离破碎的记录。她能读到的只有这些——我们来自这样一个地方，那里高楼林立，雄伟壮观，白色的房屋前方随处可见挺拔如塔楼的树木；那里有一条宽广的、走不到尽头的大道，在这条道路上，有时卷起两股潮流——一股是步行的人

1 glint /glɪnt/　vi.　闪耀，闪闪发光
2 imprint /'ɪmprɪnt/　n.　深刻的印象
3 obliterate /ə'blɪtəreɪt/　vt.　擦掉……的痕迹
4 occasion /ə'keɪʒn/　vt.　促成
5 chronicle /'krɒnɪkl/　n.　编年史
6 stately /'steɪtli/　adj.　庄严肃穆的
7 spire /spaɪə(r)/　n.　塔楼

endlessly long, down which on certain days rolled two tides: one of people on foot, brightly clad[1] with shining silks, delicate bonnets[2] with feathers and roses, scarves fluttering, little parasols[3] gay as tulips[4]; and the other of carriages rolling along rapid and quiet. Indeed, all was quiet in this walk — it was a mysterious place, full of people but without noise.

We had lived in a house with slippery floors and no carpets; a house with many mirrors and many windows. In this house I know there was a hall with a door of red and violet[5] glass, glowing brilliant in the shade of that end opposite the entrance. The bright portal[6] opened into a garden, small but green, where there was turf[7], many flowers, and one tree. What chiefly made it green and filled it with leaf was the curtain of vines concealing the high walls — vines I know they were, because I remember both the grapes and the curled tendrils[8].

With whom did we live? To this question I can only reply — with my father; and of him I have twenty reminiscences[9], but they are all scant[10] and fragmentary. My father — papa, as I called him — was the origin of all the

1 clad /klæd/ adj. 穿着……的
2 bonnet /'bɒnɪt/ n. 女帽
3 parasol /'pærəsɒl/ n. 阳伞
4 tulip /'tjuːlɪp/ n. 郁金香
5 violet /'vaɪələt/ adj. 紫罗兰色的
6 portal /'pɔːtl/ n. 入口
7 turf /tɜːf/ n. 草皮
8 tendril /'tendrɪl/ n. 蔓
9 reminiscence /ˌremɪ'nɪsns/ n. 回忆的往事
10 scant /skænt/ adj. 不足的

们，他们穿着鲜艳的丝绸服装，戴着插有羽毛和玫瑰花的帽子，披巾飘动着，小阳伞像郁金香一样赏心悦目；另一股是轻快的、静悄悄的马车的潮流。确实，在那条马路上一切都是静悄悄的——那是一块神秘的地方，到处都是人，但并不嘈杂。

我们住在一幢地板光滑、没铺地毯的房子里，里面有许多镜子和窗户。我知道，在这幢房子里，有一个门上镶有紫红色玻璃的大厅，它那色彩斑斓的反光投射在门对面的阴影中。出了这道明亮的通道口是一个小巧的绿色花园，那里有草皮、许多鲜花和一棵大树。使花园变得充满绿色、到处挂满叶子的主要还是那些遮住了高高围墙的葡萄藤——我知道是它们，因为我记得那一串串葡萄和弯弯曲曲的卷须。

我们跟谁住在一起？对于这个问题我只能回答——跟我的父亲。我只能记起二十件关于他的事，但都支离破碎。我的父亲——我当时叫他爸爸——是我童年时代所受到的一切惩罚的根源。我总是不合情理地想要和他经常在一起。为了达到这个目的，每当看管我的保姆转过身去，我便会偷

punishments I had in those early days. I had an unreasonable wish to be always with him; and to this end, whenever the nurse who had charge of me turned her back, I was apt to escape from the nursery and seek the study. Then I was caught, shaken, and sometimes whipped, which I well deserved.

Whether my father knew how much I prized his presence I cannot pronounce[1]. He was much engaged all day, frequently out, and when at home other gentlemen were with him; but it often happened of an evening that he would suddenly enter the nursery, come up to me as I sat in my little chair, stand a moment looking down at me, and as I held up my arms, full of pleasure, he would stoop. Lift me, take me to his heart and say, "Polly may come downstairs now and be papa's little visitress."

Papa had a wonderfully interesting style of conversation, intelligible[2] to my childish brain, delightful to my childish heart. He charmed while he taught me. I think he had a quick, fiery temper: his brain was indeed gentle for me, but not always for others. I remember him both hasty and stern, but never with me. I never irritated[3] him, never feared to do so.

How I liked to stroke his dark face with my hands, to stand on his knees and comb his hair, to rest my head against his shoulder and thus fall asleep!

偷溜出看护室去找他的书房。后来我就被逮住，身子被摇晃着，有时还挨了打，不过那都是我自找的。

我不敢断言，爸爸是否知道我多么珍视与他在一起的时光。他整天都很忙，经常外出，即使回到家，身边也总是带了很多人。不过，黄昏时他会随时突然进入看护室，来到我坐的小椅子边，站上一会儿，眼睛朝着我看。当我兴高采烈地伸出手臂时，他会俯身把我抱上他的胸口，说道："波莉现在可以下楼做爸爸的小客人了。"

爸爸有一种巧妙而有趣的谈话方式，很容易被幼稚的头脑所理解，让我天真的心灵感到欣慰。当他教育我时，他很具魅力。我觉得他的性情有点暴躁。他对我确实很和蔼，但他对别人并不经常如此。我记得他既性急又严厉，但对我却不这样。我从来不惹他生气，从来不担心他会生气。

我多么想用我的小手抚摩他黝黑的脸庞，站在他的膝盖上，梳梳他的头发，或者把头枕在他的肩膀上呼呼地睡上一觉。

1 pronounce /prə'naʊns/ vi. 断言
2 intelligible /in'telidʒəbl/ adj. 可理解的
3 irritate /'iriteit/ vt. 惹怒

含英咀华

《童年回忆》是一份未发表的《维莱特》手稿。本文开头写道的"举家迁移",是因为夏洛蒂的父亲要去哈沃斯(Haworth)担任副牧师,所以全家搬去了那里。夏洛蒂五岁的时候,她的妈妈因癌症去世,八岁的时候被送进了女子教会学校,所以她的童年记忆中也就只有支离破碎的父亲和保姆。虽然文章中回忆的场景是色彩斑驳、情趣盎然的,但作者在写这些文字的时候,她的生命已经危在旦夕,姐妹们已故,只和父亲住在荒原深处。所以透过美好的回忆,作者真正表达的是无限的哀思

Helen Keller

海伦·凯勒

海伦·凯勒 (1880—1968)，是美国盲聋女作家和残障教育家。她在17个月的时候因为一次急性脑充血丧失了视力和听力。接着，她又丧失了语言表达能力。然而就在这黑暗而又寂寞的世界里，她在导师安妮·沙利文的帮助和努力下学会了读书和说话，并开始和其他人沟通。她以优异的成绩毕业于美国拉德克利夫学院，成为一个掌握英、法、德、拉丁、希腊五种文字的著名作家和教育家。她的主要作品有《我的一生》(The Story of My Life, 1903)、《我生活的世界》（The World I Live In，1908）、《冲出黑暗》（Out of the Dark, 1913）等。

The Most Important Day in My Life

我生命中最重要的那一天

The most important day I remember in all my life is the one on which my teacher, Anne Mansfield Sullivan, came to me. I am filled with wonder when I consider the immeasurable[1] contrasts between the two lives which it connects. It was the third of March, 1887, three months before I was seven years old.

On the afternoon of that eventful[2] day, I stood on the porch, dumb[3], expectant. I guessed vaguely from my mother's signs and from the hurrying to and fro[4] in the house that something unusual was about to happen, so I went to the door and waited on the steps. The afternoon sun penetrated[5] the mass of honeysuckle[6] that covered the porch, and fell on my upturned face. My fingers lingered almost unconsciously on the familiar leaves and blossoms which had just come forth to greet the sweet southern spring. I did not know what the future held of marvel[7] or surprise for me. Anger and bitterness had preyed upon me continually for weeks and a deep languor[8] had succeeded this passionate struggle.

Have you ever been at sea in a dense fog,

1 immeasurable /i'meʒərəbl/ adj. 不可计量的，无边无际的，广大的
2 eventful /i'ventfl/ adj. 重要的
3 dumb /dʌm/ adj. 沉默寡言的，不愿说话的
4 to and fro 往复地，来回地
5 penetrate /'penitreit/ vt. 穿透，透过
6 honeysuckle /'hʌnisʌkl/ n. 金银花，一种植物
7 marvel /'maːvl/ n. 令人惊奇的事物
8 languor /'læŋgə(r)/ n. 倦怠

我能回想起的生命中最重要的一天就是安妮·曼斯菲尔德·沙利文老师来到我家里的那天。每当我回想起那一天之前和之后的我那截然不同的生活，我不由得感慨万千。那是1887年3月3日，离我七岁生日还有三个月。

那是改变我命运的一天。那天下午，我站在走廊上，一声不响，满怀期待。从母亲的手势和其他人来回奔忙的样子，我模糊地猜到一定是有什么不寻常的事。因此我走到门口，站在台阶上等待着。午后的阳光透过门廊上的一大片金银花，照在我仰起的脸上。我几乎是无意识地把手指放在那熟悉的花叶上留恋不去，抚摸着那些为了迎接可爱的南国春天而绽放的花朵。我不知道未来会有什么奇迹和惊喜等待着我。愤怒和痛苦几周来不停地折磨着我，我的心灵早已失去了激情而变得疲惫不堪了。

你可曾有过在浓雾弥漫的海面上航行的经历？眼前是一片伸手不见五指的白茫茫的世界，你紧张地驾驶着一条大船，

when it seemed as if a tangible[1] white darkness shut you in, and the great ship, tense and anxious, groped her way toward the shore with plummet[2] and sounding-line[3] and you waited with beating heart for something to happen? I was like that ship before my education began, only I was without compass or sounding-line, and had no way of knowing how near the harbour was. "Light! give me light!" was the wordless cry of my soul, and the light of love shone on me in that very hour.

I felt approaching footsteps. I stretched out my hand as I supposed to my mother. Some one took it, and I was caught up and held close in the arms of her who had come to reveal all things to me, and, more than all things else, to love me.

The morning after my teacher came she led me into her room and gave me a doll. The little blind children at the Perkins Institution had sent it and Laura Bridgman had dressed it; but I did not know this until afterward. When I had played with it a little while, Miss Sullivan slowly spelled into my hand the word "d-o-l-l". I was at once interested in this finger play and tried to imitate it. When I finally succeeded in making the letters correctly I was flushed[4] with childish pleasure and pride. Running downstairs to

靠着测铅和探深线，谨慎地向对岸驶去。你的心怦怦直跳，总担心会有什么事情发生。在接受教育之前，我就像那只大雾中的航船，只是我既没有指南针，也没有探深线，无法知道还要航行多久才能靠岸。"光明！快给我光明！"我在心中无声地呐喊。恰在此时，爱的光明照亮了我的生命。

我觉得有脚步向我走来，我以为是母亲，立刻伸出双手。这时有人握住了我的手，把我紧紧地抱在怀里，她就是让我领悟人生的真谛，更重要的是让我体会爱的力量的人——安妮·沙利文老师。

第二天早晨，沙利文老师把我带到她的房间，给了我一个洋娃娃。后来我才知道，这个洋娃娃是铂金斯盲童学校的小学生送给我的，洋娃娃的衣服是劳拉·布里奇曼亲手穿上的。我玩了一会儿洋娃娃，沙利文小姐拉起我的手，在手掌上慢慢地拼写"doll"这个词。这个举动让我对手指游戏产生了兴趣，我尽力模仿她的样子在手掌上写。当我最后能正确地拼写这个词时，我自豪极了，高兴得满脸通红。我立刻跑到楼下去，找到母亲，伸出手拼写"doll"这个词给她看。然

---

1 tangible /'tændʒəbl/ *adj.* 切实的
2 plummet /'plʌmɪt/ *n.* 铅锤，测铅
3 sounding-line /'saʊndɪŋlaɪn/ 测深线
4 flushed /flʌʃt/ *adj.* 兴奋的，激动的

my mother I held up my hand and made the letters for doll. I did not know that I was spelling a word or even that words existed; I was simply making my fingers go in monkey-like imitation. In the days that followed I learned to spell in this uncomprehending way a great many words, among them pin, hat, cup and a few verbs like sit, stand and walk. But my teacher had been with me several weeks before I understood that everything has a name.

One day, while I was playing with my new doll, Miss Sullivan put my big rag[1] doll into my lap also, spelled "d-o-l-l" and tried to make me understand that "d-o-l-l" applied to both. Earlier in the day we had had a tussle[2] over the words "m-u-g" and "w-a-t-e-r". Miss Sullivan had tried to impress it upon me that "m-u-g" is mug and that "w-a-t-e-r" is water, but I persisted in confounding[3] the two. In despair she had dropped the subject for the time, only to renew it at the first opportunity. I became impatient at her repeated attempts and, seizing the new doll, I dashed it upon the floor. I was keenly delighted when I felt the fragments of the broken doll at my feet. Neither sorrow nor regret followed my passionate outburst. I had not loved the doll. In the still, dark world in which I lived there was no strong sentiment of tenderness. I felt my teacher sweep the fragments to one side of the hearth[4],

---

1 rag /ræg/　n.　碎布
2 tussle /'tʌsl/　n.　争执，争辩
3 confound /kən'faʊnd/　vt.　混淆
4 hearth /hɑːθ/　n.　炉子

而，我并不知道这就是在写字，甚至也不知道世界上有文字这种东西；我不过是模仿沙利文老师的样子而已。从此以后，我以这种不求甚解的方式学会了拼写好些单词，像"针"、"帽子"、"茶杯"什么的，还有一些动词，像"坐"、"站"、"走"。老师教了我几个星期后，我才慢慢明白，原来世间万物皆有名称。

一天，我正在玩我的新娃娃，沙利文小姐把我原来那个大布娃娃拿来放在我的膝上，然后在我手上拼写"doll"这个词，想让我明白我的新娃娃和布娃娃一样都叫做"doll"。那天早上，我们才为"杯"和"水"这个词闹过别扭。她想让我懂得"杯"是"杯"，"水"是"水"，可我老是把两者混淆。她无计可施，只好暂时丢开这个问题，等以后有机会再解决。于是，当她让我重新练习拼写"doll"这个词时，我实在有些不耐烦了，一把抓起洋娃娃狠狠地摔在地上。摸着地上洋娃娃的碎片，我心里特别痛快。拿洋娃娃撒气，我一点儿也不惭愧后悔。我对洋娃娃没有爱。在我那个寂静而黑暗的世界里，根

and I had a sense of satisfaction that the cause of my discomfort was removed. She brought me my hat, and I knew I was going out into the warm sunshine. This thought, if a wordless sensation may be called a thought, made me hop[1] and skip with pleasure.

We walked down the path to the well-house, attracted by the fragrance of the honeysuckle with which it was covered. Someone was drawing[2] water and my teacher placed my hand under the spout[3]. As the cool stream gushed[4] over one hand she spelled into the other the word water, first slowly, then rapidly. I stood still, my whole attention fixed upon the motions of her fingers. Suddenly I felt a misty[5] consciousness as of something forgotten — a thrill of returning thought; and somehow the mystery of language was revealed to me. I knew then that "w-a-t-e-r" meant the wonderful cool something that was flowing over my hand. That living word awakened my soul, gave it light, hope, joy, set it free! There were barriers still, it is true, but barriers that could in time be swept away.

本没有温柔和同情。我听到沙利文小姐把可怜的洋娃娃的碎片扫到炉子边，那个给我带来麻烦的东西被处理掉了，我心满意足。沙利文小姐把我的帽子递给我，我知道又可以到外面沐浴和煦的阳光了。这样一想——假如说这种无言的感受也能够叫做"想"的话——我立刻高兴得蹦蹦跳跳起来。

我们沿着小路散步，扑鼻而来的芳香把我们带到了井房，那里的房顶上有一大片盛开的金银花。有人正在那里提水，沙利文老师把我的一只手放在喷水口下。一股清凉的水在我手上流过，她在我的另一只手上拼写"water"——"水"字。起先写得很慢，然后逐渐加快。我静静地站着，全神贯注地感受她手指的动作。突然间我隐隐约约地感到心中某种迄今为止被我遗忘的东西被唤醒了——恍然大悟的美妙感觉让我心神激荡。我一下子领悟了语言文字的奥秘，知道了"水"这个字就是正在我手上流过的这种清凉而奇妙的东西。这个活生生的词语唤醒了我的灵魂，并赋予我光明、希望、快乐和自由。诚然，障碍依然存在，但这些障碍随着时间的推移终究会被消除的。

1 hop /hɒp/ *vi.* （人）单足跳
2 draw /drɔ:/ *vt.* 汲取
3 spout /spaʊt/ *n.* 喷水口，管口
4 gush /ɡʌʃ/ *vi.* 喷，涌
5 misty /ˈmɪsti/ *adj.* 模糊的

含英咀华

本文节选自海伦·凯勒的自传《我的一生》第四章，文章讲述了安妮·沙利文用她的智慧和爱心带领小海伦走出黑暗和孤寂的故事。安妮·沙利文老师帮助小海伦领悟了语言文字的奥秘，仿佛在黑暗中给小海伦带来了光明。因此，初遇老师的这天成了小海伦生命中最重要的一天。

Suzanne Chazin

苏珊·查新

苏珊·查新（1982~），美国作家，侦探小说"追击纵火犯"系列(*Georgia Skeehan mystery series*)的作者。生于纽约，毕业于西北大学。曾任《读者文摘》（*Reader's Digest*）的高级主编，在职期间多次获得国家级奖项。2001年时推出"追击纵火犯"系列中的第一部小说《第四天使》（*The Fourth Angel*），一举成名并成为新兴小说家。之后推出第二本小说《火狐》（*Flashover, 2002*）和第三本《玩火》（*Fireplay, 2003*）。

My Mother's Gift

I grew up in a small town where school was only a ten-minute walk from my house and in an age, not so long ago, when children could go home for lunch and find their mothers waiting.

At the time, I did not consider this a luxury, although today it certainly would be. I took it for granted that mothers were the sandwich-makers, the finger-painting appreciators and the homework monitors. I never questioned that this ambitious, intelligent woman, who had had a career before I was born and would eventually return to a career, would spend almost every lunch hour throughout my primary school years just with me.

I only knew that when the lunch-time bell rang, I would race breathlessly home. My mother would be standing at the top of the stairs, smiling down at me with a look that suggested I was the only important thing she had on her mind. For this, I am forever grateful.

Some sounds bring it all back: the high-pitched squeal¹ of the kettle, the rumble² of

---

1 **squeal** /skwiːl/   *n.*   长而尖的声音
2 **rumble** /'rʌmbl/   *n.*   隆隆声

母亲的礼物

我在一个小镇上长大，从家里走到学校只需花上十分钟。在那个距今还不太久远的年代，学生们可以回家吃午饭，他们的妈妈则会早早地等在家里。

这一切对如今的孩子来说，无疑是一种奢望了，但那时候的我却并不以为然。我觉得母亲为孩子做三明治，鉴赏指画，检查家庭作业都是些理所当然的事。我从没想过，像我妈妈这样一个有抱负并很聪明的女人，在我出生前拥有一份工作，而且后来她又谋了个差事，但在我上小学的那几年，她却几乎每天陪着我吃午饭。

我只记得每当午餐时间的铃声一响，我就一口气跑回家。母亲总会站在最高的门阶上笑盈盈地望着我，那神情分明在说：我是她心目中唯一最重要的东西。为此，我一辈子都感谢我的母亲。

如今，一些声音总是会勾起我对往事的回忆，像水烧开时水壶发出的尖叫声，洗衣机的隆隆声，还有我那条狗跳下台阶欢迎我时它脖子上的吊牌发出的撞

the washing machine, the jangle of my dog's collar tags as she bounded down the stairs to greet me. Our time together seemed devoid of the contrived[1] schedules that now pervade[2] my life.

One lunchtime when I was about eight will stay with me always. I had been picked to be the princess in the school play, and for weeks my mother had painstakingly rehearsed my lines with me. But no matter how easily I delivered them at home, as soon as I stepped on stage, every word disappeared from my head.

Finally, my teacher took me aside. She explained that she had written a narrator's part to the play, and asked me to switch roles. Her words, kindly delivered, still stung, especially when I saw my part go to another girl.

I didn't tell my mother what had happened when I went home for lunch that day. But she sensed my unease, and instead of suggesting we practise my lines, she asked if I wanted to walk in the garden.

It was a lovely spring day and the climbing rose on the trellis[3] was turning green. Under the huge elm trees, we could see yellow dandelions[4] popping through the grass in bunches, as if a painter had touched our landscape with dabs[5]

击声。和母亲在一起的岁月，全然没有如今充斥于我生活中的、事先排定虚假情意的日程表。

我永远不会忘记我快到八岁时的一顿午餐。我被选中要在学校话剧中扮演公主的角色，一连几周妈妈都不辞辛劳地陪我一起背诵台词。但是不论我在家背得如何滚瓜烂熟，只要一上舞台我的脑子里就一片空白。

终于，老师把我叫到了一边。她解释说，她已经写好了这部话剧的旁白部分，想把我替换下来做旁白。尽管老师的话温柔和善，可还是刺痛了我的心，尤其是在我看到另一个女孩顶替了我的角色的时候。

那天我回家吃午饭时没把这件事告诉妈妈。但是妈妈感觉到了我的不安，她没提背台词的事，而是问我是否愿意到花园里走走。

那可真是个可爱的春日，格架上的蔷薇正在泛青。在高大的榆树下，我们可以看到一簇簇黄色的蒲公英在草丛中喷涌而出，仿佛是一位画家为我们眼前

1 contrived /kən'traɪvd/ *adj.* 人为的
2 pervade /pə'veɪd/ *vt.* 充斥
3 trellis /'trelɪs/ *n.* 格架
4 dandelion /'dændɪlaɪən/ *n.* 蒲公英
5 dab /dæb/ *n.* 少量

of gold.

I watched my mother casually bend down by one of the clumps. "I think I'm going to dig up all these weeds," she said, tugging¹ a blossom up by its roots. "From now on, we'll have only roses in this garden."

"But I like dandelions," I protested, "All flowers are beautiful — even dandelions."

My mother looked at me seriously. "Yes, every flower gives pleasure in its own way, doesn't it?" she asked thoughtfully. I nodded, pleased that I had won her over. "And that is true of people too," she added. "Not everyone can be a princess, but there is no shame in that."

Relieved that she had guessed my pain. I started to cry as I told her what had happened. She listened and smiled reassuringly² .

"But you will be a beautiful narrator," she said, reminding me of how much I loved to read stories aloud to her. "The narrator's part is every bit as important as the part of a princess."

Over the next few weeks, with her constant encouragement, I learned to take pride in the role. Lunchtimes were spent reading over my lines and talking about what I would wear.

---

1 **tug** /tʌg/ *vt.* 拉，拽
2 **reassuringly** /riːəˈʃʊərɪŋli/ *adv.* 安心地，可靠地

的美景着上了点点金色。

我看到母亲在一簇花丛边漫不经心地弯下身。"我看得把这些杂草都拔了，"她一边说，一边使劲把一丛蒲公英连根拔出。"从今以后，我们的园子就只种蔷薇花。"

"但是我喜欢蒲公英，"我抗议道，"凡是花都好看——即便是蒲公英。"

母亲认真地看着我。"这么说，每种花都自有它令人赏心悦目的方式喽？"她若有所思地问道。我点点头，很满意自己说服了母亲。"那人也是一样啊，"母亲接着说道，"不是每个人都能做公主，但不能当公主也没什么丢脸的。"

母亲猜到了我的苦处使我的情绪安定了下来。我边哭边告诉她事情的经过。母亲听着，脸上挂着安详的微笑。

"但你会是一名特别棒的解说员，"她说，并提醒我有多喜欢大声朗诵故事给她听。"从哪一点来说，解说员的角色都和公主的角色同样重要。"

在接下来的几周时间里，母亲不断地鼓励我，我渐渐地对这个角色感到骄傲。我们利用午饭时间念台词，讨论到时候我该穿什么衣服。

Backstage on the night of the performance, I felt nervous. A few minutes before the play, my teacher came over to me. "Your mother asked me to give this to you," she said, handing me a dandelion. Its edges were already beginning to curl and it flopped[1] lazily from its stem. But just looking at it, knowing my mother was out there and thinking of our lunchtime talk, made me proud.

After the play, I took home the flower I had stuffed in the apron[2] of my costume. My mother pressed it between two sheets of kitchen towel in a dictionary, laughing as she did it that we were perhaps the only people who would press such a sorry looking weed.

I often look back on our lunchtimes together, bathed in the soft midday light. They were the commas in my childhood, the pauses that told me life is not savored in premeasured increments[3], but in the sum of daily rituals and small pleasures we casually share with loved ones. Over peanut-butter sandwiches and chocolate-chip cookies, I learned that love, first and foremost, means being there for the little things.

A few months ago, my mother came to

---

1 flop /flɒp/ *vi.* 耷拉
2 apron /'eɪprən/ *n.* 围裙
3 increment /'ɪŋkrəmənt/ *n.* 增加

演出那天晚上，我进入后台时还是感到紧张。离演出还有几分钟的时候，老师朝我走了过来。"你妈妈让我把这个交给你，"说着，她递给我一朵蒲公英。花的边缘已经开始打蔫，花瓣有气无力地耷拉在茎上。但是看看它，知道母亲就在外面，想着我们午饭时的谈话，我变得自信起来。

演出过后，我把塞在演出服装围裙里的蒲公英带回了家。母亲把它放在两张纸巾中间夹进了一本字典里，她一边忙碌着，一边笑着说，也许只有我们会珍藏这样一朵蔫了的野草花。

我经常回想起那些沐浴在和暖阳光中和母亲一起度过的午餐时光。他们是我童年时代的一个个小插曲，告诉我一个道理：人生的滋味，就在于和我们所爱的人在一起不经意地共度的日常生活、分享的点点滴滴的欢乐，而不在于某种事先测量好的"添加剂"。在享用母亲做的花生酱三明治和巧克力碎末小甜饼的时候，我懂得了，这些细微之处最能体现爱之所在。

几个月之前，母亲来看我。我请了一天假，请母亲吃午饭。饭店里熙熙攘攘，做生意的人忙着交易，不时地看着手表。

visit. I took a day off work and treated her to lunch. The restaurant bustled with activity as businesspeople made deals and glanced at their watches. In the middle of all this sat my mother, now retired, and I. From her face I could see that she relished[1] the pace of the work world. "You must have been terribly bored staying at home when I was a child," I said.

"Bored? Housework is boring. But you were never boring."

I didn't believe her, so I pressed. "Surely children are not as stimulating as a career."

"A career is stimulating," she said. "I'm glad I had one. But a career is like an open balloon. It remains inflated only as long as you keep pumping. A child is a seed. You water it. You care for it the best you can. And then it grows all by itself into a beautiful flower."

Just then, looking at her, I could picture us sitting at her kitchen table once again, and I understood why I kept that flaky[2] brown dandelion in our old dictionary pressed between two crumpled[3] bits of paper towel.

如今已经退休的妈妈和我就坐在他们当中。从母亲的表情中我可以看出，她喜欢上班族的生活节奏。"我小时候，你一直在家待着肯定很烦吧，"我说。

"烦？做家务是很心烦。但是你从来没有让我心烦过。"

我不相信她说的话，所以继续说道，"看孩子肯定没有工作带劲儿吧。"

"工作是很富有刺激性，"她说。"很高兴我有过工作。但是工作好比开着口的气球。你只有不停地充气它才会保持膨胀。而一个孩子却像是一粒种子，你给它浇水，全心全意照管它，然后它就能独立开出美丽的花朵来。"

就在那个时刻，看着我的母亲，我的脑海里又浮现出以前我们共坐在厨房餐桌旁的情景，我也明白了为什么我还珍藏着夹在我们那本旧字典里、用两片皱巴巴的纸巾压平的那朵棕褐色蒲公英。

---

1 relish /ˈrelɪʃ/　*vt.*　喜欢
2 flaky /ˈfleɪki/　*adj.*　薄片的
3 crumpled /ˈkrʌmpld/　*adj.*　有褶皱的

含英咀华

　　在这篇文章中，作者回忆了童年时和妈妈一起度过的午餐时光，并讲述了关于蒲公英的一个小故事。这篇文章之所以受到读者喜爱，是因为作者通过这样的一件小事告诉我们：伟大的母爱体现在平常生活的点滴中，一个细小的动作，一个小小的叮咛，都渗透着母亲崇高而无私的爱。

Dylan Thomas

狄兰·托马斯

狄兰·托马斯（1914—1953），威尔士诗人、作家。出版的诗集有《诗18首》(18 Poems, 1934)、《诗25首》(Twenty-Five Poems, 1936)、《爱情的地图》(The Map of Love, 1939)、《死亡与出路》(Deaths and Entrances, 1946)等。他被许多文学学者公认为二十世纪最具影响力的抒情诗人，并始终位居各时代最佳抒情诗人之首。托马斯的诗作大体属于超现实主义流派，其诗中所蕴含的内容较具有梦幻色彩，通过对于意象的描绘堆砌，托马斯所创造出来的诗境往往引人入胜。另外，托马斯很注重押韵，其诗以善于朗诵闻名。虽然狄兰主要是位诗人，他亦出版电影剧本和短篇小说，并公开演出自己的作品及在电台播音。

Memories of Christmas

One Christmas was so much like another, in those years, around the sea-town corner now, and out of all sound except the distant speaking of the voices I sometimes hear a moment before sleep, that I can never remember whether it snowed for six days and six nights when I was twelve or whether it snowed for twelve days and twelve nights when I was six; and Mrs Griffiths complained, and we threw a snowball at her niece, and my hands burned so, with the heat and the cold, when I held them in front of the fire, that I cried for twenty minutes and then had some jelly[1].

It was on the afternoon of the day of Christmas Eve, and I was in Mrs Prothero's garden, waiting for cats, with her son Jim. It was snowing. It was always snowing at Christmas. December, in my memory, is white as Lapland, though there were no reindeers. But there were cats. Patient, cold and callous, our hands wrapped in socks, we waited to snowball the cats. Sleek[2] and long as jaguars[3] and terrible-whiskered, spitting and snarling, they would slink[4] and sidle[5] over the white back-garden walls, and

1 jelly /'dʒeli/   n. 果冻
2 sleek /sliːk/   adj. 光滑的
3 jaguar /'dʒægjʊə(r)/   n. 美洲虎
4 slink /slɪŋk/   vi. 偷偷地走
5 sidle /'saɪdl/   vi. 悄悄贴近

圣诞回忆

年复一年，圣诞节总是如此，如今在这个海边小镇的一角，有时候在睡前那一刻，除了那些遥远的对话我听不到任何声音。我已经记不清到底是我十二岁的那年圣诞连续下了六天六夜的雪，还是我六岁那年的圣诞连续下了十二天十二夜的雪了。可我记得格利菲斯夫人的抱怨，我们朝她的侄女扔雪球，我把手放在火上取暖时，冷热交加，把我的手灼得疼痛难忍，我哭喊了二十分钟后得到了一些果冻吃。

那是一个圣诞夜的下午，我在普罗塞罗夫人的园子里和她的儿子吉姆一起等着猫的出现。那时正下着雪。那时的圣诞节总是在下雪。在我的记忆中，十二月份就像拉普兰那地方一样白雪飘飞了，虽然看不到驯鹿，但总能看到一些猫。我们等着用雪球打那些猫。它们像美洲虎一样皮毛光滑，身体高大，长着吓人的胡须。看到我们，它们发出低沉的怒嚎，它们通常会从园子的白色后墙那儿悄悄逃走。眼光犀利的猎人们——吉姆和我，戴

the lynx-eyed[1] hunters, Jim and I, fur-capped and moccasined[2], would hurl our deadly snowballs at the green of their eyes. The wise cats never appeared. We never heard Mrs Prothero's first cry from her igloo[3] at the bottom of the garden. Or, if we heard it at all, it was, to us, like the far-off challenge of our enemy and prey, the neighbour's Polar Cat. But soon the voice grew louder. "Fire!" cried Mrs Prothero, and she beat the dinner-gong. And we ran down the garden, with the snowballs in our arms, towards the house, and smoke, indeed, was pouring out of the dining-room, and the gong was bombilating[4], and Mrs Prothero was announcing ruin like a town-crier in Pompeii[5]. This was better than all the cats in Wales standing on the wall in a row. We bounded into the house, laden with snowballs, and stopped at the open door of the smoke-filled room. Something was burning all right; perhaps it was Mr Prothero, who always slept there after midday dinner with a newspaper over his face; but he was standing in the middle of the room, saying "A fine Christmas!" and smacking at the smoke with a slipper.

"Call the fire-brigade[6]," cried Mrs Prothero as she beat the gong.

"They won't be there," said Mr Prothero, "it's

---

1 lynx-eyed /ˈlɪŋksˈaɪd/   眼光锐利的
2 moccasin /ˈmɒkəsɪn/   *n.* 鹿皮鞋
3 igloo /ˈɪɡluː/   *n.* 圆顶建筑
4 bombilate = bombinate /ˈbɒmbɪleɪt/   发嗡嗡声
5 Pompeii /pɒmˈpeɪi/   庞贝，意大利古都，公元79年全城淹没在维苏韦火山的一次喷发中
6 fire-brigade /ˈfaɪə brɪˈɡeɪd/   *n.* 消防队，火警

着皮帽子，穿着鹿皮鞋，会准准地把我们威力无穷的雪球扔向它们的绿眼珠儿。狡猾的猫从没出现过。我们也没听见普罗塞罗夫人在园子最里面的圆顶建筑里发出的第一声叫喊。或者说，即便我们确实听见了，那声音对我们来说，也像是我们的敌人和猎物——邻居家那只南极猫远远发出的挑战。但是很快声音变得越来越大，"着火拉！"普罗塞罗夫人边敲着晚餐锣边喊道。我们手里拿着雪球，朝着在园子的尽头的房子跑去。事实上，烟是从饭厅里冒出来的，锣还震天动地地响着，普罗塞罗夫人像庞贝古城的街头公告员一样宣告着一切都完了。这可比威尔士所有的猫都列队站在墙上还过瘾哩。我们带着雪球冲进了房子，在满是浓烟的那个房间的敞开的门前停了下来。什么东西正烧着，可能是普罗塞罗先生，他总是在午饭后睡在那儿，脸上盖张报纸。但是他正站在屋子的中央，边说着"好一个圣诞节啊！"边用拖鞋拍打着烟。

"打电话叫消防队，"普罗塞罗夫人边敲锣边喊道。

"他们不会上班的，"普罗塞罗先生说，"这可是圣诞

Christmas."

There was no fire to be seen, only clouds of smoke and Mr Prothero standing in the middle of them, waving his slipper as though he were conducting.

"Do something," he said.

And we threw all our snowballs into the smoke — I think we missed Mr Prothero — and ran out of the house to the telephone-box.

"Let's call the police as well," Jim said.

"And the ambulance."

"And Ernie Jenkins, he likes fires."

But we only called the fire-brigade, and soon the fire engine came and three tall men in helmets brought a hose into the house and Mr Prothero got out just in time before they turned it on. Nobody could have had a noisier Christmas Eve. And when the firemen turned off the hose and were standing in the wet and smoky room, Jim's aunt, Miss Prothero, came downstairs and peered in at them. Jim and I waited, very quietly, to hear what she would say to them. She said the right thing, always. She looked at the three tall firemen in their shining helmets, standing among the smoke and cinders[1] and dissolving[2] snowballs, and she said: "Would you like something to

---

1 cinder /'sɪndə(r)/ n. 灰烬
2 dissolving /dɪ'zɒlvɪŋ/ adj. 融化了的

节啊。"

看不见有明火，只有滚滚的浓烟，普罗塞罗先生站在当中挥舞着拖鞋，好像他在指挥一个乐队。

"做点什么，"他说道。

我们把所有的雪球都扔向了那些烟——我认为我们没打到普罗塞罗先生——然后跑出屋子，直奔电话亭。

"我们也给警察打电话吧，"吉姆说。

"还要叫救护车。"

"还有欧尼·詹金丝，他喜欢火。"

但是我们只打了消防队的电话。不一会消防车就来了，三个带着头盔的高个子男人带了一根管子进了房子，普罗塞罗先生在他们开始打开水管前刚好来得及从房子里出来。没人曾经度过一个比这还吵闹的圣诞夜。正当消防员关了水管子，站在湿漉漉还冒着烟的房间里时，吉姆的阿姨——普罗塞罗小姐从楼上走了下来，并盯着那些消防员。我和吉姆静静地等着，看她要对他们说些什么。她总是一语中的。看着三个高个子消防员带着亮闪闪的头盔站在烟雾、灰烬和已经消融的雪球中间，她说道：

read?"

Christmas morning was always over before you could say Jack Frost[1]. And look! Suddenly the pudding was burning! Bang the gong and call the fire-brigade and the book-loving firemen!

And I remember that on the afternoon of Christmas Day, when the others sat around the fire and told each other that this was nothing, no, nothing, to the great Christmas when they were children, I would go out, school-capped and gloved and mufflered[2], with my bright new boots squeaking, into the white world on to the seaward[3] hill, to call on Jim and Dan and Jack and to walk with them through the silent snowscape[4] of our town.

We went padding through the streets, leaving huge deep footprints in the snow, on the hidden pavements.

"I bet people'll think there're been hippos ."

"What would you do if you saw a hippo[5] coming down Terrace Road?"

"I'd go like this, bang! I'd throw him over the railings[6] and roll him down the hill and then I'd tickle him under the ear and he'd wag his tail…"

Or we walked on the white shore.

"Can the fishes see it's snowing?"

---

1 Jack Frost　霜冻或严寒天气
2 muffler /ˈmʌflə(r)/　n.　围巾
3 seaward /ˈsiːwəd/　adj.　面朝大海的
4 snowscape /ˈsnəʊskeɪp/　n.　雪景
5 hippo /ˈhɪpəʊ/　n.　河马
6 railing /ˈreɪlɪŋ/　n.　栏杆

"你们想读点什么吗？"

圣诞节的早晨总是在严寒到来之前就过去了。看！布丁突然着火了！把锣敲起来！把消防队叫过来！还有那些爱读书的消防员！

我还记得那个圣诞节的下午，其他人围坐在火炉旁，互相讲着现在的圣诞节和他们小时候的简直没法比时，我出去了。像去上学一样，戴上帽子、手套和围巾，穿着吱呀作响、漂亮神奇的新皮靴，去面朝大海那座小山上的白色世界，叫上吉姆、丹和杰克，和他们一起走过我们镇上宁静的雪景。

我们踏过街道，在覆盖着厚厚的积雪的人行道上留下又大又深的脚印。

"我打赌，人们会认为河马来过这儿了。"

"如果你看到一只河马从泰勒思路上朝你走来，你会怎么做？"

"我会这么做，砰！我会把它扔到栏杆那边，让它滚下山，然后我会在它耳朵下搔痒，它就会朝我摆尾巴。"

或者我们在白色的沙滩上散步。

"鱼会看到现在正在下雪吗？"

"They think it's the sky falling down."

And I remember that we went singing carols once, a night or two before Christmas Eve, when there wasn't the shaving of a moon to light the secret, white-flying streets. At the end of a long road was a drive[1] that led to a large house, and we stumbled up the darkness of the drive that night, each one of us afraid, each one holding a stone in his hand in case, and all of us too brave to say a word. The wind made through the drive-treed noises as of old and unpleasant and maybe web-footed[2] men wheezing in caves. We reached the black bulk of the house.

"What shall we give them?" Dan whispered.

"Hark the Herald?" "Christmas comes but Once a Year?"

"No," Jack said: "We'll sing Good King Wenceslas. I'll count three."

One, two, three, and we began to sing, our voices high and seemingly distant in the snow-felted darkness round the house that was occupied by nobody we knew. We stood close together, near the dark door.

Good King Wenceslas looked out
On the Feast of Stephen.

And then a small, dry voice, like the voice

---

1 drive /draɪv/ *n.* 快车道
2 web-footed /web fʊtɪd/ 脚趾间有膜的

"它 们 会 认 为 天 塌 下 来 了。"

我还记得一次我们出去唱圣诞颂歌。这是圣诞夜前一两天的一个晚上，没有一丝月光照在神秘的、大雪纷飞的街上，路的尽头有一条快车道通向一所大房子。那天晚上，我们在黑暗中跌跌绊绊地走在那条快车道上，每个人都很害怕，手里都握了块石头以防万一，没一个人有胆量说句话。风穿过路边树木的声音，就像是个讨厌的，可能脚趾间还有薄膜的老男人在山洞里发出的喘息声。我们走到了房子黑色的躯体面前。

"我们给他们唱什么？"丹低声说。

"《使者哈克》？"

"《一年一次的圣诞节》？"

"不，"杰克说："我们要唱《好国王文西斯劳斯》，我数三下。"

"好国王文西斯劳斯向外望，
在斯蒂芬的宴会上。"

一、二、三；我们开始唱。我们的声音很尖，在那所不知何人居住的房子周围被雪覆盖的黑暗中，听上去异常遥远。我们靠近大门，紧紧地站在一起。

of someone who has not spoken for a long time, suddenly joined our singing: a small, dry voice from the other side of the door: a small, dry voice through the keyhole. And when we stopped running we were outside our house; the front room was lovely and bright; the gramophone[1] was playing; we saw the red and white balloons hanging from the gas-bracket; uncles and aunts sat by the fire; I thought I smelt our supper being fried in the kitchen. Everything was good again, and Christmas shone through all the familiar town.

"Perhaps it was a ghost," Jim said.

"Perhaps it was trolls[2]," Dan said, who was always reading.

"Let's go in and see if there's any jelly left," Jack said. And we did that.

Always on Christmas night there was music. An uncle played the fiddle, a cousin sang "Cherry Ripe," and another uncle sang "Drake's Drum." It was very warm in the little house. Auntie Hannah, who had got on to the parsnip[3] wine, sang a song about Bleeding Hearts and Death, and then another in which she said her heart was like a Bird's Nest; and then everybody laughed again; and then I went

1 gramophone /ˈɡræməfəʊn/ n. 留声机
2 troll /trəʊl, trɒl/ n. 轮唱
3 parsnip /ˈpɑːsnɪp/ n. （植物）荷兰防风草

就在那时，一个微弱的、干哑的声音，像是一个很久没有说过话的人发出的声音，突然间加入了我们的合唱。这是一个从门里面传来的微弱的、干哑的声音，一个从钥匙孔里传来的微弱的、干哑的声音。当我们停止奔跑的时候，我们已经在自己家门外了。前厅可爱、明亮；留声机正在播放音乐；我们看到煤气灯支柱上挂着红色和白色的气球；叔叔婶婶们在火炉旁坐着；我以为自己闻到了厨房里正烧着的晚餐的香气。一切重又变得美好，圣诞照亮了整个熟悉的小镇。

"说不定那是鬼，"吉姆说。

"有可能是轮唱，"读过很多书的丹说。

"我们进屋去看看还有没有剩下的果冻吧，"杰克说道。我们就照他的话做了。

圣诞夜总是有歌声的。一位叔叔演奏小提琴，一个表兄演唱《熟樱桃》，另一位叔叔演唱《公鸭的鼓》。小房子里其乐融融。汉娜阿姨喝了些防风草酒，唱了一首关于滴血的心和死亡的歌，在接下来的另一首歌中，她又唱到她的心像一个鸟窝；于是大家都笑了起来；然后我回到了自己的床

to bed. Looking through my bedroom window, out into the moonlight and the unending snow, I could see the lights in the windows of all the other houses on our hill. I turned the gas down, I got into bed.

上。透过房间的窗向外望，在月光下和无垠的雪地里，我能看到我们这个小山上所有其他人家窗子里的灯光。我关掉油气灯，钻进了被窝。

含英咀华

托马斯这篇有关圣诞节的回忆是一曲幼年往事的优美乐章。作者以如诗的笔触为人们描绘了一个妙趣横生的童心世界。全文充盈着童真和童趣，仿佛把我们也带回到自己的童年。

怀人思远

William Makepeace Thackeray
威廉·梅克皮斯·萨克雷

威廉·梅克皮斯·萨克雷（1811—1863），英国19世纪杰出的批判现实主义小说家，曾就读于剑桥大学。他继承和发扬了英国18世纪由斯威夫特(Jonathan Swift, 1667—1745)、菲尔丁(Henry Fielding, 1707—1754)、斯特恩(Laurence Sterne, 1713—1768)等人开创的讽刺小说传统，以英国有教养的绅士所特有的机智幽默甚至玩世不恭的态度无情地展示生活的真实。著名的作品有特写集《势利眼集》(The Book of Snobs, 1848)，长篇小说《名利场》(Vanity Fair, 1848)，历史小说《亨利·埃斯芒德》(The History of Henry Esmond, 1852)、《潘登尼斯》(Pendennis, 1848—1850)等，其中《名利场》是萨克雷的成名作和代表作。这部小说篇幅宏大，场面壮观，情节复杂，心理刻画深入，其尖锐泼辣的讽刺风格更为精彩。

The Last Manuscript

With a feeling much akin to that with which I looked upon the friend's — the admirable artist's — unfinished work, I can fancy many readers turning to the last pages which were traced by Charlotte Brontë's hand. Of the multitude[1] that have read her books, who has not known and deplored the tragedy of her family, her own most sad and untimely fate? Which of her readers has not become her friend? Who that has known her books has not admired the artist's noble English, the burning love of truth, the bravery, the simplicity, the indignation[2] at wrong, the eager sympathy, the pious[3] love and reverence[4], the passionate honor, so to speak[5], of the woman? What a story is that of that family of poets in their solitude yonder on the gloomy northern moors! At nine o'clock at night, Mrs. Gaskell tells, after evening prayers, when their guardian and relative had gone to bed, the three poetesses — the three maidens[6], Charlotte, and Emily, and Anne[7] — Charlotte being the "motherly friend and guardian to the other two" —"began, like restless wild animals, to

最后的手稿

当许多读者看到这些残篇——夏洛蒂·勃朗特手书的最后残篇时，我可以想象得出，他们的心情会十分近似我看着我的那位朋友——那位可敬佩的艺术家的未完成的作品时的心情。众多读过她的小说的人，谁不知道、谁不叹息她的家庭悲剧和她自己过早辞世的悲惨命运？她的哪位读者没有和她成为朋友？哪一位了解她著作的人不钦佩她典雅华贵的语言，以及自作品中渗透着的她对真理炽热的爱、她的勇敢和纯洁、她对邪恶的愤恨、她热切的同情心、她虔诚的爱和尊重，以及她激越的荣誉感？在北方阴郁的荒原上，那个家庭的诗人们生活在孤寂之中，这是一个多么凄凉的故事啊！盖斯凯尔夫人告诉我们，每晚九点钟，做过晚祷之后，当她们的家人亲眷们都已上床睡觉之际，三位女诗人——夏洛蒂、艾米利和安妮三位少女，夏洛蒂是"另两位少女慈母般的朋友和保护者"——"开始像焦躁不安的野兽似地

---

1 **multitude** /ˈmʌltɪtjuːd/ *n.* 许多
2 **indignation** /ˌɪndɪɡˈneɪʃn/ *n.* 愤怒，愤慨，义愤
3 **pious** /ˈpaɪəs/ *adj.* 虔诚的，笃信的
4 **reverence** /ˈrevərəns/ *n.* 敬爱，崇敬，敬畏
5 **so to speak** 可以说，可谓
6 **maiden** /ˈmeɪdns/ *n.* 少女，处女
7 **Charlotte, and Emily, and Anne:** 勃朗特姐妹，有夏洛特、艾米利、安妮三姐妹，均为英国小说家。她们的作品在首次出版时都引起了很大的轰动，并被认为是英国文学中的传世佳作

pace up and down their parlor, 'making out' their wonderful stories, talking over plans and projects, and thoughts of what was to be their future life."

One evening, at the close of 1854, as Charlotte Nicholls[1] sat with her husband by the fire, listening to the howling of the wind about the house, she suddenly said to her husband, "If you had not been with me, I must have been writing now." She then ran up stairs, and brought down, and read aloud, the beginning of a new tale. When she had finished, her husband remarked, "The critics will accuse you of repetition." She replied, "Oh! I shall alter that. I always begin two or three times before I can please myself." But it was not to be. The trembling little hand was to write no more. The heart newly awakened to love and happiness, and throbbing[2] with maternal[3] hope, was soon to cease to beat; that intrepid[4] outspeaker and champion of truth, that eager, impetuous[5] redresser[6] of wrong, was to be called out of the world's fight and struggle, to lay down[7] the shining arms, and to be removed to a sphere[8] where even a noble indignation cor ulterius nequit lacerare[9], and where truth complete, and right triumphant, no longer need to wage war.

1 **Charlotte Nicholls** 夏洛蒂·勃朗特婚后的姓名
2 **throb** /θrɒb/ *vi.* （心脏、脉搏等）跳动，悸动
3 **maternal** /mə'tɜːnl/ *adj.* 母亲的，母性的
4 **intrepid** /ɪn'trepɪd/ *adj.* 勇敢的，大胆的，无畏的，坚忍不拔的
5 **impetuous** /ɪm'petʃuəs/ *adj.* 性急的，热切的
6 **redresser** /rɪ'dresə(r)/ *n.* 纠正者，矫正者，革除者
7 **lay down** 放下
8 **sphere** /sfɪə(r)/ *n.* 范围，领域
9 **cor ulterius nequit lacerare**：（拉丁文）大意是"不会把心撕裂"

在客厅里来回踱步，'创造'她们奇妙的故事，谈论她们的计划和打算，以及关于她们未来生活的种种设想。"

1854年年末的一个傍晚，夏洛蒂·尼科尔斯同丈夫坐在火炉边，听着狂风在屋子四周的呼号，忽然她对丈夫说："要不是你跟我在一起，我现在一定在写东西呢。"说着她跑上楼，取下她新小说的开头，开始大声朗读。读完后，她丈夫说道："评论家会指责你重复过去写过的东西。"她回答说："噢！那个我还要修改呢。开头时我总是要写上两三遍，才能让自己满意。"可这话却没有实现。那只颤抖着的小手再也不能写什么了。那颗刚刚被爱情和幸福唤醒、怀着做母亲的愿望的心，不久就停止了跳动；那个无所畏惧的宣扬真理、捍卫真理的人，那个急不可耐的斧正时弊的人，即将被召唤去，远离世间的争斗，放下闪闪发光的武器，被转移到这样一个去处：在那儿，即使是高尚的愤怒也不会把心撕裂；在那儿，真理是完美的，正义赢得胜利，再也无需战斗。

我只能就我所看到的谈

I can only say of this lady, vidi tantum[1]. saw her first just as I rose out of an illness from which I had never thought to recover. I remember the trembling little frame, the little hand, the great honest eyes. An impetuous honesty seemed to me to characterize the woman. Twice I recollect she took me to task for what she held to be errors in doctrine[2]. Once about Fielding[3] we had a disputation. She spoke her mind out. She jumped too rapidly to conclusions. (I have smiled at one or two passages in the "Biography", in which my own disposition or behavior forms the subject of talk.) She formed conclusions that might be wrong, and built up whole theories of character upon them. New to the London world, she entered it with an independent, indomitable[4] spirit of her own; and judged of contemporaries, and especially spied out arrogance or affectation, with extraordinary keenness of vision. She was angry with her favorites if their conduct or conversation fell below her ideal. Often she seemed to me to be judging the London folk prematurely: but perhaps the city is rather angry at being judged. I fancied an austere little Joan of Arc[5] marching in upon us, and rebuking our easy lives, our easy morals.

论这位女士。第一次见她时，我刚好从一场自以为不治的病中恢复过来。我记得她那战栗着的弱小身躯，那只小手，那双真诚的大眼睛。在我看来，冲动的真诚似乎可以概括她的性格。我记得，有两次她为了她认为关乎信念对错的事情责备我。一次是关于菲尔丁，我们有过争论。她直言不讳地说了自己的看法。她过于急促地下了结论。（《夏洛蒂·勃朗特传》中的一两段不禁使我微笑，那里面把我的一些态度和行为当成了话题。）她的结论可能有误，但她在这些结论上面却引申出整套人物性格的理论。她带着特有的独立、不屈的精神，初入伦敦世界。品评时人，她尤其能以非凡的敏锐洞察力辨出傲慢与虚伪。如果发现她欣赏的人的行为言谈没能达到她的期望，她就会对他们生气。我常觉得，她好像对伦敦人作出了欠成熟的判断；不过，也许伦敦城对它自己遭人评头论足也颇为恼火吧。我想象，一位疾言厉色的小贞德朝我们大步走来，她谴责我们懒散的生活方式和不羁的道德风尚。在我的印象中，她是一个非常纯洁、崇高、品格高尚

1 vidi tantum（拉丁文）大意是"就我所看到的那么多"
2 doctrine /'dɒktrɪn/ n. 主义，信条，政策
3 Fielding 菲尔丁（1707—1754），英国小说家、剧作家、散文家
4 indomitable /ɪn'dɒmɪtəbl/ adj. 不屈服的
5 Joan of Arc 贞德（1412—1431），法国女民族英雄

She gave me the impression of being a very pure, and lofty, and high-minded person. A great and holy reverence of right and truth seemed to be with her always. Such, in our brief interview, she appeared to me. As one thinks of that life so noble, so lonely — of that passion for truth — of those nights and nights of eager study, swarming fancies, invention, depression, elation[1], prayer; as one reads the necessarily incomplete, though most touching and admirable history of the heart that throbbed in this one little frame — of this one amongst the myriads[2] of souls that have lived and died on this great earth — this great earth? — this little speck in the infinite universe[3] of God, — with what wonder do we think of to-day, with what awe await to-morrow, when that which is now but darkly seen shall be clear!

As I read this little fragmentary sketch, I think of the rest. Is it? And where is it? Will not the leaf be turned some day, and the story be told? Shall the deviser of the tale somewhere perfect the history of little EMMA'S grieves and troubles? Shall TITANIA[4] come forth complete with[5] her sportive court, with the flowers at her

---

1 elation /ɪˈleɪʃn/ n. 兴高采烈
2 myriad /ˈmɪrɪəd/ n. 无数
3 infinite universe /ˈɪnfɪnət ˈjuːnɪvɜːs/ 无限全域
4 TITANIA: 莎士比亚戏剧《仲夏夜之梦》里的仙后
5 complete with: 连同

的人。她似乎总是对正义和真理怀着崇高而神圣的敬意。这就是她在我们短暂的会见中给我留下的印象。当我们想到她的一生是如此崇高、孤独，怀着追求真理的热忱，在那些夜晚里，她热切地研读着，各种各样的念头云集在头脑中，她构思着作品，情绪上历经着低落与高涨，祈祷着上帝的福佑；当我们读着那颗在这样一个瘦小的躯体里跳动着的心灵史时，她那一段让人无可奈何没有写完但感人至深令人钦佩的历史，在这个庞大的地球上——庞大的地球？它只不过是上帝创造的无限寰宇的一粒尘埃而已——生生死死不计其数的心灵中她的心灵的历史时，我们会怀着怎样的惊奇思考今天发生的事情，怀着怎样的敬畏等待明天的到来，那时候，我们现在看来晦暗的事情将会变得清晰！

当我读着这短短的手稿残篇时，我想到了它未完成的部分。它存在么？它又在哪里？书页是否会在某天被翻过，故事就又延续了呢？这个故事的缔造者是否将在某个地方完成小爱玛悲伤烦扰的历史？泰坦尼亚是否会连同她嬉戏的王宫

feet, the forest around her, and all the stars of summer glittering overhead?

How well I remember the delight, and wonder, and pleasure with which I read "Jane Eyre", sent to me by an author whose name and sex were then alike unknown to me; the strange fascinations of the book; and how with my own work pressing upon me, I could not, having taken the volumes up, lay them down until they were read through! Hundreds of those who, like myself, recognized and admired that master-work of a great genius, will look with a mournful interest and regard and curiosity upon the last fragmentary sketch from the noble hand which wrote "Jane Eyre".

一起出现，脚下鲜花盛开，周围森林环绕，夏夜的繁星在头顶闪烁？

我十分清楚地记得，当一位不知姓名、性别的作者把《简·爱》寄给我时，我是怀着多么兴奋、惊奇、愉悦的心情来读它。我记得那本书的奇异魅力。我记得虽然我自己有一大堆工作要做，可我一旦拿了那本书就再也放不下，直到我一口气把它读完！成千上万像我这样的读者，那些承认并钦慕那位伟大天才的杰作的人，会在悲哀之余怀着兴趣、关怀和好奇，来阅读这部末了之作，它出自曾写过《简·爱》的那只高贵的手。

怀人思远

含英咀华

　　夏洛蒂·勃朗特素来钦佩萨克雷，还把自己的《简·爱》(Jane Eyre)献给他。文坛猜测《简·爱》中的男主角正是以萨克雷为原型，因为他正巧有个精神失常的妻子被关在阁楼上。所以，勃朗特死后，萨克雷一反他平时的玩世不恭，于1860年4月在《康希尔杂志》（The Cornhill Magazine）发表了这篇深情的散文悼念她，介绍其因病未完成的长篇小说Emma（《爱玛》，1855）。文中作者通过自己的切身体会，把着重点放在对夏洛蒂的性格描写上，突出表现了她纯洁热诚的心灵。

Thomas De Quincey
托马斯·德·昆西

托马斯·德·昆西(1785—1859)，英国著名散文家和批评家，被誉为"少有的英语文体大师"，作品受到D·H·劳伦斯(David Herbert Lawrence, 1885—1930)及弗吉尼亚·吴尔芙(Virginia Woolf, 1882-1941)等诸多后世文坛大家的赞誉。在他七岁时，父亲去世，德·昆西由他天赋极高却十分严厉的母亲抚养成人。十六岁时逃离就读的文法学校，漫游威尔士；十七岁时在伦敦流浪了一个严冬。早年风餐露宿的经历令他成为一个生活阴暗面的深刻洞察者，也使他罹患终生未愈的胃病和牙痛。为缓解病痛，他按当时流行的疗法服用鸦片酊，成为终生的瘾君子。《瘾君子自白》(Confessions of an English Opium-Eater, 1821)是托马斯·德·昆西最负盛名的著作，作者将服用鸦片成瘾前后的经历和感受，以自白的形式示之于众，具有忏悔录般的真挚坦诚及思想的穿透力。这部真实而玄妙的幻想曲，展现出英国浪漫主义文学的大家风范，给历代读者留下了难以磨灭的印象。

Ann in My Memory

Another person there was, at that time, whom I have since sought to trace, with far deeper earnestness[1], and with far deeper sorrow at my failure. This person was a young woman, and one of the unhappy class who subsist upon[2] the wages of prostitution[3]. I feel no shame, nor have any reason to feel it, in avowing[4], that I was then on familiar and friendly terms with many women in that unfortunate condition. The reader needs neither smile at this avowal, nor frown[5]; for, not to remind my classical readers of the old Latin proverb, "Sine Cerere[6]," etc., it may well be supposed that in the existing state of my purse my connection with such women could not have been an impure one. But the truth is that at no time of my life have I been a person to hold myself polluted by the touch or approach of any creature that wore a human shape. On the contrary, from my very earliest youth, it has been my pride to converse familiarly with all human beings, — man, woman, and child, — that chance might fling in my way: a practice

我记忆中的安

那时候还有另外一个人，我真诚地寻找她，并且为未能找寻到她而感到深深的抱歉。这个人是位年轻的姑娘，她是以卖淫为生的不幸阶层中的一个。坦白讲，我当时正处在落魄生涯中，同很多女性关系都很亲密、友好，我并不以此为耻，我没有理由这样想。读者不必讥笑我的坦白，也不必紧蹙眉头。因为，大可不必提醒读者这句古老的拉丁谚语"没有酒肉，爱情也要渐渐冷却"。可以设想，从我的口袋的落魄程度看，我和这些女性的关系不可能是不纯洁的。但事实上，我一生中从未因接触或接近哪一个衣冠禽兽而使心灵受到污染。与此相反，自我少年时期起，我即能与所有人自如交谈，无论男人、女人，还是孩子，这一点颇令我引以

---

1 earnestness /'ɔːnɪstnɪs/ *n.* 认真，诚挚
2 subsist upon /səb'sɪst/ 活下去，维持生活
3 prostitution /ˌprɒstɪ'tjuːʃn/ *n.* 卖淫
4 in avowing /ə'vauɪŋ/ 坦白讲
5 frown /fraun/ *vi.* 皱眉，表示不满
6 Sine Cerere （拉丁语）意为"没有酒肉，爱情也要渐渐冷却"

which is friendly to the knowledge of human nature, to good feelings, and to that frankness of address which becomes a man who would be thought a philosopher: for a philosopher should not see with the eyes of the poor limitary creature calling himself a man of the world, and filled with narrow and self-regarding prejudices of birth and education, but should look upon himself as a catholic[1] creature, and as standing in an equal relation to high and low, to educated and uneducated, to the guilty and the innocent.

Being myself, at that time, of necessity, a peripatetic[2], or a walker of the streets, I naturally fell in, more frequently, with those female peripatetics who are technically called street-walkers. Many of these women had occasionally taken my part against watchmen who wished to drive me off the steps of houses where I was sitting. But one amongst them, — the one on whose account[3] I have at all introduced this subject, — yet no! let me not class thee[4], oh noble-minded Ann —, with that order of women; — let me find, if it be possible, some gentler name to designate[5] the condition of her to whose bounty[6] and compassion-ministering to my necessities when all the world had forsaken me — I owe it that I am at this time alive. For

自豪。可能是命运将这些人抛掷在我的人生之途，让我与他们相遇。它有助于使我认识人类本性，使我了解什么是美好的情操，使我了解作为一个人（而且公认为是个哲人）的真诚态度。因为一个哲人不应该以那种可怜的、有局限性的自称为世间之人的生物的眼光去观察万物，也不应抱有先天和后天的狭隘利己偏见，而应看待自己为一个能够宽容他人的人，无论地位高低、知识多寡、有罪与否，都应平等视之。

那时候，由于我自己就是一个到处游荡的家伙或是街道闲逛者，自然经常遇到那些被专门称为妓女的闲荡女性。很多这类妇女，偶尔同我联合起来反抗那些不准我坐在房角阶梯上而要赶我走的巡查人员，其中有一个就因为她的缘故，我才撰写关于那个阶层的女性的这篇文章。——不，也并非如此！让我不要把你划入任何等级！哦，品德高尚的安。

---

1 catholic /'kæθlık/　adj.　宽容的，开明的
2 peripatetic /ˌperɪpə'tetɪk/　n.　走来走去的人，游荡的人
3 on one's account　为了某人
4 thee /ðiː/　pron.　you 的古英语写法
5 designate /'dezɪgneɪt/　vt.　把……定名为，称呼
6 bounty /'baʊnti/　n.　慷慨，大方

many weeks, I had walked at nights, with this poor friendless girl, up and down Oxford Street, or had rested with her on steps and under the shelter of porticoe[1]. She could not be so old as myself: she told me, indeed, that she had not completed her sixteenth year. By such questions as my interest about her prompted, I had gradually drawn forth[2] her simple history. Hers was a case of ordinary occurrence (as I have since had reason to think), and one in which, if London beneficence[3] had better adapted its arrangements to meet it, the power of the law might oftener be interposed to protect and to avenge. But the stream of London charity flows in a channel which, though deep and mighty, is yet noiseless and underground; not obvious or readily accessible to poor, houseless wanderers, and it cannot be denied that the outside air and framework of London society is harsh, cruel, and repulsive[4]. In any case, however, I saw that part of her injuries might easily have been redressed; and I urged her often and earnestly to lay her complaint before a magistrate[5]. Friendless as she was, I assured her that she would meet with immediate attention; and that English justice, which was no respecter of persons[6], would speedily and amply avenge her on the brutal

如果可能的话，我还要寻找其他的词汇来赞赏她的仁慈与热情。当我被社会抛弃时，是她解救了我的困窘。我现在能够再生，全都归功于她。多少个星期，我曾经同这个可怜的并没交情的姑娘，每晚游荡在牛津街头，或者和她在门廊台阶上面或隐蔽处所过夜，她的年龄比我要小。她说，还不到十六岁。通过这些了解，我对她逐渐产生兴趣，也就了解到她的简单经历。如果伦敦的慈善机构能够采取适当措施，法律力量能经常插手保护民众，并为民众雪清冤屈，那她的情况不过是一件普通无奇的案件（我从来都是这么想的）。但是，伦敦的慈善河流，尽管深邃而宽广，但都一起悄悄地、秘密地涌泻到阴沟下面。对于那些无家可归的可怜流浪者，他们态度暧昧，全无恻隐之心。不可否认的是，伦敦的外在气氛与体制则是如此严酷、残忍，拒人于千里之外。然而，不论怎样，我所见到的

1　portico /ˈpɔːtɪkəʊ/　n.　门廊，柱廊
2　draw forth　引出，唤出
3　beneficence /bɪˈnefɪsns/　n.　慈善机构
4　repulsive /rɪˈpʌlsɪv/　adj.　排斥的，相斥的
5　magistrate /ˈmædʒɪstrət, -streɪt/　n.　地方法官，治安推事
6　be no respecter of persons　对任何人一视同仁

ruffian[1] who had plundered[2] her little property. She promised me often that she would; but she delayed taking the steps I pointed out, from time to time; for she was timid and dejected to a degree which showed how deeply sorrow had taken hold of her young heart; and perhaps she thought justly that the most upright judge and the most righteous tribunals[3] could do nothing to repair her heaviest wrongs. Something, however, would perhaps have been done; for it had been settled between us, at length[4], — but, unhappily, on the very last time but one that I was ever to see her, — that in a day or two we should speak on her behalf[5]. This little service it was destined, however, that I should never realize.

Meantime, that which she rendered to me, and which was greater than I could ever have repaid her, was this: one night, when we were pacing slowly along Oxford Street, and after a day when I had felt unusually ill and faint, I requested her to turn off with me into Soho Square. Thither we went; and we sat down on the steps of a house, which, to this hour, I never pass without a pang[6] of grief and an inner act of homage[7] to the spirit of that unhappy girl, in memory of the noble act which she there performed. Suddenly, as we sat, I grew much

---

1 ruffian /ˈrʌfiən/ n. 流氓，恶棍
2 plunder /ˈplʌndə(r)/ vt. 抢劫
3 tribunal /traɪˈbjuːnl/ n. 法官
4 at length 最后，终于
5 on one's behalf 为某人
6 pang /pæŋ/ n. 悲痛
7 homage /ˈhɒmɪdʒ/ n. 敬意

这个姑娘所遭受的伤害，总是不难纠正的。所以，我鼓励她经常诚恳地到官吏面前申诉。虽然她的表现很冷漠，但仍会留心这种忠告，这一点我很肯定。我认为，英国的司法机关（对任何人都一视同仁）将会迅速地、广泛地追缉掠夺了她微薄财物的暴徒。她经常答应我，她会去申诉，但对于我为她指出的步骤，却又总是犹豫不决。因为她如此懦弱，如此失望，以致愁苦完全笼罩了她的一颗年轻的心灵；或者，她恰恰考虑到最正直的裁判者、最公正的法官都对她深重的冤屈无计可施。虽然，有些事也许是本可以完成的，我们两人最后已决定一两天内为她的事情就去申诉，但是，不幸的是，自此以后我再也没有见到过她。命中注定，这次微薄的施助竟再也没有实现的机会。

当时，她报答我的比我给予她的更多：一天夜里，我们沿着牛津街散步，整日奔走，使我感到特别疲惫不适，我要她同我转入索荷广场；我们走到那里，坐在一所房子的台阶上，直到现在，我一直怀着悲痛的心情与对这位不幸的姑娘的衷心敬意，纪念她在当

worse. I had been leaning my head against her bosom, and all at once, I sank from her arms and fell backwards on the steps. From the sensations I then had, I felt an inner conviction of the liveliest kind, that without some powerful and reviving stimulus I should either have died on the spot, or should, at least, have sunk to a point of exhaustion from which all re-ascent[1], under my friendless circumstances, would soon have become hopeless. Then it was, at this crisis of my fate, that my poor orphan companion, who had herself met with little but injuries in this world, stretched out a saving hand to me. Uttering[2] a cry of terror, but without a moment's delay, she ran off into Oxford Street, and in less time than could be imagined returned to me with a glass of port-wine and spices, that acted upon my empty stomach (which at that time would have rejected all solid food) with an instantaneous[3] power of restoration[4]; and for this glass the generous girl, without a murmur, paid out of her own humble[5] purse, at a time, be it remembered, when she had scarcely wherewithal[6] to purchase the bare necessaries of life, and when she could have no reason to expect that I should ever be able to reimburse[7] her. Oh, youthful benefactress!

How often, in succeeding years, standing

时所表现的高尚行为。我们正坐着时，我的病情突然加重。我本来头靠在她的胸脯上，却一下子从她的怀抱中跌落，向后倒在台阶上，从我当时的知觉说，我完全相信，如果没有她坚强的扶助，我会死在那个地方，或者，至少由于精疲力竭，在无依无靠中，也毫无恢复健康的希望。在这生死攸关的时刻，就是这位孤苦伶仃、经历坎坷的伙伴向我伸出援助之手。她惊叫了一声，毫无半点迟疑，便跑出牛津街，而又立即带着一杯加有香料的葡萄酒回到我的身边，酒入空肠（这时我已不能进食固体食物），马上显示了起死回生的力量。这杯酒是这位慷慨的姑娘毫不犹豫从她可怜的钱包中掏钱买的——一定要记住啊！她那时几乎买不起生活必需品，而我也无力回报她。啊，多么仁慈的年轻恩人。

在接下来的几年里，我常站立在一些幽僻之地，带着悲伤的心情与深厚的爱意想念

---

1 re-ascent / rɪəˈsent/ *n.* 重新恢复
2 utter/ˈʌtə(r)/ *vt.* 发出（声音等），说，讲，表达
3 instantaneous /ˌɪnstənˈteɪnɪəs/ *adj.* 瞬间的，实时的
4 restoration /restəˈreɪʃn/ *n.* 恢复
5 humble /ˈhʌmbl/ *adj.* 粗糙的，简陋的，这里意味着"没什么钱的"
6 wherewithal /ˈweəwɪðɔːl/ *n.* 必要的资金
7 reimburse /ˌriːɪmˈbɜːs/ *vt.* 偿还

in solitary places, and thinking of thee with grief of heart and perfect love, — how often have I wished that, as in ancient times the curse of a father was believed to have a supernatural power, and to pursue its object with a fatal necessity of self-fulfillment, — even so the benediction[1] of a heart oppressed with gratitude might have a like prerogative[2]; might have power given to it from above to chase, to haunt, to waylay, to overtake, to pursue thee into the central darkness of a London brothel[3], or (if it were possible) into the darkness of the grave, there to awaken thee with an authentic message of peace and forgiveness, and of final reconciliation[4]!

你。在远古洪荒时代，人类祖先的咒语具有超自然的力量，其所追寻的目标命中注定会得以实现。不知多少次，我多么希望充满着感激之情者的祈祷也能具有这样一个同样的特权，也许上天会赋予我一种特别的力量，让我进入伦敦的黑暗中心——妓院——寻觅、逗留、拦截、搜索，去追随你。倘若可能，直至进入坟墓的黑暗深处，在那里，带着平静、宽容以及对人世的和解，唤醒你。

1 benediction /ˌbenɪˈdɪkʃn/ *n.* 祝福
2 prerogative /prɪˈrɒɡətɪv/ *n.* 特权
3 brothel /ˈbrɒθl/ *n.* 妓院
4 reconciliation /ˌrekənsɪliˈeɪʃn/ *n.* 和谐，一致

含英咀华

　　选文内容为作者对一位女性朋友安的怀念。安虽误落风尘，但心地良善，在作者因病垂危之际，是她慷慨解囊，施以援手，倾其菲薄可怜的一点钱为作者买来了一杯葡萄酒，终使作者转危为安。作者行文走笔之处，无不流露出对安的不幸遭遇的同情和对安的不求回报的品德的赞颂。

Ann Beattie
安·贝蒂

安·贝蒂（1947— ），美国80年代著名作家，29岁开始她的创作生涯，笔调清新自然、细腻感人，发表过长篇小说《冬天凄凉的景色》(Chilly Scenes of Winter, 1976)、《就位》（Falling in Place，1980）等，均获成功。

Like Glass

恍如玻璃

In the picture, only the man is looking at the camera. The baby in the chair, out on the lawn, is looking in another direction, not at his father. His father has a grip on a collie[1] — trying, no doubt, to make the dog turn its head toward the lens. The dog looks away, no space separating its snout[2] from the white border.

The collie is dead. The man with a pompadour[3] of curly brown hair and with large, sloping shoulders was alive, the last time I heard. The baby grew up and became my husband, and now is no longer married to me. I am trying to follow his line of vision in the picture.

I have a lot of distinct memories of things that happened while I was married, but lately I've been thinking about two things that are similar, although they have nothing in common[4]. We lived on the top floor of a brownstone. When we decided to separate and I moved out. By then it was winter, and cold leaked in my windows. I had my daughter, and other things, to think about. In the cold, though, walking around the apartment

照片里，只有那个男人在看着相机。草坪上坐在椅子里的婴儿并没有望着他的父亲，而是看着另一边。他的父亲紧紧抓着一只牧羊犬——毫无疑问，他正试图让那条狗看镜头。狗还是看着别处，鼻子就贴着照片的白边。

那只牧羊犬已经死了。那个把棕色卷发往后梳的男人，肩膀宽大倾斜，上次我听人说起他时，他还活着。照片中的婴儿已经长大成人并成了我的丈夫，不过现在我们已经不再是夫妻了。我试图追随他在照片中的目光。

婚后发生的许多事情都历历在目，但是最近，有两件事一直萦绕在我心头，虽然它们之间没有共同之处，但却很相似。我们住在一栋褐色砂石建筑的顶层。我们决定分手时我就搬了出来。那时候已经是冬天了，寒气从窗子钻进屋子里。我想起女儿和其他一些事情。尽管天寒地冻，但当我穿一件多数人们认为足以抵御户

1 collie /ˈkɒli/　*n.*　一种高大聪明长毛的牧羊犬
2 snout /snaʊt/　*n.*　鼻子
3 pompadour /ˈpɒmpədɔː(r), -dʊə(r)/　*n.*　一种往后梳的发型
4 have nothing in common　毫无共同之处

in a sweater most people would have thought thick enough to wear outside, or huddling[1] on the sofa under an old red-and-brown Afghan[2], I would start feeling romantic about my husband.

One afternoon — it was February 13, the day before Valentine's Day — I had a couple of drinks and put on my long green coat with a huge hood that made me look like a monk[3] and went to the window and saw that the snow had melted on the sidewalk: I could get away with wearing my comfortable rubber-soled[4] sandals with thick wool socks. So I went out and stopped at Sheridan Square to buy Hamlet[5] and flipped through[6] until I found what I was looking for. Then I went to our old building and buzzed Larry. He lives in the basement — what is called a garden apartment. He opened the door and unlocked the high black iron gate. Larry was surprised to see me. I acted slightly humbly and apologetic and smiled to let him know that what I was asking was a silly thing: could I stand in his garden for a minute and call out a poem to my husband? Larry laughed. How could my husband hear me, he asked. It was February. There were storm windows[7]. But he let me in, and I walked down his long, narrow hallway, through the back

外寒冷的毛衣在公寓附近散步，或是披着一条旧红棕色的阿富汗毯子蜷缩在沙发上时，对丈夫那种浪漫的情感就会自心头涌起。

一天下午——二月十三号，情人节的前一天——我喝了几杯酒，然后穿上那件让我看上去像个僧人的有个大帽子的绿色长外套，走到窗边，看到人行道上的积雪已经融化了——我穿那双舒服的有厚厚羊毛内里的胶底鞋就不怕了。于是我出门去谢里丹广场买了本《哈姆雷特》快速翻阅起来，直到翻到了我要找的东西。随后，我去了我们原来住的房子，按了拉里的门铃。他住在底搂——那种被人们称为"花园公寓"的房子。他打开房门和高高的黑色大铁门，看见我很吃惊。我举止笨拙地向他道歉，笑着让他知道我要求的不过是件愚蠢的小事：我能在他的花园里站一会给我丈夫念首诗吗？拉里笑着问，我丈夫怎么可能听到。时值寒冬二月，又装着防风雪的护窗。但他还是让我进去了，我走过他狭长的走廊，穿过他当做办公室的后室，来到通往后花园的门前。我推开门，他的那条灰

1　huddle /ˈhʌdl/　vi.　蜷缩
2　Afghan /ˈæfgæn/　n.　一种阿富汗毛毯
3　monk /mʌŋk/　n.　僧人
4　rubber-soled /ˈrʌbəˈsəuld/　adj.　橡胶底的
5　Hamlet　《哈姆雷特》，莎士比亚著名悲剧
6　flip through　（口语中的用法）浏览
7　storm window　遮挡风雪的护窗

room that he used as an office, to the door that led out to the back garden. I pushed open the door, and his gray poodle came yapping up to my ankles.

I picked up a little stone, and threw it at my husband's fourth-floor bedroom window, and hit it—tonk[1]!—on the very first try. Blurrily, I watched the look of puzzlement on Larry's face. My real attention was on my husband's face, when it appeared at the window, full of rage, then wonder. I looked at the torn-out page and recited, liltingly. Ophelia's[2] song: "tomorrow is Saint Valentine's day,/ All in the morning bed time,/ And I a maid at your window,/ To be your Valentine. "

"Are you insane?" Paul called down to me. It was a shout, really, but his voice hung thin in the air. It floated down.

I could smell jasmine[3] when the wind blew. I had put on too much perfume. Even if he did take me in, he'd back off; he'd never let me be his valentine. What he noticed, of course, when he'd come downstairs to lead me out of the garden, seconds later, was the Scotch[4] on my breath.

"This is all wrong," I said, "I only had two Scotches, I just realized when the wind blew that I smell like a flower garden."

色狮子狗叫着扑向我的脚踝。

我捡了一个小石子，朝着五楼我丈夫的卧室扔去，"当"，一击即中！隐约间，我看见了拉里脸上迷惑的表情。我真正的注意力在我丈夫的脸上，他出现在窗前，满脸的愤怒很快变成了迷惑不解。我看着自书中撕下来的那一页，轻快地吟诵起奥菲莉娅的诗句："明天即为情人节，我是个少女，将在清晨起床时，等候于你的窗前，作你的情人。"

"你疯了吗？"保罗冲我吼道。那真的是高声呵斥，但他的声音在空中显得那样单薄，轻轻地飘了下来。

风吹过时我闻到了茉莉花香，我喷了太多的香水。即使他让我进去，也会再把我赶出来。他永远不会让我成为他的情人。几秒钟后他下楼把我领出花园时，注意到的当然是我呼吸中威士忌的酒气。

"这完全是个错误，"我说，"我只喝了两杯威士忌，刚才风吹过我才知道我闻上去像个开满花的园子。"

---

1 tonk /tɒŋk/ n. 拟声词，当
2 Ophelia 莎士比亚剧作《哈姆雷特》中的女主人公
3 jasmine /ˈdʒæzmɪn/ n. 茉莉
4 Scotch /skɒtʃ/ n. 苏格兰威士忌

"You bet it's all wrong," he said, squeezing my hand so hard it almost broke. Then he shook off my hand and walked up the steps, went in and slammed the door behind him. I watched a hairline crack[1] leap across all four panes[2] of glass at the top of the door.

The other thing happened in happier times, when we were visiting my sister, Karin. It was the first time we had met Dan, the man she was engaged to, and we had brought a bottle of champagne. We drank her wine first, and ate her cheese and told stories and heard stories and smoked a joint, and sometime after midnight my husband went to the refrigerator and got out our wine — Spanish champagne, in a black bottle. He pointed the bottle away from him, and we all squinted[3], silently watching. At the same instant that the cork[4] popped, as we were all saying "Hooray!" or "That does it!" — whatever we were saying — we heard glass raining down, and Paul suddenly crouched, and then we looked above him to see hole in the skylight, and through the hole black sky.

I've just told these stories to my daughter, Eliza, who is six. Now she wants me to tell her the point of the two stories — well, I don't know what the point is.

1 hairline crack /'heəlain/ /kræk/　毛发细的裂缝
2 pane /pein/　n.　（窗户或门上的）一块玻璃
3 squint /skwint/　vi.　斜着眼睛看
4 cork /kɔːk/　n.　软木塞

"这当然完全是个错误，"他使劲攥着我的手说着，几乎要把它捏碎了。然后他丢开我的手，上楼了，进了屋，"砰！"的一声关上了门。我看见发丝一样的裂纹出现在门上边的四块玻璃上。

另一件事发生在一个较为快乐的场合，当时我们正在看望我的妹妹凯林。那是我们第一次见到凯林的未婚夫丹，他们已经订婚了，我们带了一瓶香槟酒。我们先是喝她的酒，吃她的奶酪，互相讲故事，还抽着烟。过了午夜的某个时候，我丈夫从冰箱里拿出了我们那瓶装在黑色瓶子里的酒——西班牙香槟。他把瓶口从朝着他自己的方向移开。我们都斜着眼，静静地看着他。与此同时，软木塞跳了出来，我们都叫着"好！"或是"干得漂亮！"不管说了什么，我们听见了玻璃撒落下来的声音，保罗一下子缩成了一团。于是我们抬头向他头上看去，只见天窗上破了个洞，透过那个洞我们看见了漆黑的天空。

我刚把这些故事告诉我六岁的女儿，伊利沙。现在她想让我告诉她，这两件事意味着什么。其实，我也不知道。

I cop out[1], too tried to think, and then tell her another part of the story to distract her: Uncle Dan and Aunt Karin told the superintendent[2] that the hole must have come from something that fell from above. He knew they were lying — nothing was above them — but what could he say?

She watches me digress. She reaches for the cologne on her night table[3] and lifts her long blond hair, and I spray[4] her neck. She takes the bottle and sprays her wrists, rubs them together, holds out her wrists for me to smell. I make a silly face and pretend to be dazed by such a wonderful smell. I strike her hair until she is silent, still moving as if I'm walking through broken glass.

我逃避了这个问题，我已经疲倦到不能思考了。于是我给她讲了故事的另一部分来分散她的注意力：丹姨夫和凯林姨妈跟管理员说，这洞一定是上面掉下来的什么东西砸出来的。他知道他们在说谎——他们上面什么也没有，但他又能说什么呢？

她注意到了我的离题。她伸手去拿放在她床头柜上的古龙水并撩起了金色的长发，我帮她喷了脖子。她接过瓶子喷在自己的手腕上，涂抹均匀，伸出手腕给我闻。我做了个滑稽相，装出为这迷人的香味陶醉的样子。我抚摸她的头发直到她安静下来，但我仿佛依然穿行于碎玻璃之中。

---

1 cop out   逃避
2 superintendent /ˌsuːpərɪnˈtendənt/   *n.* 负责人，管理人
3 night table 床头柜
4 spray /spreɪ/   *vt.* 喷

含英咀华

　　本文中作者回忆了一直萦绕在心头的两件事，一件是与丈夫离婚后的一个情人节，去他的窗下为他念莎士比亚剧中的情诗，希望再次做他的情人，却被他赶走。另一件是离婚前，两人在姐姐家小聚，开香槟时发生的趣事。故事虽平淡无奇，可是却淋漓尽致地表达出作者对前夫的无限思念，和对往昔日子的怀念。作者将玻璃作为题目与线索，无论是有裂纹的玻璃或是破碎的玻璃，作者是想借以表达自己仿佛是在玻璃中游走，心绪模糊迷惘。

Edmund Gosse
埃德蒙·戈斯

埃德蒙·戈斯（1849—1928），英国散文家、评论家，早年在英国博物馆供职，曾任剑桥三一学院英国文学讲师。他首先介绍和翻译易卜生作品，从而闻名于英国文坛。1884至1885年在美国讲学。一战后，埃德蒙长期为《星期日泰晤士报》(Sunday Times)撰稿，每周一篇新书评论。同时积极从事文学翻译，把一些法国作家和画家的作品介绍给英国读者。其代表作《父与子两种气质的研究》（Father and Son: A Study of Two Temperaments, 1907）揭示了宗教信仰和怀疑态度与科学精神和求知态度之间的矛盾，反映出维多利亚时代的特点。他的其他作品还有《图书馆闲话》（Gossip in a Library, 1913）、《亨利克·易卜生传》（Life of Ibsens, 1908）、《十八世纪文学史》（A History of Eighteenth-Century Literature, 1889）等多种。

A Visit to Walt Whitman[1]

When I was in Boston, in the winter of 1884, I received a note from Whitman asking me not to leave America without coming to see him. My first instinct was promptly to decline the invitation. Camden, New Jersey, was a very long way off[2]. But better counsels[3] prevailed[4], curiosity and civility[5] combined to draw me, and I wrote to him that I would come. It would be fatuous[6] to mention all this, if it were not that I particularly wish to bring out the peculiar magic of the old man, acting not on a disciple[7], but on a stiff-necked[8] and forward unbeliever.

To reach Camden, one must arrive at Philadelphia, where I put up on the 2nd of January, 1885, ready to pass over into New Jersey next morning. The distance being considerable, I started early on the 3rd, crossed the broad Delaware River, where blocks of ice bumped and crackled around us, and saw the flat shores of New Jersey expanding in front, raked by the broad morning light. I was put ashore[9] in a crude

惠特曼访问记

1884年冬天，我在波士顿收到惠特曼一封便签，叫我离开美国之前去看看他。我最初的本能反应是婉言谢绝，新泽西的坎姆登离这儿可谓千里迢迢。可踌躇再三，出于礼貌，也出于好奇，我还是写信告之，我将应约前往。如若不是为了展示老人奇特的魅力，它不仅深深影响其追随者，同时也强烈打动了我这个傲岸刚愎、不轻易相信别人的人，我提及这些琐事，未免显得愚蠢狂妄。

去卡姆敦要经过费城。1885年1月2日我抵达费城住下，准备次日上午乘船去新泽西。两地相距甚远，3号一早我就动身了，当船穿越宽阔的德拉沃河时，河面上浮冰碰撞，其声不绝于耳。晨曦微

---

1 Walt Whitman: 沃尔特·惠特曼（1819—1892），美国诗人，著有《草叶集》(Leaves of Grass, 1855)
2 way off 有很大的距离
3 counsel /ˈkaʊnsl/ n. 想法
4 prevail /prɪˈveɪl/ vi. 占了上风
5 civility /səˈvɪləti/ n. 礼貌
6 fatuous /ˈfætjʊəs/ adj. 愚昧的
7 disciple /dɪˈsaɪp(ə)l/ n. 信徒
8 stiff-necked /ˈstɪfˈnekɪd/ adj. 顽固的
9 ashore /əˈʃɔː(r)/ adv. 向岸，上陆地

and apparently uninhabited[1] village, grim[2] with that concentrated ugliness that only an American township in the depth of winter can display. I wandered aimlessly[3] about[4], and was just ready to give all I possessed to be back again in New York, when I discovered that I was opposite No. 328 Mickle Street, and that on a minute[5] brass plate was engraved[6] "W. Whitman". I knocked at this dreary[7] little two-storey tenement house[8], and wondered what was going to happen. A melancholy[9] woman opened the door. But before I could speak, a large figure, hobbling[10] down the stairs, called out in a cheery voice, "Is that my friend?" Suddenly, by I know not what magnetic[11] charm, all wire-drawn[12] literary[13] reservations faded out of being, and one's only sensation was of gratified satisfaction as being the "friend" of this very nice old gentleman.

There was a good deal of greeting on the stairs, and then the host, moving actively, though clumsily[14], and with a stick, advanced to his own dwelling-room[15] on the first storey. The opening

露，普照大地，新泽西平坦的河岸渐渐展现眼前。我在一个小村落下船登岸。这是个稀见人迹的简陋村庄，显出隆冬季节美国小镇惯有的阴森恐怖。我漫无目的地游荡着，正准备用我所有的钱回纽约的时候，我发现自己就在米克大街328号的对面，一块小铜牌上刻着"沃·惠特曼"。我敲了敲这栋冷清矮小的二层公寓楼的大门，想着接下来会发生什么。一位面色忧郁的妇人开了门。可没等我开口，一位高大的身影蹒跚着走下楼来，欢快地叫了出来："是我的朋友吗？"突然间，不知出于何种魔力，我的所有文人顾忌荡然无存，只觉得与这么个和蔼可亲的老人做朋友，真是万分荣幸。

在楼梯上一阵寒暄之后，主人拄着拐棍笨拙但十分精神

1 uninhabited /ˌʌnɪnˈhæbɪtɪd/ adj. 杳无人迹的
2 grim /grɪm/ adj. 阴森可怖的
3 aimlessly /ˈeɪmlɪsli/ adv. 漫无目的地
4 wandered about /ˈwɒndəd/ 游荡
5 minute /ˈmɪnɪt/ adj. 小的
6 engrave /ɪnˈgreɪv/ vt. 刻
7 dreary /ˈdrɪəri/ adj. 冷清的
8 tenement house /ˈtenəmənt/ 公寓
9 melancholy /ˈmelənkəli/ adj. 忧郁的
10 hobble /ˈhɒbl/ vi. 蹒跚
11 magnetic /mægˈnetɪk/ adj. 有磁性的
12 wire-drawn adj. 琐碎拘泥的
13 literary /ˈlɪtərəri/ n. 文人
14 clumsily /ˈklʌmzili/ adv. 笨拙地
15 dwelling-room /ˈdwelɪŋruːm/ 居室

impression was, as the closing one would be, of extreme simplicity[1]. But all the room, and the old man himself, clean in the highest degree, raised to the nth power of stainlessness[2], scoured[3] and scrubbed[4] to such a pitch that dirt seemed defied for all remaining time. Whitman, in particular, the whole man sandwhite with spotlessness, like a deal[5] table that has grown old under the scrubbing-brush[6].

Whitman sat down in the one chair with a small poker[7] in his hand and spent much of his leisure in feeding and irritating the stove. I cleared some papers away from off a box and sat opposite to him. When he was not actively engaged upon the stove his steady attention was fixed upon his visitors, and I had a perfect opportunity of forming a mental picture of him. He sat with a very curious pose of the head thrown backward, as if resting it one vertebra[8] lower down the spinal column[9] than other people do, and thus tilting[10] his face a little upwards. With his head so poised and the whole man fixed in contemplation of the interlocutor he seemed to pass into a state of absolute passivity, waiting for remarks or incidents, the glassy eyes

地朝他一楼的卧室走去。第一印象和离开时的印象一样，都是极为朴素的。但整个房间和惠特曼本人却十分干净，简直到了一尘不染的n次方，似乎擦洗到灰尘这辈子再也不敢沾染的地步。尤其是惠特曼，全身上下沙白得一尘不染，像一张因刷洗而变旧了的松木桌子。

惠特曼坐在唯一一把椅子里，手中拿着一个小拨火棍，大部分空闲的时间都在拨弄炉火，给它加柴。我理清了一个箱子上的一些纸张，坐在他对面。当他不是一个劲地拨弄炉火时，他专注的注意力就都集中在来访者身上。我正好利用这个机会在脑中仔细勾画他的形象。他的坐姿十分特别，头向后仰，和别人比起来，头好像靠在脊柱更低一节的脊椎骨上，因此脸微微上翘。他的头就这样仰着，整个人凝神地注视着我，他似乎进入了一种完全被动的状态，在等着我发话

---

1 simplicity /sɪmˈplɪsəti/ *n.* 朴素
2 stainlessness /ˈsteɪnlɪsnɪs/ *n.* 无尘
3 scour /ˈskaʊə(r)/ *vi.* 冲洗
4 scrub /skrʌb/ *vi.* 擦净
5 deal /diːl/ *n.* 松木
6 scrubbing-brush /ˈskrʌbɪŋˈbrʌʃ/ *n.* 硬毛刷
7 poker /ˈpəʊkə(r)/ *n.* 拨火棍
8 vertebra /ˈvɜːtɪbrə/ *n.* 脊椎骨
9 spinal column /ˈspaɪnl ˈkɒləm/ 脊柱
10 tilt /tɪlt/ *vi.* 翘起

half closed, the large knotted hands spread out before him. So he would remain, immovable for a quarter of an hour at a time; even the action of speech betraying no movement, the lips hidden under a cascade[1] of beard.

His talk was elemental[2], like his writings. It had none of the usual ornaments[3] or irritants of conversation. It welled out naturally, or stopped; it was innocent of every species of rhetoric[4] or epigram[5]. It was the perfectly simple utterance[6] of unaffected[7] urbanity[8]. So, I imagine, an Oriental sage[9] would talk, in a low uniform tone, without any excitement or haste, without emphasis, in a land where time and flurry[10] were unknown. Whitman sat there with his great head tilted back, smiling serenely[11], and he talked about himself. He mentioned his poverty, which was patent[12], and his paralysis[13];those were the two burdens beneath which he crouched, like Issachar[14], he seemed to be quite at home[15] with both of them, and scarcely heeded[16] them. I think

或出现什么小插曲，两支没有神采的眼睛半闭着，一双骨节突起的大手伸在胸前。他每次竟能这样一动不动地坐上一刻钟，即使说话也纹丝不动，因为他浓密的胡子遮住了双唇。

他的谈话像他的作品一样原始、自然。没有华丽辞藻，也没有狂言妄语。它自然地涌出或是停顿，不浮夸修饰，也不引经据典。那是一种毫无造作的儒雅风范。我想象在那片不知道时间和匆忙为何物的土地上的东方哲圣，就是这样谈话的，音调始终低沉，不温不火，不抑扬也不顿挫。惠特曼坐在那儿，朝后仰着大脑袋，安详地笑着，谈论关于自己的事情。他提到了他的贫困（这是大家都知道的事）和他的瘫痪。它们成了压垮他的两个重

---

1 cascade /kæs'keɪd/ n. 小瀑布
2 elemental /ˌeli'mentl/ adj. 原始的，自然的
3 ornament /'ɔ:nəmənt/ n. 矫饰
4 rhetoric /'retərɪk/ n. 浮夸的修辞
5 epigram /'epɪgræm/ n. 警句
6 utterance /'ʌtərəns/ n. 说话，讲话
7 unaffected /ˌʌnə'fektɪd/ adj. 不造作的
8 urbanity /ɔ:'bænɪti/ n. 文雅
9 sage /seɪdʒ/ n. 圣贤
10 flurry /'flʌri/ n. 慌张
11 serenely /sɪ'ri:nli/ adv. 安详地
12 patent /'pætnt, 'peɪtnt/ adj. 公开的，明白的
13 paralysis /pə'rælɪsɪs/ n. 瘫痪
14 Issachar: 以萨迦，《圣经》中人物，他父亲雅各在埃及临终前为他祝福"以萨迦是头强壮的驴，卧在羊圈之间。他看安息之处为佳，看那地为美，便低肩背重，成为服苦的仆人"
15 at home 习以为常的
16 heed /hi:d/ vt. 在意

I asked leave to move my box, for the light began to pour in at the great uncurtained window; and then Whitman said that someone had promised him a gift of curtains, but he was not eager for[1] them, he thought they "kept our some of the light". Light and air, that was all he wanted; and through the winter he sat there patiently waiting for the air and light of summer, when he would hobble out again and bask[2] his body in a shallow[3] creek he knew "back of Camden". Meanwhile he waited with infinite patience, uncomplaining, thinking about the sand, and the thin hot layer of water over it, in that shy New Jersey creek. And he winked away in silence, while I thought of the Indian poet Valmiki, when, in a trance[4] of voluptuous[5] abstraction[6], he sat under the fig-tree[7] and was slowly eaten of ants.

It might be supposed, and I think that even admirers have said, that Whitman had no humour. But that seemed to me not quite correct. No boisterous[8] humour, truly, but a gentle sort of sly fun, something like Tennyson's[9], he certainly showed. For example, he told me of some tribute[10] from India, and added, with a twinkling smile, "You see, I 'sound my barbaric[11]

1 eager for 渴望
2 bask /bɑːsk/ vt. 晒太阳
3 shallow /'ʃæləu/ adj. 浅的
4 trance /trɑːns/ n. 恍惚
5 voluptuous /və'lʌptʃuəs/ adj. 欢欣的
6 abstraction /æb'strækʃn/ n. 遐思
7 fig-tree /fig triː/ 无花果树
8 boisterous /'bɔistərəs/ adj. 嬉闹的，喧嚷的
9 Alfred Tennyson 阿尔弗莱德·丁尼生，英国维多利亚时代诗人
10 tribute /'tribjuːt/ n. 颂辞
11 barbaric /bɑː'bærik/ adj. 野蛮的

负，就像是以萨迦，他似乎对两者都习以为常了，几乎不在意它们。我想我当时要求挪动一下箱子，因为阳光开始从没挂窗帘的窗子上倾泻进来。惠特曼便说曾经有人许诺送他窗帘，但他并不急着想要，他认为窗帘会"遮住一些阳光"。阳光和空气，是他想要的一切。整个冬天他都耐心地坐在那儿，等待夏天的空气和阳光。到了夏季，他又可以蹒跚而出，全身沉浸在他熟悉的"坎姆登后院"一处浅浅的小溪里晒太阳。他就是这样，想着偏僻的新泽西小溪的沙滩和沙石上浅浅的温水，耐心地、毫无怨言地等待着。他静静地出神，那情景不禁令我想起印度诗人瓦尔米基，端坐在无花果树下，沉浸于浑然忘我的遐思之中，全然不觉周身布满了蚂蚁。

或许可以假定，我想就连那些他的崇拜者也说过，惠特曼并不幽默。但我并不认同此种说法。是的，虽然没有哗众取宠的幽默，却不乏狡黠的风趣，有点丁尼生的风格。比如说，当提到印度诗坛对他的赞誉时，他狡黠地笑着补充说，"你看，我'仰天长啸，响彻世界屋脊。'"但这是很少见的：大多数时候，他似乎沉浸于往昔朦胧的田园生活

yawp[1] over the roofs of the world[2].'" But this was rare: mostly he seemed dwelling in a vague[3] pastoral[4] past life, the lovely days when he was young, and went about with "the boys" in the sun. He read me many things; a new "poem", intoning[5] the long irregular lines of it not very distinctly; and a preface to some new edition. All this has left, I confess, a dim impression, swallowed up in the serene[6] self-unconsciousness, the sweet, dignified urbanity[7], the feline[8] immobility.

As I passed from the little house and stood in dull, deserted Mickle Street once more, my heart was full of affection for this beautiful old man, who had just said in his calm accents, "Good-bye, my friend!" I felt that the experience of the day was embalmed[9] by something that a great poet had written long ago, but I could not find what it was till we started once more to cross the frosty Delaware; then it came to me, and I knew that when Shelley[10] spoke of

Peace within and calm around,
And that content, surpassing wealth,
The sage in meditation found,
And walk'd with inward glory crown'd.

中，他年轻的美好岁月里，在阳光下和"小伙子们"东奔西跑。他给我读了很多东西，包括一首句子长短不一的新"诗"和某个新版的序言，朗读的语调已不很清晰。我承认，所有这些都只给我留下了模糊的印象，都淹没于他那平和坦然、温文儒雅、庄严宁静的风范中。

我穿过小屋，再一次站在沉闷荒凉的米克大街上时，心中充满了对这位优雅的老人的仰慕之情，他刚用平静的语调对我说："再见，我的朋友！"我感觉这一天的经历已经铭记于一位伟大诗人很久以前的作品中，但是直到再次动身渡过风霜严寒的特拉华河时，我才想起来这篇诗作出自雪莱之口：

内心平和四周静谧，
这种满足财富难敌，
贤哲在沉思中洞彻，
满怀荣耀悠悠前行。

1 yawp /jɔːp/ n. 叫喊
2 You see, …world. 惠特曼的名句，出自《我自己的歌》
3 vague /veɪg/ adj. 朦胧的
4 pastoral /ˈpɑːstərəl/ adj. 田园的
5 intone /ɪnˈtəʊn/ vt. 吟咏
6 serene /sɪˈriːn/ adj. 平静的
7 urbanity /əːˈbænɪti/ n. 文雅
8 feline /ˈfiːlaɪn/ adj. 猫一样的
9 embalm /ɪmˈbɑːm/ vt. 铭记
10 Shelley 雪莱（1792—1882），英国浪漫主义诗人

He had been prophesying[1] of Walt Whitman, nor shall I ever read those lines again without thinking of the old rhapsodist[2] in his empty room, glorified by patience and philosophy.

雪莱简直就是预言了惠特曼，以后再读这些诗句，我一定会情不自禁地想起陋室里的这位老诗人，他的坚韧与达观令他熠熠生辉。

1 prophesy /ˈprɒfəsaɪ/ vt. 预言
2 rhapsodist /ˈræpsədɪst/ n. 游吟诗人

含英咀华

本文是埃德蒙与惠特曼唯一一次见面的回忆录，作者的笔触细腻独到，人物描写十分饱满，让我们如见其人、如闻其声，仿佛切身体会到了伟大诗人惠特曼的儒雅风范。

Maxwell Maltz

麦克斯韦·莫尔茨

麦克斯韦·莫尔茨是美国世界闻名的整形外科医生。他的励志书《心理控制术》(*Psycho-Cybernetics*)自1960年出版以来已销售了几千万册，在这本书中他介绍了用更积极的心态面对人生，养成成功的习惯，培养真正的心理健康与快乐的方法。

The Most Unforgettable Character I've Met

一位最难忘的人物

When I got to my office that morning Mrs. Julia Cremona was waiting for me. Though many years had passed since I had seen her, I recognized her immediately.

"The doctor says Benny's only got a few days left," She said. "Benny wants you to come see him. Maybe you can — today?"

To hear that Benuto Cremona was nearing the end of the long, colorful road that had been his life was a shock. Heart trouble, his wife told me, as we drove downtown.

The mystery, she went on, was why Benny wanted to see me, for he knew I was a plastic surgeon[1], not a heart man. I, too, wondered why he had asked for me. Simply to say good-bye to one of "his boys"? But there would be so many to say good-bye to!

As we drove to New York's tenement[2] district my mind went back to the years when I had known Benuto Cremona. He had a one-chair barbershop[3] in the neighborhood where I was born and brought up. In that brawling[4] neighborhood, a tough tenement jungle, a

那天早上我到诊所的时候，朱丽亚·克莱莫纳夫人正在那等着我。虽然多年不见，我一眼就认出了她。

"医生说班尼没几天好活了，"她说，"班尼想让你去看看他。今天行吗？"

听到一生多姿多彩的本努特·克莱莫纳将要去世了，真是晴天霹雳。克莱莫纳夫人在我们开往市区的路上告诉我，他得的是心脏病。

她又说，她不明白为什么班尼想见我，因为他明明知道我是整形外科医生，不是心脏病专家。我也不明白他为什么要找我。是为了向我这位老朋友道别吗？那他要道别的人可太多了！

在我们驱车前往纽约的经济公寓区的路上，我不禁想起了当年认识本努特·克莱莫纳时的情形。在我出生、成长的那块地方，他开了一间只有一个座位的理发店。那一片喧嚣嘈杂的街区，到处都建着杂乱无章的廉价公寓房，那里的住户来自不同的

1　plastic surgeon /'plæstɪk/ /'sɜːdʒən/　整形外科医生
2　tenement /'tenəmənt/　n.　贫民窟，群租房
3　barbershop /'bɑːbəʃɒp/　n.　理发店
4　brawl /brɔːl/　vi.　争吵，怒骂

cockpit[1] of different nationalities and customs and feuds[2], Mr. Cremona's barbershop was an oasis of beauty and good will.

He scorned the usual barbershop trappings[3] of those days: the racy[4] calendars, the crime-and-sex gazettes[5]. "The way I'm working," he would say, "I'm always looking down at heads. A man's got to have something to look up to, too." When we youngsters had our hair cut we gazed on reproductions of the Mona Lisa[6], the Winged Victory[7], the Adoration of the Magi[8], Michelangelo's[9] David[10]. We learned who Dante[11] was, and Shakespeare[12], by hearing for the first time the splendid, gleaming lines of poetry.

Mr. Cremona was a round butter-ball of a man with an enormous, flowing black mustache, and he acted out everything he told us. He was versatile[13] with his scissors. You came into the shop shaggy and frayed[14]; you went out feeling handsome and respectable, newly aware of the wide, wonderful,

民族，习俗各异，矛盾不断。然而，克莱莫纳先生的理发店却像是沙漠里的一块绿洲，是一个充满美好和善意的去处。

那时候的理发店里常悬挂着庸俗的招贴画，比如猥亵的挂历、刊登有犯罪和色情绯闻的报纸，他对此嗤之以鼻。他总是说，"我给人理发，总是低头看着顾客的脑袋。但一个人也要抬头来看些东西。"我们这些年轻人去理发时，会盯着看一些名画的复制品，如《蒙娜丽莎》、《胜利女神》、《三王朝拜图》、米开朗琪罗的《大卫》等。我们在他那儿初次听到美妙瑰丽的诗句之后，才知道了但丁和莎士比亚。

克莱莫纳先生是个大腹便便、圆滚滚的胖子，蓄着浓黑的胡须，说起话来比手画脚，一把剪刀妙用无穷。我们

1 cockpit /ˈkɒkpɪt/ n. 频繁发生争吵的地方
2 feud /fjuːd/ n. 不和，争执
3 trapping /træpɪŋ/ n. 装饰，摆设
4 racy /ˈreɪsɪ/ adj. 猥亵的
5 gazette /ɡəˈzet/ n. 报纸
6 Mona Lisa 蒙娜丽莎，达·芬奇所画的著名人像画
7 Winged Victory 希腊胜利女神像，1836年在爱琴海东北部萨莫色雷斯岛上发现
8 Adoration of the Magi 三王朝拜，法布里亚诺1423年所作，被公认为德国哥特式风格绘画的杰作之一
9 Michelangelo 米开朗琪罗，意大利文艺复兴时期成就卓著的科学家、艺术家
10 David 米开朗琪罗的传世雕塑
11 Dante 但丁，意大利诗人，著有《神曲》（Divina Commedia）等
12 Shakespeare 莎士比亚，英国剧作家、诗人，有37部戏剧，154首十四行诗和两首长诗
13 versatile /ˈvɜːsətaɪl/ adj. 多才多艺的，多面手的
14 frayed /freɪd/ adj. 不整洁的

challenging world, so inspiring were the stories you had heard of great men, great deeds, and great works of art.

If you didn't have the 15 cents for haircut and obviously were in desperate need of one, Mr. Cremona beckoned[1] you in off the street, cut your hair and then said, "Tell your mama to send me down some of her raisin cookies, next time she makes them. But wait — that's worth more than 15 cents! We got to give you your change." The tiny cash register would go bing! — and there was dime[2] sparkling gaily in your hand.

He really couldn't afford such largesse[3], considering his own growing family. Nor could he afford to adopt Donny, a six-year-old whose parents were killed when an antiquated[4] tenement collapsed one night, but Mr. Cremona couldn't bear to see the sad-eyed, pale little boy marched off to an institution.

The realm[5] of Mr. Cremona's special love was the youth on our block. But this plump little man with the bald head and huge mustache was also keenly conscious of the woes[6] and troubles of our elders. I don't know how many ancient feuds he settled, how many bewildered newcomers he introduced gently and patiently to

进他的理发店时总蓬头垢面，出来时不仅觉得自己漂亮有气派了，还初次知道了还有一个广大辽阔、奇妙无穷、充满挑战的世界。我们听到了伟大人物、丰功伟业、艺坛杰作的故事，都如此振奋人心。

如果哪家孩子没有一角五分钱理发，而头发又到了非理不可的程度，克莱莫纳先生就会把他从街上招呼进去，给他理发，然后说："告诉你妈妈，下次做葡萄干松饼的时候，带一点儿来给我。啊，等一等，那可不只一角五分！我们找钱给你。"小钱柜叮的一声响——孩子手里多了一枚亮晶晶的一角硬币。

照他一家人口增多的情形来说，他实在没能力这样大方。他也没有余力收养六岁的东尼，东尼的父母在一天夜里因破旧的公寓倒塌而丧生，而克莱莫纳先生实在不忍心看这个脸色苍白的孩子眼泪汪汪地到孤儿院去。

克莱莫纳先生对我们这里的小孩子固然尤其爱护，但是这位秃顶大胡子的矮胖子，对大人的困苦也很关切。我不知道他化解了多少冤仇，指导了多少新来的移民，他们初到

1 beckon /'bekən/ *vt.* 招手，召唤
2 dime /daɪm/ *n.* 美国一角硬币
3 largesse /lɑːˈdʒes/ *n.* 慷慨
4 antiquated /ˈæntɪkweɪtɪd/ *adj.* 陈旧的
5 realm /relm/ *n.* 领域
6 woe /wəʊ/ *n.* 悲哀

the customs of this strange new land.

Now that I was going to see Mr. Cremona for the last time, I thought how much I owed him — he who had given so many of us our first taste of beauty, who had told so many of us that poverty and the slums[1] need not stand in out way if we aimed high[2] enough. As I drove into the old neighborhood I blamed bitterly for not having returned long ago to show him that I hadn't forgotten him. There were so many changes here — great new apartment houses with lawns and trees around them; hideous[3] old eyesores[4] removed; broad new playgrounds. I realized that much of this was due to him, for he had always fought for green things and space for children to play, and more than one of "his boys" had grown up to have a hand in the rehabilitation[5] of the neighborhood.

When his wife took me into the bedroom, I saw that Mr. Cremona had changed, too — he had grown very thin and his face had the pallor[6] of porcelain[7]. Only the dark merry eyes and the huge flowing mustache were the same.

He pushed himself up a little in the bed. I couldn't say anything just then; I just held his hand.

1 **slum** /slʌm/ *n.* 贫穷
2 **aim high** 胸怀大志
3 **hideous** /ˈhɪdɪəs/ *adj.* 丑陋的，讨厌的
4 **eyesore** /ˈaɪsɔː/ *n.* 丑陋的东西，眼中钉，此处指 "旧日的破建筑等"
5 **rehabilitation** /ˌriːəˌbɪlɪˈteɪʃn/ *n.* 改善，兴建
6 **pallor** /ˈpælə(r)/ *n.* 因疾病而脸色苍白
7 **porcelain** /ˈpɔːsəlɪn/ *n.* 瓷器

这陌生的地方，他温和而又耐心地教他们适应这里的风俗习惯。

现在我就要见克莱莫纳先生最后一面了，我想自己应该感谢他的地方实在太多。他让我们许多孩子第一次领略到美。他告诉我们，一个人只要胸怀大志，贫穷和贫民窟也无法阻止他。车子开进了旧日的街区，我深深自责，为什么不早早回来，让他知道我并没有忘记他。这里的变化非常大——有许多新的公寓大楼，周围有草地和树木；丑陋的破房子被拆除了；还新建了好几个宽阔的运动场。我知道有许多变化都应该归功于克莱莫纳先生，因为他一直在要求植草种树，为儿童争取游乐场地，而且他的 "老朋友" 有些已经长大成人，为这一带的建设出了力。

他的太太带我进了卧室，我发现克莱莫纳先生也变了。他变得瘦骨嶙峋，脸像瓷器一样白。只有乌黑欢快的眼睛和浓密飘散的胡须还和原来一样。

他在床上稍稍撑起身来。我一时说不出话，只是握着他的手。

"Maxie," Mr. Cremona said, "you're this kind of doctor who can take scars off people?" I nodded. "Maybe you'll think I've gone foolish in the head, but in Sicily when I was a young man I was very wicked, very wild. I had a fight with someone, with knives, and I cut him up bad. He cut me in one place, and it left a scar. Maxie" — he leaned closer — "pretty soon now I'm going to see the good Lord. He can see through anything, and I don't want Him to see me with something I'm ashamed of. Will you take that scar off?"

He lifted up a corner of the great mustache. "See the mark on the lip and cheek?"

I stared at him. That, then, was the secret of the mustache — grown to cover a scar! "How long is it since you looked at it, Mr. Cremona?" I asked.

"A long time. Why, Maxie?"

"Because it looks as if the Lord's been taking care of it for you." And I brought a hand mirror and showed him.

It cannot be denied that in old age the skin becomes fragile and contracts, erasing and concealing old marks, but I prefer to believe that all through the years, with each of Mr. Cremona's acts of compassion and kindness, the scar was made smaller, bit by bit, until at last none of it was left at all.

"麦克斯，"克莱莫纳先生说，"你是能把人们身上伤疤去掉的医生对吧？"我点点头。"或许你会认为我头脑不清醒了，但是我年轻时在西西里，我特别坏，特别疯。我和人打架，动了刀子，我狠狠地给了他几刀。他也戳了我一刀，留下了一个伤疤。麦克斯"——他又凑近些——"很快我就要去见上帝了。他什么都看得清清楚楚，我不想让他看到我的疤，因为我觉得羞耻。你能帮我把这伤疤去掉吗？"

他扯起大胡子的一角，"看到了吧，在嘴唇和脸上？"

我仔细地看了看。原来这就是他胡子的秘密——用来遮住伤疤！"克莱莫纳先生，你上次看它是什么时候？"我问道。

"很久了。怎么了，麦克斯？"

"因为上帝好像已经帮你把它处理掉了。"我递给他一面镜子，好让他看清楚。

无可否认，老年人皮肤虚弱收缩，旧疤会无形中消失。但是我宁愿相信，这么多年来，克莱莫纳先生做了这么多关爱同情别人的好事，刀疤跟着一点一点越变越小，终于不留丝毫痕迹。

含英咀华

　　从文章来看，作者具有良好的心态，并告知读者也要积极面对人生。文中所写到的这位克莱莫纳先生无疑是他的启蒙老师。克莱莫纳让作者第一次感受到美好的事物，并竭尽一生帮助别人，爱护孩子们，这对作者产生了很大的影响。

Arthur Gordon
亚瑟·戈登

亚瑟·戈登(1912—2002)，美国作家、杂志撰稿人，曾任《读者文摘》（Reader's Digest）、《好主妇》（Good Housekeeping）、《妇女家庭杂志》（Ladies Home Journal）、《大都会》（Cosmopolitan）等杂志的专栏作家。

The Stranger Who Taught Magic

教魔法的陌生人

That July morning, I remember, was like any other, calm and opalescent[1] before the heat of the fierce summer sun. I was 13; sunburned, shaggy-haired, a little aloof[2], and solitary[3]. In winter I had to put on shoes and go to school like everyone else. But summers I lived by the sea, and my mind was empty and wild and free.

On this particular morning, I had tied my rowboat[4] to the pilings[5] of an old dock[6] upriver from our village. There, sometimes, the striped sheepshead[7] lurked[8] in the still, green water. I was crouched, motionless as a stone, when a voice spoke suddenly above my head: "Canst thou draw out leviathan with a hook or his tongue with a cord which thou lettest down[9]?"

I looked up, startled, into a lean[10], pale face and a pair of the most remarkable eyes I had ever seen. It wasn't a question of color; I'm

我记得那是七月里一个无异于往日的早晨，盛夏的燥热还未降临，一切宁静明亮。我那时十三岁，皮肤晒得黝黑，头发凌乱，有点孤僻，也有点孤独。冬天里，我必须得和别的孩子一样穿上鞋子去上学。但在夏天里，由于住在海边，我可以了无牵挂，随意遐想，自由自在。

这天早晨，我把小船拴在村庄上游一个旧码头的木桩上。有时候，那里平静碧绿的河水中可以看见带条纹的红鲈时隐时现。我一动不动，蹲在河边，忽然听到有人在头顶说："你能用鱼钩钓上龙吗？能用绳子压下他的舌头吗？"

我一惊，抬起头来，看见了一张消瘦苍白的脸和一双我生平见过的最不同寻常的眼睛。不是眼睛的颜色特殊；我现在已经想不起这双眼睛的颜色了，而是目光中所包含的丰富的情感：温暖、幽默、关怀、机警。还有"深邃"，我觉得用这个词描绘他的目光最

1 **opalescent** /ˌəupəˈlesnt/ *adj.* 乳白色的
2 **aloof** /əˈluːf/ *adj.* 孤僻的
3 **solitary** /ˈsɒlətri/ *adj.* 孤独的
4 **rowboat** /ˈrəubəut/ *n.* 小船
5 **piling** /ˈpaɪlɪŋ/ *n.* 木桩
6 **dock** /dɒk/ *n.* 码头
7 **sheepshead** /ˈʃiːpʃed/ *n.* 红鲈鱼
8 **lurk** /lɜːk/ *vi.* 忽隐忽现
9 **Canst thou draw out leviathan with a hook or his tongue with a cord which thou lettest down?** 圣经中的一段话：你能用鱼钩钓上龙吗？能用绳子压下他的舌头吗？canst=can；thou=you；leviathan，圣经中象征邪恶的海中怪兽
10 **lean** /liːn/ *adj.* 消瘦的

not sure, now, what color they were. It was a combination of things: warmth, humor, interest, alertness. Intensity—that's the word, I guess—and, underlying it all, a curious kind of mocking sadness.

He saw how taken aback[1] I was. "Sorry," he said. "It's a bit early in the morning for the Book of Job[2], isn't it?" he nodded at the two or three fish in the boat. "Think you could teach me how to catch those?"

Ordinarily, I was wary of[3] strangers, but anyone interested in fishing was hardly a stranger. I nodded, and he climbed down into the boat. "Perhaps we should introduce ourselves," he said. "But then again, perhaps not. You're a boy willing to teach. I'm a teacher willing to learn. That's introduction enough. I'll call you 'Boy', and you call me 'Sir'."

Such talk sounded strange in my world of sun and salt water. But there was something so magnetic about the man and so disarming[4] about his smile, which I didn't care.

I handed him a hand line[5] and showed him how to bait[6] his hooks with fiddler crabs[7]. He kept losing baits[8], because he could not recognize a sheepshead's stealthy tug, but he seemed

恰当不过了，隐匿于深邃之中的还有一种难以形容的睥睨尘世的忧郁。

他看出我的吃惊。"对不起，"他说。"大清早念《约伯记》未免太早了一点，是不是？"他看见船里有两三条鱼，点点头。"你可以教我钓鱼吧？"

通常我对陌生人存有戒心，但是对钓鱼有兴趣的人就不能视之为陌生人了。我点点头，他爬下船来。"也许我们应该彼此介绍一下，"他说。"不过话又说回来，也许不必。你是个愿意教人的孩子。我是个愿意学习的老师。这样介绍就够了。我喊你'小朋友'、你就喊我'先生'吧。"

在我的阳光与海水的世界里，这样的话听起来很奇怪。但是这个人有不可抗拒的魔力，他的笑让人轻松释然，因此我就不在意了。

我递给他一根手钓线，告诉他怎样把招潮蟹串在钩上作饵。但他的饵总是白白地被吃了，因为红鲈轻轻吞饵时，他察觉不出；然而钓不到鱼，他好像也满不在乎。他告诉我他在码头后面租了套旧房子。

---

1 take aback 惊吓
2 Book of Job 圣经《约伯记》，旧约中讲述约伯向神诉苦以及神的回答的篇章
3 be wary /ˈweəri/ of 提防
4 disarming /dɪsˈɑːmɪŋ/ adj. 使人放松的
5 hand line 手钓线
6 bait /beɪt/ vt. 把饵装上
7 fiddler crab /ˈfɪdlə(r) /kræb/ 招潮蟹
8 bait /beɪt/ n. 饵

content not to catch anything. He told me he had rented one of the weathered bungalows[1] behind the dock. "I needed to hide for a while," he said. "Not from the police or anything like that. Just from friends and relatives. So don't tell anyone you've found me, will you?"

I was tempted to ask where he was from; there was crispness in the way he spoke that was very different from the soft Georgia[2] accents I was accustomed to. But I didn't. He had said he was a teacher, though, and so I asked what he taught.

"In the school catalogue[3] they call it English," he said. "But I like to think of it as a course in magic — in the mystery and magic of words. Are you fond of words?"

I said that I had never thought much about them. I also pointed out that the tide was ebbing[4], that the current was too strong for more fishing, and that in any case it was time for breakfast.

"Of course," he said, pulling in his line. "I'm a little forgetful about such things these days." He eased himself back onto the dock with a little grimace[5], as if the effort cost him something. "Will you be back on the river later?"

I said that I would probably go casting for shrimp at low tide[6].

"我得避一避，"他说。"不是躲避警察或是诸如此类的什么。只是避亲戚朋友。所以别告诉别人你看到我了，好不好？"

我很想问问他是哪里人。他的语调清脆，和我听惯了的柔软的佐治亚音很不一样。不过我没有问。既然他说过他是老师，那我就问他教的是什么。

"学校的课程表上，他们称之为英文，"他说。"不过我把它看做一门魔术课，专门研究文字的奥妙和魔力。你喜欢文字吗？"

我告诉他，我从来没怎么留心过文字。我还提醒说，潮水已经退了，水流太急，不宜再钓鱼。何况到了吃早饭的时候了。

"当然，"他说，收起了他的钓线。"最近我对这些事有点健忘。"他皱着眉，爬上码头，似乎有些费力。"一会儿你还会回到河边吗？"

我告诉他，我可能会在退潮的时候来捉虾。

"顺便来我这儿吧，"他

---

1 bungalow /ˈbʌŋgələʊ/ *n.* 平房
2 Georgia /ˈdʒɔːdʒə/ 美国南部佐治亚州
3 catalogue /ˈkætəlɒg/ *n.* 课程表
4 ebb /eb/ *vi.* 退
5 grimace /ˈgrɪməs, grɪˈmeɪs/ *n.* 皱眉
6 at low tide 退潮的时候

"Stop by[1]," he said. "We'll talk about words for a while, and then perhaps you can show me how to catch shrimp."

So began a most unlikely friendship, because I did go back. To this day, I'm not sure why. Perhaps it was because, for the first time, I had met an adult on terms that were in balance. In the realm of words and ideas, he might be the teacher. But in my own small universe of winds and tides and sea creatures, the wisdom belonged to me.

Almost every day after that, we'd go wherever the sea gods or my whim[2] decreed[3]. Sometimes up the silver creeks, where the terrapin[4] skittered down the banks and the great blue herons[5] stood like statues. Sometimes along the ocean dunes[6], fringed[7] with graceful sea oats[8], where by night the great sea turtles crawled and by day the wild goats browsed. I showed him where the mullet[9] swirled and where the flounder[10] lay in cunning[11] camouflage[12]. I learned that he was incapable of much exertion: even pulling up the anchor seemed to exhaust

说。"我们可以讨论一会儿文字，然后也许你可以教我怎么捉虾。"

我果真再去找他了，一段最意想不到的友谊就这样开始了。直到今天，我还不明白是什么理由。也许是因为我第一次结识了一个感情上与我平起平坐的成年人。在文字和思想方面他固然是老师。但是风向、潮汐、蟹龟鱼虾是我的小天地，在这方面他得向我请教。

此后，我们几乎每天都在一起，听任风向潮汐的安排，或者依我一时的高兴，随处遨游。有时去银波闪烁的海湾，看水龟轻快地窜下堤岸，看大蓝鹭如雕像般站立着。有时徜徉在海边沙丘之间，沙丘周围长着婀娜多姿的海燕麦，晚上大海龟在此爬来爬去，白天野山羊则在此啃食。我指给他看，鲻鱼在什么地方回旋，比目鱼在什么地方巧妙地伪装躲藏。我发觉他不能过分操劳，甚至连起锚都会把他累得精疲力竭。不过他从不抱怨，一直滔滔不绝地讲个不停。

1 stop by   顺便访问
2 whim /wɪm/   *n.*   一时兴起
3 decree /dɪˈkriː/   *vi.*   改变
4 terrapin /ˈterəpɪn/   *n.*   乌龟
5 heron /ˈherən/   *n.*   苍鹭
6 dune /djuːn/   *n.*   沙丘
7 fringe /frɪndʒ/   *vi.*   布满……的边缘
8 oat /əut/   *n.*   燕麦
9 mullet /ˈmʌlɪt/   *n.*   鲻鱼
10 flounder /ˈflaundə(r)/   *n.*   比目鱼
11 cunning /ˈkʌnɪŋ/   *adj.*   巧妙的
12 camouflage /ˈkæməflɑːʒ/   *n.*   伪装

him. But he never complained. And, all the time, talk flowed from him like a river.

Much of it I have forgotten now, but perhaps something deep inside me did. In any case, I listened.

I listened, too, when he read from the books he sometimes brought: Kipling[1], Conan Doyle[2], Tennyson's Idylls of the King[3]. Often he would stop and repeat a phrase or a line that pleased him.

But the magic that he taught was not confined to words; he had a way of generating in me an excitement about things I had always taken for granted. He might point to a bank of clouds. "What do you see there? Colors? That's not enough. Look for towers and drawbridges[4]. Look for dragons and griffins[5] and strange and wonderful beasts."

Or he might pick up an angry, claw-brandishing[6] blue crab, holding it cautiously by the back flippers as I had taught him. "Pretend you're this crab," he'd say. "What do you see through those stalk-like eyes? What do you feel with those complicated legs? What goes on in your tiny brain? Try it for just five seconds. Stop being a boy. Be a crab!" And I would stare in

1 **Kipling** 吉卜林（1865—1936），英国作家，1907年诺贝尔文学奖获得者
2 **Conan Doyle** 柯南道尔（1859—1930），英国医师、小说家、推理小说家，创造了私人侦探福尔摩斯的形象
3 **Idylls of the King** 《亚瑟王之歌》，一卷共十二篇叙事诗，讲述的是亚瑟王和他的骑士们的传说
4 **drawbridge** /ˈdrɔːbrɪdʒ/ n. 吊桥
5 **griffin** /ˈɡrɪfɪn/ n. 希腊神话中鹰头狮身有翅的怪兽
6 **brandish** /ˈbrændɪʃ/ vt. 挥舞

他讲的话我现在多半已经忘记，不过在我内心深处的有些话也许是难以忘怀的。无论如何，他讲话时我都在听着。

有时候他带些书念给我听，我也静静地听着。像吉卜林、柯南道尔、丁尼生的《亚瑟王之歌》他都念过，如果他欣赏其中的某一警句或某一行，常常会停下来再念一遍。

不过，他教的魔法并不限于文字。对一些我一向认为毫不稀奇的东西，他也有办法激起我的兴趣。他指着一片云，问："你看见了什么？看见五颜六色吗？这不够。要找尖塔、吊桥，要找云龙、飞狮，要找千奇百怪的野兽。"

或者，他会抓起一只张螯舞爪的怒蟹，照我教他的办法，小心翼翼地抓住后脚。"设想一下你就是这只蟹吧，"他说："用麦秆似的眼睛，你看到了什么？用乱七八糟的脚，你碰到了什么？你的小脑袋里想到了什么？试试看，只要五秒钟就行了。不要把自己当成男孩，把自己当成蟹！"于是我会新奇地盯着那只狂怒的螃蟹，本来心安理得的内心，受这个怪念头的影响，发生了动摇。

amazement at the furious creature, feeling my comfortable identity lurch[1] and sway under the impact of the idea.

So the days went by. Our excursions became less frequent because he tired so easily. He brought two chairs down to the dock and some books, but he didn't read much. He seemed content to watch me as I fished, or the circling gulls, or the slow river coiling[2] past.

A sudden shadow fell across my life when my parents told me I was going to camp for two weeks. On the dock that afternoon I asked my friend if he would be there when I got back. "I hope so," he said gently.

But he wasn't. I remember standing on the sun-warmed planking[3] of the old dock, staring at the shuttered bungalow and feeling a hollow sense of finality and loss. I ran to Jackson's grocery store — where everyone knew everything —and asked where the school-teacher had gone.

"He was sick, real sick," Mrs. Jackson replies. "Doc phoned his relatives to come get him. He left something for you — he figured you'd be asking after him."

She handed me a book. It was a slender[4] volume of verse, Flame and Shadow, by someone I had never heard of: Sara Teasdale[5]. The corner

---

1 lurch /lɔːtʃ/ vi. 动摇
2 coil /kɔɪl/ vi. 盘绕
3 planking /ˈplæŋkɪŋ/ n. 木板
4 slender /ˈslendə(r)/ adj. 薄的
5 Sara Teasdale: 沙拉·蒂斯代尔（1884—1933），美国诗人

日子就这样过去了，我们出游的次数越来越少，因为他动不动就累了。他搬两把椅子到码头，带几本书，但却不怎么看。他看我钓鱼、看海鸥盘旋在天际、看缓缓的河水蜿蜒而去，似乎就觉得满足了。

当父母亲要我去夏令营待两个星期的时候，我的生活突然蒙上了一层阴影。那天下午在码头上，我问我的朋友，等我回来时，他会不会还在这里。"希望我还在，"他温和地回答道。

但是他不在了。我还记得，我站在旧码头上被太阳晒热的木板上，盯着那栋门窗紧闭的房子，旧日难寻，我不由感到怅然若失。我跑去杰克逊的杂货店——那里的人消息最灵通——去问那位老师去哪儿了。

"他病了，病得厉害，"杰克逊太太说。"医生打电话给他亲戚来把他接回去了。他有点东西留给你——他知道你会来找他。"

她递给我一本书。是一本薄薄的诗集《火焰与阴影》，作者是我从来没听说过的沙拉·蒂斯代尔。有一页书角是折着的，上面有一首诗的旁边标了个铅笔画的星号。我至今

of one page was turned down, and there was a penciled star by one of the poems. I still have the book, with that poem, "On the Dunes[1]."

If there is any life when death is over,

There tawny[2] beaches will know much of me,

I shall come back, as constant and as changeful,

As the unchanging, many-colored sea.

If life was small, if it has made me scornful,

Forgive me; I shall straighten like a flame

In the great calm of death, and if you want me

Stand on the sea-ward dunes and call my name.

Well, I have never stood on the dunes and called his names. For one thing, I never knew it; for another, I'd be too self-conscious. And there are long stretches[3] when I forget all about him. But sometimes — when the music or the magic in a phrase makes my skin tingle[4], or when I pick up an angry blue crab, or when I see a dragon in the flaming sky — sometimes I remember.

保存着这本书，那首诗的名字叫《沙丘上》。

人死了以后假如还有生命，

这褐色海滩会理解我的心意。

我将重来，如大海般永恒而多姿，

不变的是大海的绚丽。

生命太贫乏我固然要抱怨，

请不要见怪；死亡是如此平静安宁，

我将如火焰升腾，如果你要找我，

请站上向海沙丘，呼唤我名。

我一直没有站在山丘上喊他的名字。一来，我根本不知道他的名字；另外，我也怕难为情。有很长时间我把他忘得一干二净。但有些时候，偶尔听到一句话的音韵或魅力使我兴奋时，当我抓起一只张牙舞爪的青蟹或在璀璨的天空看见一条龙时，我就会情不自禁地想起他。

---

1 **dune** /'dju:n/ *n.* 沙丘
2 **tawny** /'tɔ:ni/ *adj.* 褐色的
3 **stretch** /stretʃ/ *n.* 一段时间
4 **tingle** /'tɪŋgl/ *vi.* 兴奋，激动

含英咀华

　　该篇美文为作者对小时候一段忘年之交的回忆。文中那位已在弥留之际的老先生，用自己最后的时光把作者引入了文学诗赋的境地，让他感受到了以前未曾留意过的美好事物。作者虽然连这位老人的名字也不知道，但却从他那永远学会了享受文学、热爱生活，学会了施展快乐的魔法。

感时伤世

Augustine Birrell
奥古斯丁·比勒尔

奥古斯丁·比勒尔（1850—1933），英国散文家、政治家、律师及学者。早年为律师并任伦敦大学法律教授。从政后曾担任教育大臣和爱尔兰事务大臣。1916年因都柏林复活节骚乱而退出政界。文学创作以散文名世。此外，他还写过夏洛蒂·勃朗特和威廉·哈兹里特等人的传记。散文集有《附论》（*Obiter Dicta, 1884*）和《附论二集》（*More Obiter Dicta, 1887*）等。文章优美雅致，富于个性而又情真意切。

Book-Buying

The most distinguished of living Englishmen who, great as he is in many directions, is perhaps inherently[1] more a man of letters than anything else, has been overheard mournfully to declare that there were more booksellers' shops in his native town sixty years ago, when he was a boy in it, than are to-day to be found within its boundaries. And yet the place "all unabashed[2]" now boasts its bookless self a city!

Mr. Gladstone[3] was, of course, referring to secondhand bookshops. Neither he nor any other sensible man puts himself out about new books. When a new book is published, read an old one, was the advice of a sound though surly[4] critic. It is one of the boasts of letters to have glorified[5] the term "second-hand", which other crafts[6] have "soiled to all ignoble[7] use[8]". But why it has been able to do this is obvious. All the best books are necessarily second-hand. The writers of to-day need not grumble. Let them "bide a wee[9]". If their books are worth anything, they, too, one

购书

在世的英国人中最有声望的一位，尽管他在许多方面十分伟大，也许他的天赋更多地表现为他是一位文人。有人无意间听说，他很忧伤地称，六十年前，他的故乡有许多书店，那时他还是个孩子，现在今不如昔了，方圆之内找不到几家书店。然而现在这个不见书本的地方居然"恬不知耻"地称自己为一座城市！

当然，这位格莱斯顿先生指的是旧书店。不论他还是其他明智的人，都不会把心思放在新书上。一本新书出版的时候，先读旧书，这是一位头脑好而脾气坏的批评家的忠告。赞颂"二手货"乃是文人的吹嘘之举，而在其他行业它"已被滥用，名声扫地"。但这样做的原因却是显而易见的。一切佳作必然都是"二手货"。

1　inherently /ɪnˈhɪərəntli/　adv.　天性地，固有地
2　unabashed /ˌʌnəˈbæʃt/　adj.　不害羞的，满不在乎的，厚脸皮的
3　Gladstone　William Ewart Gladstone: (1809—1898)，英国政治家，于1868年—1894年间四度任英国首相
4　surly /ˈsɜːli/　adj.　脾气坏的，乖戾的，粗鲁的，不友好的
5　glorified /ˈɡlɔːrɪfaɪd/　adj.　美其名曰的
6　craft /krɑːft/　n.　行业，职业
7　ignoble /ɪɡˈnəʊbl/　adj.　卑鄙的，不光彩的，可耻的
8　soiled to all ignoble use: 出自丁尼生《悼念诗》，原诗为 "soil'd with all ignorable use"
9　bide a wee: 忍耐一下，出自瓦尔特·斯哥特《老死》，原句为 " 'Bide a wee, bid a wee,' said Cuddie"

day will be second-hand. If their books are not worth anything there are ancient trades still in full operation amongst us — the pastry cooks[1] and the trunk makers — who must have paper.

But is there any substance in the plaint that nobody now buys books, meaning thereby secondhand books? The late[2] Mark Pattison[3], who had 16,000 volumes, and whose lightest word has therefore weight, once stated that he had been informed, and verily believed, that there were men of his own University of Oxford who, being in uncontrolled possession of annual incomes of not less than £500, thought they were doing the thing handsomely if they expended £50 a year upon their libraries. But we are not bound to[4] believe this unless we like. There was a touch of morosity[5] about the late Rector[6] of Lincoln which led him to take gloomy views of men, particularly Oxford men.

No doubt arguments a priori[7] may readily be found to support the contention[8] that the habit of book-buying is on the decline. I confess to knowing one or two men, not Oxford men either, but Cambridge men (and the passion of Cambridge for literature is a byword[9]), who,

当今的作家不必愤然不平。且让他们"忍耐一下"吧。如果他们的书真有什么价值的话，有朝一日也会变成"二手货"；如果他们的书毫无价值的话，也还有些古老的行当盛行于我们中间，如糕点师和箱子工，他们总要用纸张。

但是，目前没有人买书，指的是买二手书籍。这种哀叹有没有道理呢？已故的马克·帕蒂森生前藏书一万六千册，所以他的片言只语也是有分量的。他曾经明言，有人告诉他，他也深信不疑，在他读书的牛津大学，有的人每年可以任意支配的收入不下五百镑，但他们认为，如果一年花费五十镑用于购书，就算出手大方了。这数字信与不信取决于我们自己。不久前离世的林肯学院院长曾流露出几分忧郁之色，以致他对人们，尤其是牛津的学人们抱以悲观之态。

购书的习惯日渐消减，这

---

1 pastry cook /'peɪstri/ 糕点工
2 late /leɪt/ *adj.* 已故的
3 Mark Pattison (1813—1884)，英国作家与牧师，曾担任英国牛津大学林肯学院的教区长，以传记著称
4 be bound to: 一定要……
5 morosity /mə'rɒsɪti/ *n.* 阴郁
6 rector /'rektə(r)/ *n.* 院长
7 a priori /ˌeɪ praɪ'ɔːraɪ/ *adj.* 推理的
8 contention /kən'tenʃn/ *n.* 观点，论点
9 byword /'baɪwɜːd/ *n.* 笑柄

on the plea of[1] being pressed with business, or because they were going to a funeral, have passed a bookshop in a strange town without so much as stepping inside, just to see whether the fellow had "anything". But painful as facts of this sort necessarily are, any damaging inference[2] we might feel disposed[3] to draw from them is dispelled by a comparison of price-lists. Compare a bookseller's catalogue of 1862 with one of the present year, and your pessimism[4] is washed away by the tears which unrestrainedly[5] flow as you see what bonnes[6] fortunes you have lost. A young book-buyer might well turn out upon Primrose Hill[7] and bemoan his youth, after comparing old catalogues with new.

Nothing but American competition, grumble some old stagers.

Well! Why not? This new battle for the books is a free fight, not a private one, and Columbia has "joined in". Lower prices are not to be looked for. The book-buyer of 1900 will be glad to buy at to-day's prices. I take pleasure in thinking he will not be able to do so. Good finds grow scarcer and scarcer. True it is that but a few short weeks ago I picked up (such is the happy phrase, most apt to describe what was indeed a

种论点的依据可以现成地经由推测性找到。我承认认识一两位人士，虽不是牛津大学的，而是剑桥大学的（剑桥酷爱文学成了笑柄），在外地的某座城市，二位以公务缠身为由或称因为要去参加丧礼，路过一书店而不入，不肯走进去"看看这家伙有点什么好书"。不过尽管这类情况必然令人心寒，只要比较一下价目单，那么我们可能不由自主地从上述情况得出的任何诽谤性推论都会消除。姑且拿1862年的书商目录跟今年的比较一下，你的悲观态度便会被泪水冲洗掉，因为当你眼看着自己失去了多少好运道，便会泪流不止。新旧目录比较之后，一个年轻的购书者很可能会登上普林姆罗斯山，叹息自己的青春消逝。

还不都是美国竞争的结果，经年老者们愤愤地嚷道。

嗯！竞争何妨？这场新的书战是自由的斗争，不是私人的角逐，就连哥伦比亚也"参与"了。不必去找更低的价钱。1900年的书商也会乐意出今天的价钱购买。一想到这是他无法办到的，我便欣然自得，因为发现好书越来越少。这是真实的情况，不过前几周

---

1 on the plea of　以……为借口
2 inference /ˈɪnfərəns/　n.　推论
3 disposed /dɪˈspəʊzd/　adj.　不由自主的，倾向……的
4 pessimism /ˈpesɪmɪzəm/　n.　悲观
5 unrestrainedly /ˌʌnrɪˈstreɪndli/　adv.　无限制地
6 bon /bɒn/　adj.　好的，相当于 good
7 Primrose Hill: 位于伦敦北部的一座小山，在其山顶可以俯瞰整个伦敦市中心。出自威廉·布莱克《耶路撒冷》

"street casualty[1]") a copy of the original edition of Endymion[2] (Keats's[3] poem — O subscriber to Mudie's[4]! — not Lod Beaconsfield's[5] novel) for the easy equivalent[6] of half-a-crown[7] — but then that was one of my lucky days. The enormous increase of booksellers' catalogues and their wide circulation amongst the trade has already produced a hateful uniformity of prices. Go where you will it is all the same to the odd sixpence[8]. Time was when you could map out the country for yourself with some hopefulness of plunder[9]. There were districts where the Elizabethan dramatists were but slenderly[10] protected. A raid into the "bonnie North Countrie" sent you home again cheered with chap-books and weighted with old pamphlets of curious interests; whilst the West of England seldom failed to yield a crop of[11] novels. I remember getting a complete set of the Brontë[12] books in the original issues at Torquay, I may say, for nothing. Those days are over.

The man who has a library of his own

1 casualty /'kaʒʊəlti/ n. 意外
2 Endymion 济慈的长诗《恩底弥翁》，描写了月亮女神 与凡人恩底弥翁相爱的故事
3 Keats 济慈，英国诗人
4 Mudie 查尔斯·艾德华·马迪，创建马迪外租图书馆
5 Lod Beaconsfield 比斯菲尔德勋爵，迪斯勒利首相，著有小说《恩底弥瓮》
6 equivalent /ɪ'kwɪvələnt/ n. 等价物
7 crown /kraʊn/ n. 克朗，欧洲某些国家货币
8 sixpence /'sɪkspəns/ n. 六便士
9 plunder /'plʌndə(r)/ n. 战利品
10 slenderly /'slendə(r)li/ adv. 微薄地，不足地
11 a crop of 一大堆
12 Brontë 勃朗特姐妹，有夏洛蒂、艾米利、安妮三姐妹，均为英国小说家。她们的作品在首次出版时都引起了很大的轰动，并被认为是英国文学中的传世佳作

我拾到（这可是个巧妙的字眼，用来形容所谓"街头意外发现"最贴切不过了）一本初版的《恩底弥翁》（是济慈的诗作——哦！是马迪外租图书馆读者的！而不是比肯斯菲尔德勋爵的小说），只花了相当于半克朗的价钱——那却是我走运的日子。书商的目录层出不穷，在行业内又大量流通，产生的结果就是书价的统一，这无疑是令人憎恶的。不管你走到哪儿，书价总是六便士左右。可以标明地点走遍全国而满怀希望捞取一把的光景已是一去不复返了。还有那么一些地区，伊丽莎白时代的戏剧家算是得到些微小的保护。去"宁静的北方乡村"劫掠一番，那些年代久远的袖珍歌谣集和稀奇古怪的小册子会让你喜不自胜地满载而归。而英格兰的西部往往可以发现大量小说。我记得在托魁弄到一整套初版的勃朗特作品集，可以说是没花几分钱。这样的日子再也不会有了。

拥有自己的藏书的人，可以客观地自我反思，并且完全有理由相信自己的存在。除他之外，任何一个人都不可能做到像他这样，拥有这么庞大纷杂的藏书。假如他有哪一方面和原本真实的他不一样的话，那么，现在的藏书就不可能存在。因此，暮色降

collection is able to contemplate[1] himself objectively, and is justified in believing in his own existence. No other man but he would have made precisely such a combination as his. Had he been in any single respect different from what he is, his library, as it exists, never would have existed. Therefore, surely he may exclaim, as in the gloaming[2] he contemplates the backs of his loved ones, "They are mine, and I am theirs."

But the eternal[3] note of sadness will find its way even through the keyhole of a library. You turn some familiar page, of Shakespeare it may be, and his "infinite variety[4]", his "multitudinous[5] mind", suggests some new thought, and as you are wondering over it you think of Lycidas, your friend, and promise yourself the pleasure of having his opinion of your discovery the very next time when by the fire you two "help waste a sullen day[6]". Or it is, perhaps, some quainter[7], tenderer fancy that engages your solitary attention.

"Death bursts amongst them like a shell,
And strews them over half the town."

They will form new combinations, lighten other men's toil[8], and soothe another's sorrow. Fool that I was to call anything mine!

临十分，当他想到自己心爱的图书的书脊时，他当然可以大声地说一句"它们属于我，我也属于它们"。

但是即使透过书楼的锁眼，永恒的忧伤也会流露进去。翻到熟悉的某一页，比如莎士比亚，他的"千变万化"，他的"汪洋襟怀"，会带给你一些新启发，正当你想要弄明白它们的时候，你想到了朋友利西达斯，于是你下定决心给自己找点乐子：下一次坐在炉火边和他"消磨沉闷的一天"时，要听听他对你的发现的看法。又或许，它是种古怪的、温馨的幻想，占据着你孤独的思想。

"死亡犹如贝壳从中冒了出来，

在城里散落得遍地皆是。"

他们将形成新的组合，减轻他人的辛劳，抚慰另一个人的悲伤。把任何东西说成是自己的是多么的愚蠢！

---

1 contemplate /'kɒntempleɪt/ *vt.* 沉思，思考
2 gloaming /'gləʊmɪŋ/ *n.* 朦胧的暮色
3 eternal /ɪ'tɜːnl/ *adj.* 永恒的
4 infinite variety /'ɪnfɪnɪt/ /və'raɪəti/ 出自《安东尼与克利佩特拉》
5 multitudinous /ˌmʌltɪ'tjuːdɪnəs/ *adj.* 由许多部分组成的，种类繁多的
6 help waste a sullen day 出自弥尔顿的十四行诗，原句为 "Where shall we sometimes meet, and by the fire Help waste a sudden day"
7 quaint /kweɪnt/ *adj.* 古雅的，奇特而有趣的
8 toil /tɔɪl/ *n.* 辛劳

含英咀华

在这篇文章中，作者认为有阅读价值的书都是旧书，因为时间会为大家去伪存真，而现在的城市中却再也觅不到旧书店的影子。作者感叹往昔买到便宜的传世佳作，与朋友切磋解闷的好时光已一去不返。

William Hazlitt
威廉·赫兹利特

威廉·赫兹利特（1778—1830），英国文学家，在文学观点上属于浪漫主义流派。作品包括文学、戏剧、艺术方面的评论，文学讲稿及随笔散文。他在论著方面的主要作品有《莎士比亚戏剧中的人物》（*Characters of Shakespeare's Plays, 1817*）、《伊丽莎白时代的戏剧文学》（*Lectures on the Literature of the Age of Elizabeth, 1817*）等；随笔集主要有《燕谈录》(*Table Talk*)等。其随笔散文在英国文学中享有很高的声誉，成就与查尔斯·兰姆相当。作品风格奔放、开朗。

On the Feeling of Immortality in Youth

The change, from the commencement[1] to the close of life, appears like a fable, after it has taken place; how should we treat it otherwise than as a chimera[2] before it has come to pass? There are some things that happened so long ago, places or persons we have formerly seen, of which such dim[3] traces remain, we hardly know whether it was sleeping or waking they occurred; they are like dreams within the dream of life, a mist, a film before the eye of memory, which, as we try to recall them more distinctly, elude[4] our notice altogether. It is but natural that the lone interval that we thus look back upon, should have appeared long and endless in prospect.

There are others so distinct and fresh, they seem but of yesterday — their very vividness might be deemed a pledge[5] of their permanence. Then, however far back our impressions may go, we find others still older (for our years are multiplied in youth); descriptions of scenes that we had read, and spoke of the race[6] of heroes that were no more; — what wonder that, seeing

1 commencement /kəˈmensmənt/ n. 开始
2 chimera /kaɪˈmɪərə/ n. 妄想
3 dim /dɪm/ adj. 模糊的
4 elude /ɪˈluːd/ vt. 躲避
5 pledge /pledʒ/ n. 保证
6 race /reɪs/ n. 家族

论青春的不朽之感

生命的演变，从开始到结束，一经发生，就好似一个神话，在它尚未发生之前，除了妄想，我们还能把它当做什么呢？有一些很久之前发生的事，我们从前去过的地方、见过的人，只留下如此模糊的印象，我们已经记不得它们发生时自己是梦是醒。它们犹如梦幻的人生之梦，又像记忆之眼前方的一层薄雾，我们越想把它们记得清楚，它们越是逃得无影无踪。我们回忆那寂寥的生命历程尚且如此，在前瞻之时，它自然就显得漫长无尽。

另一些事则又如此历历在目、记忆犹新，像是昨日之事——它们的栩栩如生也许能作为它们能持久的保证。于是，无论追溯多么久远的记忆，我们都能发现更加古老的事情（因为我们青年时候的岁月是要成倍计算的）。我们仰望已逝伟人的英明，他们声望不灭、流芳千古；我们对这些如此心仪神往，那我们不知不

this long line of being pictured in our minds, and reviving as it were in us, we should give ourselves in voluntary credit for an indeterminate[1] period of existence?

In the Cathedral at Peterborough[2] there is a monument to Mary, Queen of Scots, at which I used to gaze when a boy, while the events of the period, all that had happened since, passed in review before me. If all this mass of feeling and imagination could be crowded into a moment's compass[3], what might not the whole of life be supposed to contain? We are heirs[4] of the past; we count upon the future as our natural reversion[5].

Besides, there are some of our early impressions so exquisitely tempered, it appears that they must always last — nothing can add to or take away from their sweetness and purity — the first breath of spring, the hyacinth[6] dipped in the dew, the mild luster[7] of the evening-star, the rainbow after a storm — while we have the full enjoyment of these, we must be young; and what can ever alter us in this respect? Truth, friendship, love, books, are also proofs against the canker[8] of time; and while we live, but for them, we can never grow old.

觉地相信自己可以无限期地活下去也就不足为奇了。

在彼得堡大教堂里，有一座苏格兰女王玛丽的纪念碑，我年少时常去瞻仰，而那个时代的事件，自那以后发生的一切，就会一一在我眼前展现。如果，这样一个瞬间可以容纳如此丰富的感情与联想，那么人的一生还有什么无法囊括呢？我们是过去的后嗣，自然也期望未来是自己的遗产。

此外，一些我们早年的印象是如此精妙，它们理当永世长存，它们的甜美与纯净，增一分则嫌多，减一分则嫌少——春天的第一丝迹象，沐浴着露珠的风信子，夜晚柔美的星光，暴风雨之后的彩虹——只要我们还能对此全心领略，我们就还年轻，如此这般，又有什么能改变我们呢？真诚、友谊、爱情、书籍，也是抵抗时间侵袭的证据。只要我们为它们而活，我们就永远不会变老。

1 indeterminate /ˌɪndɪˈtɜːmɪnət/ *adj.* 无限期的
2 the Cathedral at Peterborough 彼得堡大教堂
3 compass /ˈkʌmpəs/ *n.* 范围，界限
4 heir /eə(r)/ *n.* 后嗣
5 reversion /rɪˈvɜːʃn/ *n.* 继承
6 hyacinth /ˈhaɪəsɪnθ/ *n.* 风信子，一种植物
7 luster /ˈlʌstə(r)/ *n.* 光泽
8 canker /ˈkæŋkə(r)/ *n.* 侵袭

We take out a new lease[1] of existence from the objects on which we set our affections, and become abstracted[2], impassive, immortal in them. We cannot conceive how certain sentiments[3] should ever decay or grow cold in our breasts; and, consequently, to maintain them in their first youthful glow[4] and vigour, the flame of life must continue to burn as bright as ever, or rather, they are the fuel that feed the sacred lamp, that kindle "the purple light of love", and spread a golden cloud around our heads!

"That time is past with all its giddy[5] raptures[6]." Since the future was barred to my progress, I have turned for consolation[7] to the past, gathering up the fragments of my early recollections, and putting them into a form that might live.

As we advance in life, we acquire a keener sense of the value of time. Nothing else, indeed, seems of any consequence; and we become misers[8] in this respect. We try to arrest its few last tottering[9] steps, and to make it linger on the brink of the grave. We can never leave off wondering how that which has ever been should cease to be, and would still live on, that we may wonder at our own shadow, and when "all the life of life is

1 lease /liːs/   n.   一段时间
2 abstracted /əbˈstræktɪd/   adj.   出神的
3 sentiment /ˈsentɪmənt/   n.   情感
4 glow /gləʊ/   n.   光辉
5 giddy /ˈgɪdi/   adj.   意乱情迷的
6 rapture /ˈræptʃə/   n.   狂欢
7 consolation /ˌkɒnsəˈleɪʃn/   n.   慰藉
8 miser /ˈmaɪzə(r)/   n.   吝啬鬼
9 tottering /ˈtɒtərɪŋ/   adj.   蹒跚的

自我们寄托感情的事物之中，我们获得了一段新生，变得心驰神往、浑然不觉，从中得到永生。我们无法理解这种情感会在我们的胸膛中衰退、冷却。于是，为了让它们保持着最初青春的光辉与朝气，生命之火必须一如既往地灿烂燃烧，抑或说，这情感是生命这盏神圣之灯的燃料，点燃起"灿烂的爱情火焰"，在我们头顶展现一片金色的云霞！

"那意乱情迷、欣喜狂欢的日子一去不返了。"既然向未来行进的路已被阻断，我只好转过去寻求慰藉，集起早时回忆的零星碎片，把它们记述下来以便使其得以延续。

我们年岁渐长，对光阴之可贵也日益敏感。别的一切都全不计较，对于时光我们却变成了吝啬鬼。竭力抓住生命最后这蹒跚的几步，让它在坟墓的边沿多停留些时日。我们总不休追索昨日之物何以不复存在，又何以长存下去，我们也许还会对自己的影子疑惑不解，待到"生命的活力都飘然而去"，我们就沉涸于对往昔的追忆之中。与之相伴的是对既得事物机械的执著，以及对眼前所见的不信任和迷惘空虚

flown", dwell on[1] the retrospect[2] of the past. This is accompanied by a mechanical tenaciousness[3] of whatever we possess, by distrust and a sense of fallacious[4] hollowness in all we see. Instead of the full, pulpy[5] feeling of youth, every thing is flat and insipid[6]. The world is a painted witch that puts us off with false shows and tempting appearances. The ease, the jocund[7] gaiety, the unsuspecting security of youth are fled: nor can we, without flying in the face of[8] common sense,

From the last dregs[9] of life, hope to receive

What its first sprightly runnings could not give.

之感。没有了青年时的充实、饱满，取而代之的每件事情都平淡无奇，索然无味。世界像一个画中的女巫，用虚假的外观和诱人的面貌来迷惑我们。轻松怡然、畅快欢乐和对永恒青春的信念已全然消逝。我们也不能公然违抗常规，而做到，

在生命的余烬中，希冀得到

生机勃发的青春无法给予的东西。

1 **dwell on** /dwel/ 细想
2 **retrospect** /ˈretrəspekt/ *n.* 回顾
3 **tenaciousness** /tɪˈneɪʃəsnɪs/ *n.* 执著
4 **fallacious** /fəˈleɪʃəs/ *adj.* 迷惘的
5 **pulpy** /ˈpʌlpi/ *adj.* 饱满的
6 **insipid** /ɪnˈsɪpɪd/ *adj.* 索然无味的
7 **jocund** /ˈdʒɒkənd, ˈdʒəʊk-/ *adj.* 快乐的
8 **fly in the face of** 公然违抗
9 **dreg** /dreg/ *n.* 余烬

含英咀华

在文中，作者纵谈人生，并由此引开，向读者倾诉了自己对人生、宇宙、历史、文学、艺术等的看法，全文汪洋恣肆、一泄无余。选段侧重于论及对往昔的回忆与颂扬美好青春的部分。

Hilaire Belloc
希拉里·贝洛克

希拉里·贝洛克（1870—1953），英国诗人、散文家，20世纪早期英国最为多产的作家之一，有现代英国散文大师之称。他虔诚信奉天主教，经常抨击时弊。他的许多作品为有感而发，并在其中流露出自己的怀旧情绪。著述包括小说、儿童文学、历史研究、随笔、诗文、评论、传记、游记等多种，代表作有《罗马之路》(The Path to Rome, 1902)、《欧洲和信仰》（Europe and the faith, 1920)、《犹太人》（The Jews, 1922）等。

Our Inheritance

How noble is our inheritance. The more one thinks of it the more suffused[1] with pleasure one's mind becomes; for the inheritance of a man living in this country is not one of this sort or of that sort, but of all sorts. It is, indeed, a necessary condition for the enjoyment of that inheritance that a man should be free, and we have really so muddled[2] things that very many men in England are not free, for they have either to suffer a gross denial[3] of mere opportunity — I mean they cannot even leave their town for any distance — or they are so persecuted[4] by the insecurity of their lives that they have no room for looking at the world, but if an Englishman is free what an inheritance he has to enjoy!

It is the fashion of great nations to insist upon some part of their inheritance, their military memories, or their letters, or their religion, or some other thing. But in modern Europe, as it seems to me, three or four of the great nations can play upon many such titles to joy as upon an instrument. For a man in Italy, or England, or France, or Spain, if he is weary of the manifold[5] literature of his own country, can

我们的遗产

我们的遗产何其壮观。愈是想象，心里就越加愉快。生活在这个国度的人们拥有的遗产丰饶富足，应有尽有。而要享受这份遗产，人们就必须是自由的，但我们着实把事情弄糟了，以至于很多的英国人并不自由，他们要么就是完全连起码的机会都没有——我指他们甚至不能离开村庄走远一点——或是他们受生活的不安全感所迫而无暇顾及外面的世界。但是，如果一个英国人是自由的，他可以享受多棒的一份遗产啊！

盛国强邦强调他们的遗产，诸如战事、文学、宗教，或者其他事物是一种风尚。但在我看来，当代欧洲的三四个强国都可以对这些话题高谈阔论，享受其中，犹如演奏乐器一般。一个意大利、英国、法国或西班牙人，如果他谈腻了本国丰富多彩的文学，可以

---

1 **suffused** /səˈfjuːzt/ *adj.* 充溢着的
2 **muddle** /ˈmʌdl/ *vt.* 弄糟
3 **denial** /dɪˈnaɪəl/ *n.* 拒绝
4 **persecute** /ˈpɔːsɪkjuːt/ *vt.* 迫害
5 **manifold** /ˈmænɪfəʊld/ *adj.* 丰富多彩的

turn to its endurance[1] under arms, or if he is weary of these military things, or thinks the too continued contemplation[2] of them hurtful to the State, he can consider the great minds which his nation has produced, and which give glory to his nation not so much because they are great as because they are national. Then, again, he can consider the landscapes of his own land, whether peaceably, as do older men, or in a riot[3] of enthusiasm as do all younger men who see England in the midst of exercising their bodies, as it says in the Song of the Man who Bicycled:

"…and her distance and her sea.

Here is wealth that has no measure,

Park and Close[4] and private pleasure

All her hills were made for me."

Then he can poke[5] about the cities, and any one of them might occupy him almost for a lifetime.

Then a man may be pleased to consider the recorded history of this country, and to inform the fields he knows with the past and with the actions of men long dead. In this way he can use a battlefield with no danger of any detestable[6] insolence[7] or vulgar[8] civilian ways, for the interest in a battlefield, if it is closely studied, becomes so keen and hot that it burns away all foolish

---

1　endurance /ɪn'djʊərəns/　n.　抵抗
2　contemplation /ˌkɒntem'pleɪʃn/　n.　专注
3　riot /'raɪət/　n.　（感情等的）爆发，放纵
4　Close /kləʊs/　n.　院子
5　poke /pəʊk/　vi.　探索
6　detestable /dɪ'testəbl/　adj.　可恶的
7　insolence /'ɪnsələns/　n.　傲慢
8　vulgar /'vʌlgə(r)/　n.　粗俗

谈本国在他国军队侵略下的顽强抵抗，假如他谈腻了这些军事上的事，或是认为过分专注于这些有伤国体，他可以夸耀本国造就的伟人，他们给祖国带来荣耀的原因倒不在于他们的伟大，而是因为他们代表了民族。再次，他可以放眼本国的山川风物，恬然沉静如阅世老者，抑或奔放绚烂如花样少年。年轻人在游历英格兰之中体质也得以锻炼，恰如《骑车人之歌》所述：

"她辽阔的土地和海洋，

蕴藏着无尽的宝藏，

公园、院子和私人领地，

所有的山峰都为我而立。"

然后，他可以去城市里寻幽探胜，任何一座城市可能都让他终生难忘。

随后，他会乐于回顾国家有记载的历史，会把他知道的战场与过去，并与早已死去的人们的功绩联系在一起。此种情形之下，他才不会以令人憎恶的狂傲神情或以村氓野夫的鄙陋眼光来描述这个战场，因对于战场的兴趣会在深入探究之中变得敏锐热切，足以驱除愚蠢无谓的暴力欲念，并且，随着

violence, and you will soon find if you study this sort of terrain[1] closely that you forget on which side your sympathies fail or succeed.

When a man tires of these there is left to him the music of his country, by which I mean the tunes. These he can sing to himself as he goes along, and if ever he tires of that there is the victuals[2] and the drink, which, if he has traveled, he may compare to their advantage over those of any other land. But they must be national. Let him take no pleasure in things cooked in a foreign way.

Some men say that whereas wealth can be accumulated and left to others when we die, this sort of inheritance can not, and that the great pleasure a man took in his own land and the very many ways in which he found that pleasure and his increase in that pleasure as his life proceeded, all die with him. This you will very often hear deplored[3]: As noble a woman as ever lived in London used to say, speaking of her father, that all she valued in him died with him, although he had left her a considerable[4] fortune. By which she meant that not only in losing him she had lost a rooted human affection and had suffered what all must suffer, because there is a doom[5] upon us, but that those particular things in which he was particularly favoured had gone away for ever.

1 terrain /teˈreɪn/　　n.　地形
2 victuals /ˈvɪtlz/　　n.　美食
3 deplore /dɪˈplɔː(r)/　　vt.　哀叹
4 considerable /kənˈsɪdərəbl/　　adj.　相当可观的
5 doom /duːm/　　n.　最后的审判

对此领域研究的细致入微，你很快将发现对于交战双方你已忘却同情所向。

当一个人厌倦了那些话题，他还有本国的音乐可作谈资，我指的是那些小调。他可以边走边哼唱，万一他对这也厌了，那还有美酒佳肴，如果他去旅行，就能拿来与异地的食物一比高下。不过那些食物必须是有民族风味的。他对异国的烹调方式不会感兴趣。

有人说，尽管财富可以聚积，并在死后传给他人，但是这类遗产可不行，祖国给一个人带来的巨大欢乐，和他在寻求那种欢乐时的种种方法，还有同年岁一同增长的快乐，全都随他逝去。你会常常听到这样的哀叹：伦敦有位高贵的夫人过去常说，谈到她父亲，她所珍视的他的一切都随他同去了，尽管他留给她一份数目可观的财产。她的意思是，她不仅失去了父亲，还丧失了一份深切的人类感情，承受了所有人必须承受的打击，因为每一个人都要面对最后的审判，并且他身上受人称羡的过人之处也永远消失了。他驾驭各种外语和本国语言的能力，他的

His power over other languages and over his own language, his vast knowledge of his own county, his acquired courtesy[1] and humour, all mellowed[2] by the world and time, these, she said, were altogether gone. And to us of a younger generation it was her work to lament[3] that we should never know what had once been in England. Now this noble woman, it seems to me, was in error, for all of us who have loved and enjoyed know not only that we carry something with us elsewhere, but leave also in some manner which I do not clearly perceive a legacy[4] to our own people. We take with us that of which Peter Wanderwide[5] spoke when he said or rather sang these lines —

"If all that I have loved and seen

Be with me on the Judgment Day[6],

I shall be saved the crowd between

From Satan[7] and his foul array[8]."

But I say that not only do we carry something with us, but that we leave something also; and this has been best put, I think, by the poet Ronsard[9] when he was dying, who said, if I have rightly translated him, this —

"Of all those vanities[10], the loveliest and most praiseworthy is glory — fame. No one of my

---

关于祖国的广博知识，他已习得的风雅与幽默，这世界和时间使之醇香的一切，她说，都一起随之而去了。依我们晚辈来看，她还要为之哀叹的是我们无从得知的英格兰的过去。在我看来，这位高贵的夫人错了，我们这些爱过幸福过的人，知道我们不仅会带去什么，还会以某种我还不知道的方式给人们留下遗赠。我们带走的东西，就如同彼得•万得韦得在他的诗句中朗诵抑或是吟唱的一样——

"如果我爱过见过的一切

在末日审判时与我同在，

我将免于堕落为

撒旦或他罪恶队伍中的一员。"

但我要说的是我们不仅会带去些什么，也会留下些东西；我认为诗人隆萨在临终时对之做的诠释最为恰当，他说——如果我翻译正确的话——

"在一切浮华中，最可爱也最值得称颂的是荣耀——名誉。在我同时代的人中，没有谁像我这样享有盛誉。在过去的时光里，我生活在其中，深爱它并为之骄傲。如今，在

---

1 courtesy /'kɔːtɪsi/ n. 风雅
2 mellow /'meləʊ/ vt. 使醇香
3 lament /lə'ment/ vt. 悲伤
4 legacy /'legəsi/ n. 遗赠
5 Peter Wanderwide 彼得•万得韦得，英国著名诗人
6 Judgment Day 上帝对人类最后审判的日子
7 Satan 撒旦，反叛天主的大天使，恶魔
8 array /ə'reɪ/ n. 队伍
9 Pierre De Ronsard 皮埃尔•德•隆萨，法国第一个近代抒情诗人，七星诗社代表人
10 vanity /'vænɪti/ n. 浮华

time has been so filled with it as I; I have lived in it and loved and triumphed in it through time past, and now I leave it to my country to garner[1] and possess it after I shall die. So do I go away from my own place as satiated[2] with the glory of this world as I am hungry and all longing for that of God."

That is very good. It would be very difficult to put it better, and if you complain that here Ronsard was only talking of fame or glory, why, I can tell you that the pleasure one takes in one's country is of the same stuff as fame. So true is this that the two commonly go together, and that those become most glorious who have most enjoyed their own land.

我死后我把它交给我的国家来保管和享有。我离开自己的地方，满足于世界上的荣耀，正如我渴望寻求上帝的荣光。"

说得好极了。很难做出超越它的诠释了，如果你会对此持有异议，认为隆萨只是提到了名誉或荣耀。那么，我可以告诉你，一个人从他的祖国那里得到的快乐与名誉是同一码事。毫无疑义，两者同时存在，最热爱祖国的人就会成为最荣耀的人。

---

1 garner /'gɑːnə(r)/　*vt.*　保管
2 satiate /'seɪʃɪeɪt/　*vi.*　满足

含英咀华

该文从英格兰丰富的民族遗产入手，认为一个自由人应该从这些遗产中得到乐趣。之后作者论及前人留下的精神财富，认为人类在继承的同时也有所创造，以使历史的遗产悠久且常新。读罢全文，不难看出作者对历史文化的怀念之情。

Evelyn Waugh
伊芙琳·沃

伊芙琳·沃（1903—1966），英国讽刺小说家。曾就读于牛津大学，当过教师。他的第一部小说《没落与堕落》（Decline and Fall, 1928）就引起了轰动，之后又出版了《行尸走肉》（Vile Bodies, 1930）、《黑色的祸害》（Black Mischief, 1932）等小说。三部曲《行伍生涯》（Men at Arms, 1952）、《军官与绅士》（Officers and Gentlemen, 1955）、《无条件投降》（Unconditional Surrender, 1961），合称《荣誉之剑》（Sword of Honour），写的是二战对人们的影响。

Take Your Home into Your Own Hands!

亲手布置你的家

I do not know who started the idea of "good taste". I strongly suspect that DORA[1] had a young brother who went to art classes at an evening polytechnic[2], and that it all began with him.

Certainly no one worried much about it in the eighteenth century, when people who were rich enough put cupids[3] all over their ceilings, and built fireplaces in a style happily based on a combination of Greek, Chinese and French Gothic[4]. Nor, I think, did it much concern our grandparents who went on accumulating the grossest kinds of bric-a-brac[5] in superb[6] disregard of all that Mr. Ruskin[7] was saying in his clever books. But quite lately, with the advent of all the other worries which gave that hunted look to Mr. Strube's[8] "Little Man", came the plague[9] of "good taste".

One has only to look around today at the bleak[10] little parlours[11] of the suburbs and the

我不知道是谁最先提出了"有品位"这个概念。我十分怀疑多拉有个晚上在工艺学校上艺术课的弟弟，这都是他弄出来的。

毫无疑问，十八世纪没人过于担心这个。那时，比较富有的人在天花板上布满了丘比特，建造的壁炉巧妙地结合了希腊、中国和法式哥特风格。我认为，这与我们祖辈的关系也不大，他们依旧积聚那些粗俗至极的小摆设，完全不顾拉斯金先生在他的聪明的书中说了些什么。但就在最近，各种烦恼纷至沓来，弄得斯特鲁布先生笔下的那些小市民一脸惊恐的表情，"有品位"的风气泛滥成灾。

今天，人们只需要看看

---

1 DORA: 多拉，英国剧作家托马斯·默顿一部剧中的人物形象，喜欢说三道四
2 polytechnic /ˌpɒlɪ'teknɪk/ *n.* 工艺学校
3 Cupid 丘比特，爱神
4 Gothic *n.* 哥特风格，尖拱式建筑
5 bric-a-brac 小古董，小玩意
6 superb /suː'pɜːb, sjuː-/ *adj.* 特别的，完全的
7 Ruskin: 约翰·拉斯金(John Ruskin, 1819—1900)，英国作家、艺术评论家，著有《现代画家》(Modern Painters, 1843—1860)等作品
8 Strube: 西德尼·斯特鲁布(Sidney Strube, 1891—1956)，英国漫画家
9 plague /pleɪg/ *n.* 灾祸
10 bleak /bliːk/ *adj.* 空荡荡的
11 parlour /'pɑːlə(r)/ *n.* 起居室

still bleaker great drawing-rooms[1] of Belgrave Square to see the havoc[2] it has caused. Some terrific voice from behind the bar seems to have said "Time, gentlemen, please," and forthwith[3] everyone began carrying away her dearest possessions to the lumber-room[4] or sending them down to a very chilly reception in the servants' hall.

In some mysterious way, for which I strongly suspect my fellow journalists in the Home Pages are largely responsible, everybody seems to have been bullied into an inferiority complex[5] about their own homes.

In Victorian[6] times people were terrified of being thought poor, and starved themselves in order to clothe[7] a second footman[8]. Nowadays we are all desperately poor and quite boastful[9] about it, but I have yet to find anyone but myself who still says with absolute complacency[10], "I don't know much about art, but I do know what I like." I say that about three times a day and it always has the profoundly shocking effect that I hoped for.

Look around your own drawing-room. Where is the fire screen with the family coat-of-arms[11]

郊区空荡荡的小起居室，和更加空旷的贝尔格拉夫广场的大客厅就能发现它已经造成的混乱。柜子后面什么可怕的声音好像说了句"时间到了，先生们，请吧，"于是每个人立刻开始把她最喜欢的东西带去杂物间，或是叫人送到下面仆人厅里冷飕飕的接待室里。

通过某种神秘的方式，我强烈地怀疑我在家庭版的杂志业同行们对此负有很大的责任，似乎人人都对自己的家太没品位而产生了自卑情结。

在维多利亚时代，人们怕别人认为自己穷，挨饿也要再雇一个男仆。现在我们都穷得叮当响，仍夸夸其谈着什么艺术品位。不过除了我自己，我还没发现其他任何人能骄傲地说："我不太懂艺术，但是我知道自己喜欢什么。"这话我一天大概说三次，每次都能达到我所期望的那种震惊效果。

环顾你自己的客厅。你阿

---

1 drawing-room /ˈdrɔːŋruːm/　客厅，休息室
2 havoc /ˈhævək/　n.　危害，混乱
3 forthwith /fɔːθˈwɪθ, -ð/　adv.　立刻
4 lumber-room /ˈlʌmbə(r)ruːm/　n.　储藏室
5 inferiority complex /ɪnˌfɪərɪˈɒrəti/ /ˈkɒmpleks/　自卑感，自卑情结
6 Victorian　维多利亚女王时代，1837年—1901年
7 clothe /kləʊð/　vt.　为……提供衣服，在此引申为"雇佣"的意思
8 footman /ˈfʊtmən/　n.　男仆
9 boastful /ˈbəʊstfl/　adj.　自夸的
10 complacency /kəmˈpleɪsnsi/　n.　自满，骄傲
11 coat-of-arms　盾形徽章

worked in coloured wools by your Aunt Agatha? And why is that horrible earthenware[1] pot, which someone else's Aunt Agatha made in a suburb of Brighton[2], sitting so coldly on the mantelpiece[3]? And do you really find it comfortable to read by that triangular lamp shade[4] which throws all the light on the ceiling? And where is the stuffed parrot?

Have you made all these changes because you really like them or because someone has been at you about "good taste"?

It may be that you really do like them, but it seems odd that Colonel Brown's wife who disagrees with you about politics and religion and how to bring up her daughters should see eye to eye with you on this point. And the vicar's[5] drawing-room is exactly like yours, although you could never bear the vicar: and so is the doctor's wife's, who, they say, drinks far more than is good for her, and wears such extraordinary hats.

If by some odd coincidence[6] you really do heartily agree with your neighbour's taste in house decoration, well and good; but if she likes to fill her window with arts-and-crafts[7] pottery bowls of crocuses[8], and you like aspidistras[9]

加沙阿姨用彩色羊毛编织的带有家庭盾形徽章的挡火隔板在哪？为什么别人的阿加沙阿姨在布莱顿郊区做的那只讨厌的陶壶冷冰冰地站在壁炉架上？在把光都照到天花板上的三角形灯罩下看书，真的舒服吗？鹦鹉标本又在哪？

你做这些改变，是因为你真的喜欢它们，还是别人老跟你说要有"品位"？

可能你真的喜欢它们。但有点奇怪的是，布朗上校夫人不同意你的政治、宗教和如何抚养她的女儿们的观点，却在这一点上和你意见相同；牧师的客厅和你的一模一样，虽然你从来都受不了这牧师；医生妻子的客厅也是如此，人们说她大量酗酒，还戴特别奇怪的帽子。

如果因为什么奇怪的巧合，你由衷地认同邻居的装修品位，那没问题。但是如果她喜欢在窗台上摆种着番红花的工艺陶盆，而你更喜欢蜘蛛抱蛋，那就在你家摆上蜘蛛抱

---

1 earthenware /'ɔːθnweə(r)/ *n.* 陶器
2 Brighton 布莱顿码头，英国南部海岸避暑胜地
3 mantelpiece /'mæntlpiːs/ *n.* 壁炉架
4 lamp shade 灯罩
5 vicar /'vɪkə(r)/ *n.* 教区牧师
6 coincidence /kəʊ'ɪnsɪdəns/ *n.* 巧合
7 arts-and-crafts: 工艺品
8 crocus /'krəʊkəs/ *n.* 番红花
9 aspidistra /ˌæspɪ'dɪstrə/ *n.* 蜘蛛抱蛋，一种花卉

better, just fill your house with aspidistras till it looks like a conservatory[1], and if you like Benares[2] brass pots, put them in those, and if you like bamboo stands, put them on them. By all means hide the tiger's head which your Uncle George shot in India, if it keeps you awake at night, but if you like it, don't be bullied[3] into putting it away by Mrs. Brown who lives next door. March round with your umbrella and tell her that her hunting prints and Staffordshire pottery are "middle class" or "bad taste".

And if you see sarcastic glances being cast on the family photograph album or the cup you won at the cycling gymkhana[4] or at the tinted photograph of the Acropolis[5] or the Landseer engravings, just you say very decisively, "I don't know much about art, but I do know what I like"; then they will see that they are beaten, and Mrs. Brown will say to the vicar's wife that it is so sad that you have no taste, and the vicar's wife will say to the doctor's wife that it really only shows what sort of people you are, but all three will envy you at heart and even perhaps, one by one, bring out from the attics[6] a few of the things they really like.

蛋，直到家里看上去像个温室，如果你喜欢贝纳勒斯的铜盆，就把花放在铜盆里，如果你喜欢竹架，就把花放在竹架上。想尽办法把你乔治叔叔在印度打的那只老虎头藏起来，如果它让你晚上睡不着觉，但如果你喜欢，也别因担心隔壁布朗夫人会说你而把它藏了起来。打着伞去她家转转，并告诉她，她的狩猎图和斯塔福德郡的陶器是"普普通通"或是"糟糕的品位"。

如果你看到有人将嘲讽的目光投向你的家庭相册，你在自行车比赛中赢回来的奖杯，雅典卫城的着色照片，或是兰西尔尔德雕像，你只管坚决地说："我不太懂艺术，但是我知道自己喜欢什么"。然后他们就知道自己输了。布朗夫人会对牧师的太太说，你没有品位真是可悲，牧师太太会对医生的妻子说，这实在只能说明你是哪一种人，但是她们三个人都打心眼里嫉妒你，甚至可能一个接一个地，从阁楼里拿出几件她们真正喜欢的东西来。

---

1 **conservatory** /kən'sɔ:vətri/ *n.* 温室
2 **Benares** 贝纳勒斯，印度东北部城市
3 **bully** /'buli/ *vt.* 威胁，吓
4 **gymkhana** /dʒɪm'kɑ:nə/ *n.* 比赛
5 **Acropolis** 雅典的卫城
6 **attic** /'ætɪk/ *n.* 阁楼

含英咀华

　　本文讽刺了现今社会上附庸风雅的风气，认为历史变迁带来了时尚的变化，而这种变化却并非出自自己真正的喜好，而只是叶公好龙而已。作者主张人们在装点居室的时候要根据自己的爱好，而不要被所谓"品位"所牵制。人们可以不懂艺术，但是要懂得自己真正喜欢什么。

Edward Verrall Lucas
爱德华·V·卢卡斯

爱德华·V·卢卡斯（1868—1938），英国多产作家、散文家、评论家，20世纪初期英国文坛知名人士。一生中曾撰写了将近一百本书，写作风格及其简练。他长期从事编辑、出版工作，同时致力于写作，著有多部讽刺随笔集和游记，其中包括《旧灯换新灯》（*Old Lamps for New, 1911*）、《漫步者的奖赏》（*Saunterer's rewards, 1933* ）等。但是人们记住他，还是因为他的《查尔斯·兰姆传略》（*The Life of Charles Lamb, 1905*）和由他收集整理的查尔斯与玛丽·兰姆的书信集。

The Windmill

Chance recently made me for a while the tenant[1] of a windmill. Not to live in , and unhappily not to grind[2] corn in, but to visit as the mood arose, and see the ships in the harbour from the topmost window, and look down on the sheep and the green world all around. For this mill stands high and white — so white, indeed, that when there is a thunder cloud behind it, it seems a thing of polished[3] aluminum.

From its windows you can see four other mills, all, like itself, idle[4] , and one merely a ruin and one with only two sweeps[5] left. But just over the next range of hills, out of sight, to the north east, is a windmill that still merrily goes, and about five miles away to the north west is another also active; so that things are not quite so bad hereabouts as in many parts of the country, where the good breezes blow altogether in vain…

Thinking over the losses which England has had forced upon her by steam and the ingenuity of the engineer, one is disposed to count the decay[6] of the windmill among the first. Perhaps in the matter of pure picturesqueness[7] the most

---

1 tenant /'tenənt/   n.   房客
2 grind /graɪnd/   vt.   碾磨
3 polished /'pɒlɪʃt/   adj.   抛了光的
4 idle /'aɪdl/   adj.   闲置的
5 sweep /swiːp/   n.   （风车的）翼板
6 decay /dɪ'keɪ/   n.   衰落
7 picturesqueness /ˌpɪktʃə'resknɪs/   n.   风景如画

风车

不久之前，一个偶然的机会曾使我成为一座风车的住客。不是真的住在里面，而且说来遗憾，也不是进去磨谷物，不过是一时兴起进去参观，从它顶端的窗口遥望港口的船只，俯视周围的羊群和原野。因为这座风车高大洁白——实际上是如此的白，每当在它身后亮起闪电时，整个风车就光亮得如同一件抛了光的铝制什物。

从它另外几个窗口，你可以看到其他四个风车，这些风车都和它一样闲置着，其中一个已成废墟，还有一个只剩下了两叶风帆。但就越过下一道山冈，视力有所不及的地方，面朝东北，有一座风车仍在那里欢快地转动着，另外西北方向距此大约五英里的地方，也有一个仍在使用的风车。所以这地方的情形还不至于像全国其他地方那样糟糕，任由好好的风全都白白吹过……

仔细想想蒸汽机以及工程师的聪明才智迫使英国丢失的种种，人们首当其冲要算上风

serious thing that ever happened to England was the discovery of galvanized[1] iron roofing; but, after all, there was never anything but quiet and rich and comfortable beauty about red roofs, whereas the living windmill is not only beautiful but romantic too: a willing, man serving creature, yoked[2] to the elements, a whirling monster, often a thing of terror. No one can stand very near the crashing sweeps of a windmill in half a gale[3] without a tightening of the heart — a feeling comparable to that which comes from watching the waves break over[4] a wall in a storm. And to be within the mill at such a time is to know something of sound's very sources; it is the cave of noise itself. No doubt there are dens[5] of hammering energy which are more shattering, but the noise of a windmill is largely natural, the product of wood striving with the good sou' wester[6]; it fills the ears rather than assaults them. The effect, moreover, is by no means lessened by the absence of the wind itself and the silent nonchalance[7] of the miller[8] and his man, who move about in the midst of this appalling racket[9] with the quiet efficiency of vergers[10].

In my mill, of course, there is no such

1 galvanized /'gælvənʌɪzd/   adj.   镀锌的
2 yoke /jəuk/   vt.   牵制
3 gale /geɪl/   n.   大风
4 break over   溢出
5 den /den/   n.   洞
6 sou' wester   西南风
7 nonchalance /'nɒnʃələns/   n.   冷淡
8 miller /'mɪlə(r)/   n.   磨房主
9 racket /'rækɪt/   n.   喧闹
10 verger /'vɜːdʒə(r)/   n.   教堂管理者

车的衰落。也许如果只从如画的景致上说，英国遭遇的最大破坏乃是锌镀铁屋顶的发明。但是，毕竟红色的屋顶不过是安详富丽、让人赏心悦目而已，但是转动着的风车不但美丽，而且也浪漫：一个心甘情愿服务于人类的创造物，受制于自然的力量，一个飞舞旋转的怪物，往往还是一个使人惧怕的东西。不论谁在风力正强的时候靠近一座风车轰鸣的风帆，心里都不会镇定自若——那感觉就像人们在暴风雨中望见水浪冲击堤岸的情景一样。而此时待在风车里会对声音的来源有些体会，因为这本身就是声音的洞穴。无疑有些洞中所发出的轰鸣声震耳欲聋，具有很大的威力，但风车的声音则大体比较自然，它们是由木头与西南风搏斗而产生，它充盈于人耳而不会震耳欲聋。而且这种效果并不因为没有风或者磨坊主人及其佣人的淡漠而有所减弱，这些人即便在震耳欲聋的喧嚣之下，也总是一副教堂管事人的文静态度，办事有条不紊。

当然，我进入的磨坊并无如此喧嚣，只偶尔听到闲置风帆上的横木有几声摆动罢了。

uproar[1]; nothing but the occasional shaking of the cross pieces[2] of the idle sails. Everything is still; and the pity of it is that everything is in almost perfect order for the day's work. The mill one day — some score[3] years ago — was full of life; the next, and ever after[4], mute and lifeless, like a stream frozen in a night or the palace in Tennyson's ballad[5] of the "Sleeping Beauty". There is no decay — merely inanition[6]. One or two of the apple wood cogs[7] have been broken from the great wheel; a few floor planks[8] have been rotted; but that is all. A week's overhauling[9] would put everything right. But it will never come, and the cheerful winds that once were to drive a thousand English mills so happily now bustle over the Channel[10] in vain.

1 uproar /'ʌprɔː(r)/　n.　喧嚣
2 cross piece　风车风帆交叉处的横梁
3 score /skɔː(r)/　n.　二十
4 ever after　从此之后一直……
5 ballad /'bæləd/　n.　歌谣
6 inanition /ˌɪnə'nɪʃn/　n.　空洞
7 cog /kɒg/　n.　楔子
8 plank /plæŋk/　n.　木板
9 overhauling /ˌəʊvə'hɔːlɪŋ/　n.　整修
10 Channel　这里指英吉利海峡

一切都如此寂静。而使人惆怅的是，一切仿佛已完全就绪，只等着当天开工。曾经这个磨房——大约二十年前——充满了生机；接着，自那以后，它将永归沉寂，毫无生气，就像夜里冰封的溪流，或是如丁尼生《睡美人》歌谣中的宫殿。这风车并没毁损——而仅是空无一物。几个苹果木的楔子已从风轮上脱落了；几根木质的地板也已腐烂；但就仅此而已。只要一周的时间就足以全部修整完毕。但这永远不会发生了，曾经使千千万万个英国风车一起欢舞的欢快的风，而今也只能匆匆地在英吉利海峡之上徒劳吹过。

含英咀华

　　本文选自作者的散文集《旧灯换新灯》，笔调闲逸有致、肃静淡雅，是作者行文风格的典型代表。风车的衰败映射了工业革命对英国传统文化的冲击。

John Steinbeck
约翰·斯坦贝克

约翰·斯坦贝克（1902—1968），美国现实主义小说家、戏剧家。他年轻时候做过许多工作，去过许多地方，这些都成了他后来写作的素材。他的作品多涉及贫苦工人与农民们生活的艰辛苦楚。代表作有剧本《人与鼠》(Of Mice and Man, 1937)获得纽约戏剧评论家奖金，被誉为"触及了真正扎根于美国生活的主题"；小说《愤怒的葡萄》（The Grapes of Wrath, 1939）获当年普利策奖金，小说《我们不满的冬天》（The Winter of Our Discontent, 1961）获诺贝尔文学奖金。

Travels with Charley

One of my purposes was to listen, to hear speech, accent, speech rhythms, overtones[1] and emphasis[2]. For speech is so much more than words and sentences. I did listen everywhere. It seemed to me that regional speech is in the process of disappearing, not gone but going. Forty years of radio and twenty years of television must have this impact. Communications must destroy localness, by a slow, inevitable process. I can remember a time when I could almost pinpoint[3] a man's place of origin by his speech. That is growing more difficult now and will in some foreseeable future become impossible. Radio and television speech becomes standardized, perhaps better English than we have ever used. Just as our bread, mixed and baked, packaged and sold without benefit of accident or human frailty[4], is uniformly good and uniformly tasteless, so will our speech become one speech.

I who love words and the endless possibility of words am saddened by this inevitability[5]. For with local accent will disappear local tempo[6].

1 **overtone** /ˈəʊvətəʊn/ n. 言外之意
2 **emphasis** /ˈemfəsɪs/ n. 重音强调
3 **pinpoint** /ˈpɪnpɔɪnt/ vt. 正确地指出
4 **frailty** /ˈfreɪltɪ/ n. 过失
5 **inevitability** /ɪnevɪtəˈbɪləti/ n. 必然性
6 **tempo** /ˈtempəʊ/ n. 步调，特色

同查利旅行

我旅行的目的之一是聆听，听谈话、口音、话语节奏、言外之意和话的重点。因为谈话的内涵要远多于单独的字句。我也确实是在四处聆听。在我看来，方言正处于消失的进程中，还没到完全消亡的地步但正在被同化。四十年无线电广播和二十年电视节目的传播必定对此产生了影响。通信一定会通过一个缓慢、不可避免的过程而使当地化销声匿迹。还记得从前，我几乎能根据一个人的谈话而准确无误地判断出他的出生地。但现在这变得越来越难，并且会在可预知的未来某个时候变得不可能。广播电视语言已成为标准的、可能比我们的现行英语更好的语言。就像我们的面包，如果在配料、烘培、包装、售卖过程中没有意外和人为过失，都无一例外地好并且都一样的食之无味，如此这般，我们说的话也会变得整齐划一。

我热爱语言，热爱语言的无尽的可能性，而这一必然趋势使我悲伤，因为地方特色

187

The idioms, the figures of speech[1] that make language rich and full of the poetry of place and time must go. And in their place will be a national speech, wrapped and packaged, standard and tasteless. Localness is not gone but it is going. In the many years since I have listened to the land the change is very great. Traveling west along the northern routes I did not hear a truly local speech until I reached Montana[2]. That is one of the reasons I fell in love again with Montana. The West Coast went back to packaged English. The Southwest kept a grasp but a slipping grasp on localness. Of course the deep South holds on by main strength[3] to its regional expressions, just as it holds and treasures some other anachronisms[4], but no region can hold out for long against the highway, the high-tension line[5], and the national television. What I am mourning is perhaps not worth saving, but I regret its loss nevertheless.

Even while I protest the assembly-line production[6] of our food, our songs, our language, and eventually our souls, I know that it was a rare home that baked good bread in the old days. Mother's cooking was with rare exceptions poor, that good unpasteurized milk[7] touched

1 figure of speech 修辞
2 Montana 蒙大拿州（美国西北部的州）
3 by main strength 奋力
4 anachronism /ə'nækrənɪzəm/ n. 过时的东西
5 high-tension line /'haɪ'tenʃn/ 高压电线
6 assembly-line production /ə'semblilaɪn/ 装配线生产
7 unpasteurized milk /ʌn'pɑːstʃəraɪzd/ 未经巴氏菌消毒的牛奶

也会随着地方语言一并消失。那些习惯用语和修辞赋予了语言地域和时代韵味，使其变得丰富多彩，而它们也会逐渐消失。取而代之的将是"普通话"，规规矩矩、标准统一、索然无味。地方特色虽未消亡但却正在消失。自我开始聆听各地的这许多年来，语言已经发生了很大的变化。沿着北部路线向西旅行，直到蒙大拿我才听到真正的方言。那是我再次爱上蒙大拿的原因之一。西海岸使用规规矩矩的英语。西北部还留有一些地方特色，但是就这些地方特色也正在渐渐消亡。当然，最南部地区还尽力保持着自己的表达方式，正如它保持并珍惜其他那些过时的东西一样，但是没有一个区域可以长时间抵制高速公路、高压电线和遍及全国的电视。也许我正为之哀伤的东西并不值得保留，尽管如此，我还是对它的消亡感到遗憾。

即使在抗议我们的食物、我们的歌曲、我们的语言甚至于我们的灵魂都是由流水线统一生产时，我知道旧日能够烘烤出美味面包的家庭也是微乎其微的。母亲那个时代的烹饪除个别家庭外，都是不敢恭

only by flies and bits of manure[1] crawled with bacteria, the healthy old time life was riddled[2] with aches, sudden death from unknown causes, and that sweet local speech I mourn was the child of illiteracy[3] and ignorance. It is the nature of a man as he grows older, a small bridge in time, to protest against change, particularly change for the better. But it is true that we have exchanged corpulence[4] for starvation, and either one will kill us. The lines of change are down. We, or at least I, can have no conception of[5] human life and human thought in a hundred years or fifty years. Perhaps my greatest wisdom is the knowledge that I do not know. The sad ones are those who waste their energy in trying to hold it back, for they can only feel bitterness in loss and no joy in gain.

As I passed through or near the great hives[6] of production — Youngstown, Cleveland, Akron, Toledo, Pontiac, Flint, and later South Bend and Gary — my eyes and mind were battered[7] by the fantastic hugeness and energy of production, a complication that resembles chaos and cannot be. So might one look down on an ant hill[8] and see no method or direction or purpose in the

---

1　manure /məˈnjuə(r)/　*n.*　肥料
2　riddle /ˈrɪdl/　*vt.*　充满
3　illiteracy /ɪˈlɪtərəsi/　*n.*　无知
4　corpulence /ˈkɔːpjuləns/　*n.*　肥胖
5　have no conception of /kənˈsepʃn/　完全不懂，无法预知
6　hive /haɪv/　*n.*　闹市
7　batter /ˈbætə(r)/　*vt.*　击打
8　ant hill　蚁丘

维的，未经高温消毒的牛奶只有苍蝇和爬在牛粪上的细菌才去碰它，往昔健康的生命常会病痛缠身或突然丧命而不明死因，而我所哀叹的甜美的乡音则出自愚昧无知的孩童之口。随着年岁增长，时间上的一个小过渡，人会反对变化，特别是好的变化，这乃是人的天性。但事实是，我们已用肥胖代替了饥饿，而两者皆可置我们于死地。许许多多的改变已经发生了。我们，至少是我自己，都无法想象一百年或五十年后的人类生活及人类思想会怎么样。也许我最大的智慧就是认识到了"我不知道"。浪费精力并试图将其挽回的人则只有独自悲伤，因为他们只能感受到失去的痛苦，而无法体会获得的欢愉。

当我驶过或是临近那些非凡的拥有制造业的闹市——扬斯敦、克利夫兰、阿克伦、托莱多、庞蒂亚克、弗林特，还有后来的南本德和加里——我被制造业不可思议的庞然硕大与充沛活力弄得头晕眼花，一个集聚着混乱喧嚣的复杂物体也不至于如此。这感受可能如同一个人低头观察一个蚁丘，看见这些行动迅速、匆忙混乱

darting[1] hurrying inhabitants[2] .

What was so wonderful was that I could come again to a quiet country road, tree-bordered, with fenced fields and cows, could pull up[3] Rocinante beside a lake of clear, clean water and see high overhead the arrows of southing ducks and geese. There Charley could with his delicate[4] exploring nose read his own particular literature on bushes and tree trunks and leave his message there, perhaps as important in endless time as these pen scratches I put down on perishable[5] paper. There in the quiet, with the wind flicking tree branches, made coffee so rich and sturdy[6] it would float a nail, and, sitting on my own back doorsteps, could finally come to think about what I had seen and try to arrange some pattern of thought to accommodate[7] the teeming[8] crowds of my seeing and hearing.

的居民毫无章法、到处乱窜、没有目的时的感受一样。

令人欣慰的是，我又能来到宁静的乡村小路。树木夹道，帐子里是庄稼和母牛，可以把罗西南特停靠在湖边，湖水清澈明晰，仰望头上南飞的禽鸟笔直的队伍。在那查利可以用它灵敏探究的鼻子，解读自己那些在灌木、树干上独特的文学，并在其上留下标记，或许永存千古与我在易于腐烂的纸上留下那些笔迹同样重要。沐浴宁静，清风拂过树枝，煮杯香浓的可以浮起钉子的咖啡，然后，坐在自己的后门阶上，开始回想我见过的东西，并设法安排思想的模式，以调整我丰富多彩的见闻。

1 darting /ˈdɑːtɪŋ/ adj. 很快的
2 inhabitant /ɪnˈhæbɪtənt/ n. 居民
3 pull up 停下
4 delicate /ˈdelɪkət/ adj. 敏锐的，灵敏的
5 perishable /ˈperɪʃəbl/ adj. 容易腐烂的
6 sturdy /ˈstɜːdi/ adj. 浓稠的
7 accommodate /əˈkɒmədeɪt/ vt. 调整
8 teeming /ˈtiːmɪŋ/ adj. 丰富的

含英咀华

在快要六十岁时，斯坦贝克觉得自己已经很久没有亲身感受这片国土了，于是他踏上了重新发现的非凡旅程，与之为伴的是一只名叫查利的出色的法国狮子狗，并用小货车载着名叫罗西南特的小船。之后他写成了这本游记《同查利旅行》(Travels with Charley: In Search of America, 1962)，这是迄今对美国最生动的描述之一。选段内容为作者对美国各地方言正被标准美语所同化的惋惜，与对以往安静、悠闲的生活的怀念。

Max Beerbohm

麦克斯·比尔波姆

麦克斯·比尔波姆（1872—1956），英国作家、漫画家、演员。曾经就读于卡尔特修道院与牛津大学。在校期间开始写作，在文艺杂志《黄皮书》（The Yellow Book）的创刊号上发表了随笔《为化妆品申辩》(Defence of Cosmetics)。之后他的作品大多发表在《星期六评论》（Saturday Review）上。代表作有《加兰的圣诞节》(A Christmas Garland, 1912)、《七个男人》(Seven Men, 1919)等。他的唯一一部小说《朱莱卡·多卜生》(Zuleika Dobson, 1911)被评为20世纪百大英文小说之一。他的文字幽默机智，文学风格和写法都有唯美主义、贵族化冷峻、反讽、戏剧化的小题大做、戏仿、优美柔弱等特点。作为演员，他擅长模仿知名作家的风格，并且也是著名的讽刺画家。他可说是20世纪最具破坏性的模仿嘲弄者之一。

The Morris[1] Dancers

It was in the wide street of a tiny village near Oxford that I saw them. Fantastic —high-fantastical — figures they did cut in their finery[2]. But in demeanour[3] they were quite simple, quite serious, these eight English peasants. They had trudged[4] hither[5] from the neighbouring village that was their home. And they danced quite simply, quite seriously. One of them, I learned, was a cobbler[6], another a baker, and the rest were farm-labourers[7]. And their fathers and their fathers' fathers had danced here before them, even so, every May-day morning. They were as deeply rooted in antiquity[8] as the elm[9] outside the inn. They were here always in their season as surely as the elm put forth its buds. And the elm, knowing them, approving them, let its green-flecked branches dance in unison with them.

The first dance was in full swing when I approached. Only six of the men were dancers. Of the others, one was the "minstrel[10]", the

---

1 Morris: 莫理斯舞，英国传统民间舞蹈，舞者通常为男子，身上系铃，装扮民间传说中的人物
2 finery /ˈfaɪnəri/ n. 华丽的服饰
3 demeanour /dɪˈmiːnə(r)/ n. 仪表
4 trudge /trʌdʒ/ vi. 跋涉
5 hither /ˈhɪðə(r)/ adv. 这里
6 cobbler /ˈkɒblə(r)/ n. 鞋匠
7 farm-labourer /ˈfɑːmleɪbərə(r)/ 农场工人
8 antiquity /ænˈtɪkwəti/ n. 古代
9 elm /elm/ n. 榆树
10 minstrel /ˈmɪnstrəl/ n. 乐手

莫里斯舞者

我是在牛津城附近一个小村子的宽阔马路上见到他们的。身着华丽的服饰，他们展示出奇妙的，应该说是十分奇妙的舞姿，但是从仪表来看，他们都十分纯朴，十分稳重。这八个英国的庄稼汉，从邻村的家中跋涉到这里。在这他们十分纯朴、十分稳重地跳着舞。我听说，他们中的一个是鞋匠，另一个是面包师，其他都是农场工人。他们的父亲，和他们父亲的父亲，每个五月一日的早晨，就这样在这里跳过舞。他们就像旅店外面的那株榆树，深深地植根于古代。他们如同榆树，到了季节就准会抽芽，总是适逢其时地来到这儿。榆树认得他们，赞许他们，摆动着嫩绿斑驳的枝丫与他们共舞。

当我走近时，第一支舞正跳到高潮。他们中只有六个舞者，另外两个则一个是"乐手"，一个是"看场的"。乐手正在吹奏长笛；我从看场人的棍子和皮袋子看出，他边四

other the "dysard[1]". The minstrel was playing a flute[2]; and the dysard I knew by the wand and leathern bladder[3] which he brandished[4] as he walked around, keeping a space for the dancers, and chasing and buffeting merrily any man or child who ventured too near. He, like the others, wore a white smock[5] decked with sundry ribands[6], and a top-hat[7] that must have belonged to his grandfather. Its antiquity of form and texture contrasted strangely with the freshness of the garland[8] of paper roses that wreathed it. I was told that the wife or sweetheart of every Morris-dancer takes special pains to deck[9] her man out more gaily than his fellows. But this pious[10] endeavour[11] had defeated its own end. So bewildering[12] was the amount of brand-new bunting[13] attached to all these eight men that no matron[14] or maiden[15] could for the life of her have determined which was the most splendid of them all. Besides his adventitious finery, every dancer, of course, had in his hands the scarves

处走动边挥舞着那两样东西，给舞者们保持够大的场地，要是大人或孩子靠得太近，他就嘻嘻哈哈地跑上去拍他几下。他也和其他人一样，穿件装饰着各色缎带的工作服，戴一顶大礼帽，那一定是他祖父曾经戴过的。它的样式和质地相当古老，上面却绕着鲜艳的纸玫瑰花环，两者形成了怪异的对比。有人告诉我，每个莫里斯舞者的妻子或心上人，都特意费一番心思把她的男人打扮得格外光鲜，以胜过他的同伴。但是这份良苦用心却适得其反。所有这八个男人都身披崭新的彩旗，使得他们这群人看上去如此让人眼花缭乱，所有主妇或是少女思来想去也无法决定其中哪个才是最风光的。除了身上那套华丽的服饰，每一位舞者，当然了，双手还拿着丝巾，连同绑在腿上的铃铛，都对他表演莫里斯舞至关重要。一面挥舞着丝巾，一面跺脚发出叮叮当当的铃响，伴着呆板的节奏，六位庄稼汉面对面地跳着，一边三个，乐手吹着长笛，看场人神气活现地走来走去。乐手的曲调至今还在我脑中萦绕——那支古怪呆板的小调让我回想起那个舞蹈

1 dysard 从dizzard一词演变而来，有jester小丑和blockhead笨蛋的意思
2 flute /fluːt/ n. 长笛
3 bladder /ˈblædə(r)/ n. 袋子
4 brandish /ˈbrændɪʃ/ vt. 挥舞
5 smock /smɒk/ n. 工作服
6 riband /ˈrɪbənd/ n. 缎带
7 top-hat /ˌtɒpˈhæt/ 大礼帽
8 garland /ˈɡɑːlənd/ n. 花环
9 deck /dek/ v. 打扮
10 pious /ˈpaɪəs/ adj. 尽责的
11 endeavour /ɪnˈdevə(r)/ n. 尽力，竭力
12 bewildering /bɪˈwɪldərɪŋ/ adj. 令人眼花缭乱的
13 bunting /ˈbʌntɪŋ/ n. 彩旗
14 matron /ˈmeɪtrən/ n. 主妇
15 maiden /ˈmeɪdən/ n. 少女

which are as necessary to his performance of the Morris as are the bells strapped[1] about the calves of his legs. Waving these scarves and jangling these bells with a stolid[2] rhythm, the six peasants danced facing one another, three on either side, while the minstrel fluted and the dysard strutted around. That minstrel's tune runs in my head even now — a queer little stolid tune that recalls vividly to me the aspect of the dance.

I wish I could hum[3] it for you on paper. I wish I could set down for you on paper the sight that it conjures up[4]. But what writer that ever lived has been able to write adequately about a dance? Even a slow, simple dance, such as these peasants were performing, is a thing that not the most cunning[5] writer could fix in words. Did not Flaubert[6] say that if he could describe a valse[7] he would die happy?

Unable to make you see the Morris, how can I make you feel as I felt in seeing it? I cannot explain even to myself the effect it had on me. My critics[8] have often complained of me that I lack "heart"; and I suppose they are right. I remember having read the death of Little Nell on more than one occasion without floods of tears. How can I explain to myself the tears that came into my eyes at sight of the Morris? They are not within the

1 strap /stræp/ vt. 绑
2 stolid /'stɒlɪd/ adj. 呆板的
3 hum /hʌm/ vt. 哼唱
4 conjure up /'kʌndʒə(r)/ 用魔法召唤
5 cunning /'kʌnɪŋ/ adj. 巧妙的
6 Flaubert 福楼拜 (1821—1880)，法国小说家
7 Valse 法语为waltz，华尔兹舞
8 critic /'krɪtɪk/ n. 评论家

的生动场景。

我希望我可以在纸上为你哼唱。我希望可以在纸上为你记录下它魔法般召唤的情景。但曾经有哪位作家可以恰如其分地描写出一支舞蹈呢？即使是一支节奏缓慢、动作简单的舞蹈，就像那些农夫表演的那支，笔法最巧妙的作家也无法用文字将其表述出来。福楼拜不是说过，如果他能描写出华尔兹舞，那他将死而无憾吗？

既然无法让你见到莫里斯舞，那我怎样才能让你体会到我观看它时的感受呢？我甚至不能为自己解释它对我产生的影响。评论家们经常指责我没有用"心"去写作——我想他们是对的。我记得自己曾经不止一次读到小聂耳的死而没有泪如泉涌。我又怎么向自己解释当我看到莫里斯舞时眼里充盈的泪水呢？答案并不在仅是注视视觉上的美景而引出的泪水这一标题下。在我看来，莫里斯舞，是奇怪、古老、原始的，无论你怎么说，也说不到美丽上。它也并不含有任何明显的哀婉。穿过伦敦某个贫民窟的时

rubric[1] of the tears drawn by mere contemplation of visual beauty. The Morris, as I saw it, was curious, antique, racy, what you will: not beautiful. Nor was there any obvious pathos[2] in it. Often, in London, passing through some slum[3] where a tune was being ground[4] from an organ[5], I have paused to watch the little girls dancing. In the swaying dances of these wan[6], dishevelled[7], dim little girls I have discerned[8] authentic beauty, and have wondered where they had learned the grace of their movements, and where the certainty with which they did such strange and complicated steps. Surely, I have thought, this is no trick of to-day or yesterday: here, surely, is the remainder of some old tradition; here, may be, is Merrie England[9], run to seed. There is an obvious pathos in the dances of these children of the gutter[10] — an obvious symbolism of sadness, of a wistful longing for freedom and fearlessness, for wind and sunshine. No wonder that at sight of it even so heartless a person as the present writer[11] is a little touched. But why at sight of those rubicund[12], full-grown, eupeptic[13] Morris-dancers

1 rubric /ˈruːbrɪk/ n. 标题
2 pathos /ˈpeɪθɒs/ n. 哀婉
3 slum /slʌm/ n. 贫民窟
4 grind /graɪnd/ vt. 演奏
5 organ /ˈɔːgən/ n. 管风琴
6 wan /wɒn/ adj. 苍白的
7 dishevelled /dɪˈʃevəld/ adj. 蓬乱的
8 discern /dɪˈsɜːn/ vt. 目睹
9 Merrie England，即为Merry England，较诙谐、仿古体的写法，是一种理想化的田园牧歌般的生活方式
10 gutter /ˈgʌtə(r)/ n. 贫民区
11 present writer: 本文作者
12 rubicund /ˈruːbɪkənd/ adj. 红润的
13 eupeptic /juːˈpeptɪk/ adj. 健康的，强壮的

候，我时常听到管风琴吹奏出的曲子，于是我就停下来看那些小女孩的舞蹈。在那些面色苍白、头发蓬乱、目光暗淡的小女孩摇摇晃晃的舞蹈中，我目睹了真正的美丽，并惊异于她们从何处习得那动作中的优雅，她们脚下奇怪复杂的舞步中的镇定又从何而来。当然，我想过，这不是今天或明天的技艺；这里，当然是某个古老传统的延续；在这，可能快乐的英格兰开始萌芽。那些贫民区的孩子们的舞蹈中就有着明显的悲凉——那是明显的象征，是悲伤，是充满希冀地渴求自由与无畏，渴求和风与阳光的象征。毫无疑问，即使一个像本文作者这样无情无义的人，看见此种场景也会为之动容。但为什么看见那些在和煦春天里大街上，红光满面、身强体壮的成年莫里斯舞者也会令我动容呢？他们自身并未弥漫着明显的哀婉。他们展现的是快活的英格兰全盛时期的风采。我想，我之所以流泪，一方面是受了这群快乐舞者的感染，流出的喜悦的泪水；另一方面，是羡慕他

on the vernal[1] highroad? No obvious pathos was diffusing itself from them. They were Merrie England in full flower. In part, I suppose, my tears were tears of joy for the very joyousness of these men; in part, of envy for their fine simplicity; in part, of sorrow in the thought that they were a survival of the past, not types of the present, and that their knell[2] would soon be tolled, and the old elm saw their like no more.

After they had drunk some ale[3], they formed up for the second dance — a circular dance. And anon[4], above the notes of the flute and the jangling of the bells and the stamping of the boots, I seemed to hear the knell actually tolling, Hoot! Hoot! Hoot! A motor came fussing[5] and fuming in its cloud of dust. Hoot! Hoot! The dysard ran to meet it, brandishing his wand of office. He had to stand aside. Hoot! The dancers had just time to get out of the way. The scowling[6] motorists vanished. Dancers and dysard, presently visible through the subsiding dust, looked rather foolish and crestfallen[7]. And all the branches of the conservative[8] old elm above them seemed to be quivering with indignation.

们简单纯粹的生活；还有就是想到他们是过去的幸存者，不能适应于当今社会，他们的丧钟不久即将敲响，那株老榆树也就再也见不到他们这样的人了。

他们喝了一些麦芽酒后，又整队准备跳第二支舞——圆圈舞。时而，长笛的曲调，铃铛的叮当声，还有皮靴的踱地声被盖住了，我似乎听到丧钟真的敲响了，嘀！嘀！嘀！一辆汽车开来，弄得乌烟瘴气。嘀！嘀！看场人迎面跑过去，挥舞着他的指挥棒。他不得不让开了。嘀！跳舞的人连忙闪开让出道路。满脸怒容的开车人不见了。此刻，透过逐渐消散的尘雾，舞者和看场人看上去都有些傻头傻脑、垂头丧气。他们头上那株守旧的老榆树上所有的枝丫仿佛都在义愤填膺地颤抖。

---

1 vernal /ˈvɜːnl/ *adj.*   和煦的
2 knell /nel/ *n.*   丧钟
3 ale /eɪl/ *n.*   麦芽酒
4 and anon /əˈnɒn/ 时而
5 fuss /fʌs/ *vi.*   忙乱
6 scowling /skaʊlɪŋ / *adj.*   满脸怒容的
7 crestfallen /ˈkrestfɔːlən/ *adj.*   垂头丧气的
8 conservative /kənˈsɜːvətɪv/ *adj.*   守旧的

含英咀华

在这篇小品文中，作者描绘了一幅乡村生活的片断。莫里斯舞源远流长，是一个世代相传的传统民俗，已经成为英国乡间节庆活动的保留节目。作者不仅回忆了观看这段表演的愉快经历，更对这一美好的文化传统正在逐渐消逝而感到无限惋惜。

Charles Lamb

查尔斯·兰姆

查尔斯·兰姆（1775—1834），英国散文家。早期重要作品有他与姐姐合著的《莎士比亚故事集》（*Tales from Shakespeare, 1807*）。兰姆最大的成就是随笔。他的随笔的最大特点是笔调亲切，富有生活气息和人情味。他的随笔大多与他的经历密切相关，有的风雅幽默，情趣横生；有的则哀婉凄切，悱恻动人。兰姆好推敲文字，爱用典故，注重细节，文体富有个人特色。他的随笔后来收为两个集子《伊利亚随笔集》（*Essays of Elia*）和《伊利亚后期随笔集》（*The Last Essays of Elia*）。这两个集子收集了他最优秀的散文。

Old China

古瓷器

I have an almost feminine partiality[1] for old china. When I go to see any great house, I enquire for the china-closet, and next for the picture gallery. I cannot defend the order of preference, but by saying, that we have all some taste or other, of too ancient a date to admit of our remembering distinctly that it was an acquired[2] one. I can call to mind the first play, and the first exhibition, that I was taken to; but I am not conscious of a time when china jars and saucers were introduced into my imagination.

I had no repugnance[3] then — why should I now have? — to those little, lawless, azure-tinctured[4] grotesques[5], that under the notion of men and women, float about, uncircumscribed[6] by any element, in that world before perspective — a china tea-cup.

I like to see my old friends — whom distance cannot diminish — figuring up in the air (so they appear to our optics[7]), yet on terra firma[8] still — for so we must in courtesy[9] interpret

我对于古瓷器有种近乎于女性的偏爱。每当进入豪门巨室，我总是首先要看它的瓷橱，然后才去观赏它的画室。我也说不出为什么会是这样的顺序，但是，我们身上都会有这样或那样的癖好，由于年长日久，我们自己也追忆不起来它是不是后天养成的。我能够回忆起观看的第一出戏和第一次画展，但瓷瓶和瓷碟是何时进入我的想象空间，我已无从追忆。

那些怪异的天蓝色的小巧形体没有规律可以琢磨，我当时就不曾反感，现在又怎么会反感呢？在常人眼中，他们在那个没有透视的世界——一个瓷茶杯上飘浮不定，不受任何局限。

我喜欢看到我的老友——距离并不能使他们变小——飘在空中（至少在我们的视觉里他们如此），然而却站立在地面上——为此，我们必须善意地解释，才说得通为什么那里凭空出现一道深蓝。我们觉得，那位谨慎的艺术家，为了

1 partiality /pɑːʃɪ'ælɪti/ n. 偏爱
2 acquired /ə'kwaɪəd/ adj. 习得的，养成的
3 repugnance /rɪ'pʌgnəns/ n. 强烈的反感
4 azure-tinctured /'æʒə(r)'tɪŋktʃəd/ adj. 染上天蓝色的
5 grotesque /grəʊ'tesk/ n. 稀奇古怪
6 uncircumscribed /ʌn'sɜːkəmskraɪbd/ adj. 不受控制的
7 optics /'ɒptɪks/ n. 视觉
8 terra firma /'terə/ /'fɜːmə/ 地面
9 courtesy /'kɜːtɪsi/ n. 好意

that speck[1] of deeper blue, which the decorous[2] artist, to prevent absurdity, has made to spring up beneath their sandals.

I love the men with women's faces, and the women, if possible, with still more womanish expressions.

Here is a young and courtly Mandarin[3], handing tea to a lady from a salver — two miles off. See how distance seems to set off respect. And here the same lady, or another — for likeness is identity on tea-cups — is stepping into a little fairy boat, moored[4] on the hither[5] side of this calm garden river, with a dainty[6] mincing foot[7], which in a right angle of incidence[8] (as angles go in our world) must infallibly[9] land her in the midst of a flowery mead[10] a furlong[11] off on the other side of the same strange stream!

Farther on — if far or near can be predicated of their world — see horses, trees, pagodas[12], dancing the hays.

Here — a cow and rabbit couchant[13], and co-extensive — so objects show, seen through the lucid[14] atmosphere of fine Cathay[15].

1　speck /spek/　n.　一道
2　decorous /'dekərəs/　adj.　谨慎的
3　Mandarin /'mændərin/　n.　官吏
4　moor /mɔː(r), mʊə(r)/　vi.　停泊
5　hither /'hɪðə(r)/　adv.　（古）这边
6　dainty /'deɪnti/　adj.　轻巧的，精致的
7　mincing foot /'mɪnsɪŋ/　碎步
8　angle of incidence /'ɪnsɪdəns/　入射角
9　infallibly /ɪn'fælɪb(ə)li/　adv.　绝对无误地
10　mead /miːd/　n.　草地
11　furlong /'fɜːlɒŋ/　n.　弗隆，浪，英国长度单位，=1/8英里
12　pagoda /pə'gəʊdə/　n.　宝塔
13　couchant /'kaʊtʃ(ə)nt/　adj.　俯伏的，蹲着的
14　lucid /'luːsɪd/　adj.　明晰的
15　Cathay /kæ'θeɪ/　n.　古语诗歌中的中国

避免荒诞，故将那抹颜色在他们脚下升起。

我喜爱瓷器上具有女性般容貌的男人，如果可能的话，我甚至更愿意这里的女子带有更加女性化的表情。

这儿是一位年轻恭敬的中国官吏，正托着茶盘向一位贵妇献茶——那位贵妇离他竟有两英里！由此可以看出在这里距离意味着尊敬。这边，同样是这位贵妇，也或许是另一位——因为茶具上的容貌是有点相似的——正款款移步，欲踏入一只小巧玲珑的船。而船停泊在这寂静的花园小溪的旁边。照她举步的精确角度推测（依照我们西方的角度原理），她那只纤足会恰恰落在一片鲜花盛开的草地上——都已经越这条奇怪溪流对岸一弗隆了呢！

更远处——如果在他们的世界里尚有远近距离可言的话——可以看见马匹、树木、高塔和舞蹈着的草儿。

这里——可以看到牛和兔子昂首蹲踞，而且大小相同——也许，在那个美丽的中国，透过澄明空气所看到的事物的模样就是如此。

我们刚买了一套与众不同

I was pointing out to my cousin last evening, over our Hyson[1] (which we are old fashioned enough to drink unmixed still of an afternoon), some of these speciosa miracula[2] upon a set of extraordinary old blue china (a recent purchase) which we were now for the first time using; and could not help remarking, how favourable circumstances had been to us of late years, that we could afford to please the eye sometimes with trifles of this sort — when a passing sentiment seemed to overshade the brows of my companion. I am quick at detecting these summer clouds in Bridget.

"I wish the good old times would come again," she said, "when we were not quite so rich. I do not mean, that I want to be poor; but there was a middle state" — so she was pleased to ramble on — "in which I am sure we were a great deal happier. A purchase is but a purchase, now that you have money enough and to spare. Formerly it used to be a triumph. When we coveted[3] a cheap luxury (and, O! how much ado[4] I had to get you to consent in those times!) — we were used to have a debate two or three days before, and to weigh the for and against, and think what we might spare it out of, and what saving we could hit upon, that should be an equivalent. A thing was worth buying then, when

的蓝色古瓷器，昨天晚上我和姐姐首次用它喝熙春茶。（我们都很怀旧，可以喝着不掺杂任何其他东西的熙春茶静静地坐一下午。）我给她指出这套茶具的一些奇异瑰丽之处，不禁感叹，我们近几年境况确有好转，才有能力购置这些零星的玩物以饱眼福。这番谈话过后，我同伴的眉头掠过一丝伤感的阴影。我善于觉察布丽姬特心中的愁云。

"我真希望过去那幸福的时光能再回来。"她说，"那时候我们不太富裕。当然我不是说我愿意生活在贫穷之中，但往往都有个中间阶段。"她滔滔不绝地往下说，"那种情形下，我们真的是比现在要快乐得多。现在你的钱足够用，买一件东西会觉得很平常，但要在以前，那可是一件了不得的大事。那时如果我们看上了一个廉价的奢侈品（想想那时要想征得你的同意我得费多大劲！），我们都得认真地讨论两三天，权衡一下买与不买的利弊，考虑一下我们能

---

1 Hyson /'haɪs(ə)n/　n.　熙春茶
2 speciosa miracula　（拉丁语）意为"怪奇伟丽，瑰丽神奇"
3 covet /'kʌvɪt/　vt.　垂涎
4 ado /ə'duː/　n.　费力

we felt the money that we paid for it.

"Do you remember the brown suit, which you made to hang upon you, till all your friends cried shame upon you, it grew so thread-bare[1]—and all because of that folio[2] Beaumont and Fletcher[3], which you dragged home late at night from Barker's in Covent Garden[4]? Do you remember how we eyed it for weeks before we could make up our minds to the purchase, and had not come to a determination till it was near ten o'clock of the Saturday night, when you set off from Islington[5], fearing you should be too late — and when the old bookseller with some grumbling opened his shop, and by the twinkling taper[6] (for he was setting bedwards) lighted out the relic[7] from his dusty treasures and when you lugged it home, wishing it were twice as cumbersome[8] — and when you presented it to me — and when we were exploring the perfectness of it (collating[9] you called it) and while I was repairing some of the loose leaves with paste, which your impatience would not suffer to be left till daybreak was there no pleasure in being a poor man? or can those neat black clothes which you wear now, and are so

1 thread-bare /ˈθredbeə(r)/ *adj.* 破旧的
2 folio /ˈfəʊliəʊ/ n. 对开本
3 Beaumont and Fletcher 博蒙和弗莱彻，他们两人合作创作出精彩的喜剧《烧火杵之王》（The Knight of the Burning Pestle）
4 Covent Garden 伦敦中部一个蔬菜花卉市场
5 Islington 伊斯灵顿，伦敦一个教区名
6 taper /ˈteɪpə(r)/ n. 微弱的光
7 relic /ˈrelɪk/ n. 宝贝，圣物
8 cumbersome /ˈkʌmbəsəm/ adj. 笨重的
9 collating /kəˈleɪtɪŋ/ n. 校勘

省出多少钱来，以及这钱该怎么省，才能勉强凑够数目。像这样的买法才值得一买，因为我们能感觉到掏出的每分钱的分量。"

"你还记得那件棕色的外衣吗？那件衣服已到了让人笑话的地步，因为它太破旧了，这不都是因为博蒙和弗莱彻的那本集子？那本一天夜里你从科文花园巴克书店拿回来的对开本？你记得我们决定要买它之前的几个星期里，不是都对它垂涎三尺，而且直到星期六晚上将近十点的时候，才下定决心要买它？接着你便从伊斯灵顿出发，还生怕晚了——那个怨气十足的书店老板把门打开，借着微弱的烛光（他准备睡觉了），从他那些尘封已久的宝贝中找到了这件宝物。你把它拖回了家，真是再重也毫无怨言——接着你把书捧给我——我们检查它的完整性（你称之为校勘）——当我用糨糊修复几张散页时，你真是迫不及待，无法等到天亮——可见贫穷人家不也乐在其中吗？再比如，我们变得富裕之后你现在穿的这些笔挺的黑色衣服，你小心对待使之光洁如新，它们能使你感到过去一半

careful to keep brushed, since we have become rich and finical, give you half the honest vanity, with which you flaunted it about in that over-worn suit — your old corbeau[1] — for four or five weeks longer than you should have done, to pacify your conscience for the mighty sum of fifteen — or sixteen shillings was it—a great affair we thought it then which you had lavished on the old folio. Now you can afford to buy any book that pleases you, but I do not see that you ever bring me home any nice old purchases now. "

"When you came home with twenty apologies for laying out a less number of shillings upon that print after Lionardo[2], which we christened[3] the 'Lady Blanch'; when you looked at the purchase, and thought of the money — and thought of the money, and looked again at the picture — was there no pleasure in being a poor man? Now, you have nothing to do but to walk into Colnaghi's[4], and buy a wilderness of Lionardos. Yet do you — "

"Then, do you remember our pleasant walks to Enfield, and Potter's Bar, and Waltham, when we had holydays, and all other fun, are gone, now we are rich — and the little hand-basket in which

---

1 corbeau *n.* （法语译音）卡薄，意为"大衣"
2 Lionardo 达·芬奇的名字为Lionardo, da Vinci，在意大利文里是from Vinci的意思，Vinci是地名。以前的文人画家都习惯把自己的名字和家乡写在一起，但由于Vinci是个小地方，Lionardo的签名又总是Lionardo da Vinci，所以后人以为da Vinci是他的姓
3 christen /'krɪsn/ *vt.* 命名为
4 Colnaghi's Bernheimer-Colnaghi 世界知名的古董商。这里破折号表示要说的意思对方已经明确，所以没有说完的必要。显然这里想说的与前一段结尾相同

的得意吗？以前你穿那件破旧外衣——那件旧卡薄的时候不也是大摇大摆神气活现的吗？并且得多穿四、五个礼拜才能买新衣服，以便安慰自己的良心，因为你已在那本古书上花了十五个先令——或者是十六个先令——这在当年可是一笔巨款。现在你喜欢什么书都能买得起，但我再没看见你买回来什么古本秘籍，传世佳作。"

"有一回，你买了一幅列奥纳多的摹本，那幅我们叫它'布朗琪夫人'的画，其实花的钱还没上回多，但是，你回来后还是连连道歉。你边看着买回来的画，边心疼花出去的钱——边心疼，又边看画——这时贫穷的人不也能乐在其中吗？而如今，你只需要到柯尔耐依跑上一趟，就能把成堆的列奥纳多的画购买回来。然而你——"

"还有，你记得在假期，我们徒步到恩费尔德、波特斯巴和沃尔瑟姆等地的快乐的旅行吗？可今天我们阔起来了，那些欢乐的旅行以及其他的种种欢乐却都统统一去不复返了。以前我常用来放一日粮（一点可口的冷羊肉和色拉）

I used to deposit our day's fare of savoury[1] old lamb and salad — and how you would pry about at noon-tide[2] for some decent house, where we might go in, and produce our store — only paying for the ale[3] that you must call for — and speculate upon the looks of the landlady, and whether she was likely to allow us a tablecloth Now, when we go out a day's pleasuring, which is seldom moreover, we ride part of the way — and go into a fine inn, and order the best of dinners, never debating the expense — which, after all, never has half the relish[4] of those chance country snaps, when we were at the mercy of uncertain usage, and a precarious welcome. "

Bridget is so sparing of her speech on most occasions, that when she gets into a rhetorical vein[5], I am careful how I interrupt it. I could not help, however, smiling at the phantom[6] of wealth which her dear imagination had conjured up[7] out of a clear income of poor — hundred pounds a year. "It is true we were happier when we were poorer, but we were also younger, my cousin. The resisting power — those natural dilations[8] of the youthful spirit, which circumstances cannot straiten[9] — with us are long since passed away. And now

---

1 savoury /ˈseɪvəri/ *adj.* 可口的
2 noon-tide /ˈnuːntaɪd/ *n.* 正午
3 ale /eɪl/ *n.* 一种啤酒
4 relish /ˈrelɪʃ/ *n.* 美味
5 get into a ... vein 对……有兴致
6 phantom /ˈfæntəm/ *n.* 幻影
7 conjured up 编造
8 dilation /daɪˈleɪʃn, dɪ-/ *n.* 膨胀
9 straiten /ˈstreɪtn/ *vt.* 限制，摧枯

的小手提篮——一到中午，你就开始四处张望，想找个体面的地方进去就餐，然后拿出来我们的存货——至于别的花费，只需要付啤酒钱就行，这是你每回必点的——然后开始研究女店主的脸色，看看她是否会给我们铺上一块桌布。然而现在，当我们外出做一日之游时（现在这种活动反而少了），我们却是出必有车，用餐必进上等饭店，而点菜又都点名贵菜肴，至于费用则在所不计。然而，尽管如此，风味却远不如一些农村的小吃。那时候我们根本不知道会遭遇何种摆布或何种接待。"

在多数场合里，布丽姬特总是沉默寡言，以至于当她兴致勃勃地慷慨陈词时，我则要对如何打断她多加小心。然而，我却对她那可爱的想象力假想出的财富幻影忍俊不禁，因为我们明明每年就只有一百英镑的微薄收入。"的确，以前穷的时候我们比现在开心，但那时我们也比现在年轻啊，我的表姐。不过，我们年轻时奋发向上的勇气——那种蓬勃旺盛、任何困境也摧压不了的青春活力——早已消失不在。而现在，还是看看瓷器上的这

do just look at that merry little Chinese waiter holding an umbrella, big enough for a bed-tester, over the head of that pretty chit of a lady in that very blue summer-house."

个快乐小巧的中国侍女吧，她擎着一把床帷般大小的巨伞，给那座蓝色凉亭下一位美丽纤弱的太太遮挡阴凉呢。"

含英咀华

本文通过作者对瓷器的喜爱，引出姐姐的看法，她分别举了买书、买画、旅行等例子，在姐姐的眼里，从前的生活充满了乐趣，她留恋从前的生活。现在的生活似乎缺少了某种东西，显得寡淡。

情牵梦萦

Dream Children: A Reverie
梦幻中的孩子们：一段奇想

On a Faithful Friend
记一位忠实的朋友

My Aunt Batty
贝蒂姨

Dream Children: A Reverie

Children love to listen to stories about their elders, when they were children; to stretch their imagination to the conception of a traditionary[1] great-uncle or grandame[2], whom they never saw. It was in this spirit that my little ones crept about[3] me the other evening to hear about their great-grandmother Field, who lived in a great house in Norfolk (a hundred times bigger than that in which they and papa lived) which had been the scene — so at least it was generally believed in that part of the country — of the tragic incidents which they had lately become familiar with from the ballad of the Children in the Wood. Certain it is that the whole story of the children and their cruel uncle was to be seen fairly carved out in wood upon the chimney-piece of the great hall, the whole story down to the Robin Redbreasts[4], till a foolish rich person pulled it down to set up a marble one of modern invention in its stead, with no story upon it. Here Alice put out one of

---

1 traditionary /trəˈdɪʃ(ə)n(ə)ri / adj. 传说的
2 grandame /ˈgrændəm/ n. 祖母
3 creep about /kriːp/ 蹑手蹑脚地走，缓慢地行进
4 robin redbreast=robin，知更鸟。据上述民谣，两个孩子死后，
   红胸知更鸟衔来树叶，覆盖在他们的尸体上

梦幻中的孩子们：一段奇想

孩子们喜欢聆听关于他们长辈们的故事，想知道他们做孩子的时候到底什么样。这样，对于一个他们从未见过面、只在大人们传说中听过的某位舅公或者祖母，孩子们愿意展开无限联想。也就是出于这点好奇心吧。一天夜里，我的两个小家伙蹑手蹑脚地来到我身边，缠着我要我给他们讲讲他们的曾祖母菲尔德：她居住在诺福克的一所大宅子里（那可比他们和爸爸住的地方要大上一百倍），那个宅子恰好又是（至少在那一带乡间，人们都这么认为）他们最近念过的歌谣《树林中的孩子们》里那段悲剧故事的发生地。其实，关于那些孩子们的故事，关于他们那狠心的叔叔的故事，以至那红胸脯的知更鸟的故事，都原原本本地雕刻在那大厅壁炉面的嵌板上，明明白白，丝毫不差。可是，之后来了一位愚蠢的阔佬，把那块雕花嵌板拆了下来，换成一面

209

her dear mother's looks, too tender to be called upbraiding[1].

Then I went on to say, how religious and how good their great-grandmother Field was, how beloved and respected by everybody, though she was not indeed the mistress of this great house, but had only the charge of it (and yet in some respects she might be said to be the mistress of it too) committed to her by the owner, who preferred living in a newer and more fashionable mansion[2] which he had purchased somewhere in the adjoining[3] county; but still she lived in it in a manner as if it had been her own, and kept up the dignity of the great house in a sort while she lived, which afterward came to decay[4], and was nearly pulled down, and all its old ornaments[5] were stripped[6] and carried away to the owner's other house, where they were set up, and looked as awkward as if some one were to carry away the old tombs they had seen lately at the abbey[7], and stick them up in Lady C.'s tawdry[8] gilt drawing-room. Here John smiled, as much as to say, "That would be foolish indeed."

And then I told how, when she came to die, her funeral was attended by a concourse[9] of all

新潮式样的大理石壁炉面，这么一来，上面什么故事都没有了。听到这里，爱丽丝不觉脸上微含嗔容，酷似她的爱母，那么温柔可爱，简直不能算做是在斥责。

接着，我继续往下说，他们的曾祖母菲尔德信教多么虔诚，为人多么善良，如何受到人人尊敬，尽管她并不是那所大宅子的主人，而只是受人之托代为看管（然而，从某种意义上说，她也能被称做是宅子的主人），因为主人在附近买了一所更时兴更讲究的住所，也就在那里定居，而把老宅子交给了她。可是她居住在那里时的神情，就好像宅子是她自己的一样。她在世的时候，总要让宅子保持着大门大户的气派。然而，宅子最终还是破败了，几乎快要塌下来，它原有的装饰品统统被拆了下来，运到主人的新宅子里去，重新安置起来。但这看起来很别扭，仿佛什么人把他们最近参观过的那些古墓从寺庙里搬走，摆放在某位贵妇人花哨俗气的客厅里。听到这里，约翰笑了，好像在说："真蠢！"

接着，我讲了，曾祖母去世的时候，方圆多少里的人都

1 upbraiding /ʌp'breɪdɪŋ / n. 责骂，训斥
2 mansion /'mænʃn/ n. 大宅，府邸
3 adjoining /ə'dʒɔɪnɪŋ/ adj. 毗邻的
4 decay /dɪ'keɪ/ vi. 衰败，衰退
5 ornament /'ɔːnəmənt/ n. 装饰品
6 strip /strɪp/ vt. 拆
7 abbey /'æbi/ n. 寺院
8 tawdry /'tɔːdri/ adj. 花哨而庸俗的，俗丽的
9 concourse /'kɒŋkɔːs/ n. 汇合，集合，合流，群集

the poor, and some of the gentry[1] too, of the neighborhood for many miles round, to show their respect for her memory, because she had been such a good and religious woman; so good indeed that she knew all the Psaltery[2] by heart, aye[3], and a great part of the Testament[4] besides. Here little Alice spread her hands.

Then I told what a tall, upright, graceful person their great-grandmother Field once was; and how in her youth she was esteemed the best dancer — here Alice's little right foot played an involuntary movement, till upon my looking grave, it desisted[5] — the best dancer, I was saying, in the county, till a cruel disease, called a cancer, came, and bowed her down with pain; but it could never bend her good spirits, or make them stoop, but they were still upright, because she was so good and religious.

Then I told how she was used to sleep by herself in a lone chamber of the great lone house; and how she believed that an apparition[6] of two infants was to be seen at midnight gliding up and down the great staircase near where she slept, but she said "those innocents would do her no harm"; and how frightened I used to be, though in those days I had my maid to sleep with me, because I was never half so good or religious

---

1 gentry /'dʒentri/ n. 贵族们，上流社会人士
2 Psaltery 指《旧约》中的《诗篇》
3 aye /aɪ/ int. 是
4 Testament 圣约书（《旧约全书》或《新约全书》）
5 desist /dɪ'zɪst, dɪ'sɪst/ vi. 停止
6 apparition /æpə'rɪʃn/ n. 幽灵，亡灵，幻影

来参加她的葬礼，穷人们都来了，也有些上流社会的人，向她的亡灵致敬，因为她是一位善良、虔诚的人。她是那么虔诚，能背下来整本赞美诗，是的，还有一大部分《新约》。听到这里，小爱丽丝佩服得摊开双手。

然后，我告诉他们：曾祖母个子很高、身材挺直、举止优雅，在她年轻的时候，大家都说她舞跳得最好——听到这里，爱丽丝那小小的右脚忍不住做了个轻快的动作，但看到我神情严肃，便停下了——我刚才正说，在全郡里她是跳舞跳得最好的，然而，一种叫做癌症的残酷疾病袭来，使她受尽痛苦。但这却并没有摧毁她顽强的意志，她在精神上仍然屹然挺立，因为她是个善良和虔诚的人。

然后我又说：她总是一个人睡在那所幽静的大宅子里一间幽静的房间里。她说有人半夜里看见两个小孩子的幽灵沿着她睡觉的房间旁边的那道长楼梯上上下下来回滑；但是她说，"那两个天真的小家伙不会伤害她的"。不过，那一阵子，尽管有女佣陪着我睡，我还是很害怕，因为我没有曾祖

as she — and yet I never saw the infants.

Then, in somewhat a more heightened tone, I told how, though their great-grandmother Field loved all her grand-children, yet in an especial manner she might be said to love their uncle, John L —, because he was so handsome and spirited a youth, and a king to the rest of us; and, instead of moping[1] about in solitary corners, like some of us, he would mount the most mettlesome[2] horse he could get, when but an imp[3] no bigger than themselves, and make it carry him half over the county in a morning, and join the hunters when there were any out — and yet he loved the old great house and gardens too, but had too much spirit to be always pent up[4] within their boundaries — and how their uncle grew up to man's estate as brave as he was handsome, to the admiration of everybody, but of their great-grandmother Field most especially; and how he used to carry me upon his back when I was a lame-footed[5] boy — for he was a good bit older than me — many a mile when I could not walk for pain; — and how in after life he became lame-footed too, and I did not always (I fear) make allowances enough for him when he was impatient, and in pain, nor remember sufficiently how considerate he had

1 mope /məup/ *vi.* 闷闷不乐
2 mettlesome /ˈmetlsəm/ *adj.* 烈性的
3 imp /imp/ *n.* 小鬼，顽童
4 pen up 把……关起来
5 lame-footed /ˈleimˈfutid/ *adj.* 脚跛的

母那样善良和虔诚——不过，我也没有亲眼看见过那两个小孩子。

接着，我略略抬高声音说，虽然他们的曾祖母菲尔德对孙子孙女全都喜欢，但特别疼爱的还是他们的约翰叔叔，因为他是那么漂亮、充满活力的小伙子，简直可以说是我们这群人里的国王；他从来不会像我们当中有的人一样，一个人闷在角落，他还不过是一个跟他们一般大的小鬼的时候，不管抓住多么烈性的马，也敢纵身跳上马背，一上午跑遍大半个郡，追上那些外出打猎的猎人——当然，他也爱那个古老的大宅子和花园，只是他的精力太饱满了，受不了它的约束——后来，他们的叔叔长大成人，英俊勇敢，人见人夸，尤其是最受他们的曾祖母菲尔德的喜爱。我还说，我小时候脚跛，他常常把我背起来——因为他大我几岁——我因为脚疼，不能走路，他就背着我走好多英里。后来他脚也跛了，但我恐怕在他痛苦、烦躁的时候，没有对他那么体谅，而过去自己跛脚、他对自己那么体贴的事情，也记不大清了。可是，他一去世，虽然刚刚过了

been to me when I was lame-footed; and how when he died, though he had not been dead an hour, it seemed as if he had died a great while ago, such a distance there is betwixt[1] life and death; and how I bore his death as I thought pretty well at first, but afterward it haunted and haunted me; and though I did not cry or take it to heart as some do, and as I think he would have done if I had died, yet I missed him all day long, and knew not till then how much I had loved him. I missed his kindness, and I missed his crossness[2], and wished him to be alive again, to be quarreling with him (for we quarreled sometimes), rather than not have him again, and was as uneasy without him, as their poor uncle must have been when the doctor took off his limb. Here the children fell a crying, and asked if their little mourning[3] which they had on was not for uncle John, and they looked up and prayed me not to go on about their uncle, but to tell them some stories about their pretty, dead mother.

Then I told them how for seven long years, in hope sometimes, sometimes in despair, yet persisting ever, I courted the fair Alice W-n[4]; and, as much as children could understand, I explained to them what coyness[5], and difficulty,

几个钟头，还是叫人感觉像是死了很久似的，因为生死之间相隔甚远。起初，对于他的死，我还能够承受，可是后来这件事在我心头反复萦绕；尽管我没有像其他人那样又哭又伤心（我想，要是我死了，他一定会哭的），但我还是成天想他，这时候我才明白自己是多么爱他。我既怀念他对我的友好，也怀念他对我发脾气，我希望他能再活过来，和我吵架也好（因为我们过去吵过架），也不愿意再也见不到他。由于失去他而心神不宁，就像他，他们可怜的叔叔，被大夫截肢以后的心情那样。听到这里，孩子们都哭了，问我他们臂上那条小小的黑纱是不是为约翰叔叔戴的。他们抬起头来，求我别再讲约翰叔叔的事情了，还是给他们讲讲他们去世的亲爱的妈妈吧。

于是我说，在七年中，有时候充满希望，有时候很沮丧，然而我没有间断地追求着爱丽丝·温顿。我用小孩子能听懂的话，向他们解释少女的着羞答答、左右为难、婉言谢绝都是什么意思——这时，我回头一看，过去那个爱丽丝的眼神却从小爱丽丝眼中活灵

1 betwixt /bɪˈtwɪkst/ *prep.* （古）在……之间，相当于**between**
2 crossness /ˈkrɒsnɪs/ *n.* 执拗，坏脾气，乖戾
3 mourning /ˈmɔːnɪŋ/ *n.* 为死者戴的黑纱，丧服
4 W-n: 此指Winterton，为兰姆年少时的情人Ann Simmons的化名，其后Ann嫁于一名为Bartrum的典当商
5 coyness /ˈkɔɪnɪs/ *n.* 羞怯

and denial meant in maidens[1] — when suddenly, turning to Alice, the soul of the first Alice looked out at her eyes with such a reality of re-presentment, that I became in doubt which of them stood there before me, or whose that bright hair was; and while I stood gazing, both the children gradually grew fainter to my view, receding[2], and still receding till nothing at last but two mournful features were seen in the uttermost distance, which, without speech, strangely impressed upon me the effects of speech: "We are not of Alice, nor of thee, nor are we children at all. The children of Alice call Bartrum father. We are nothing; less than nothing, and dreams. We are only what might have been, and must wait upon the tedious shores of Lethe[3] millions of ages before we have existence, and a name" — and immediately awaking, I found myself quietly seated in my bachelor armchair[4], where I had fallen asleep, with the faithful Bridget unchanged by my side — but John L. (or James Elia[5]) was gone forever.

活现地显露出来，我真是说不出站在我面前的是哪一个爱丽丝，也说不清那闪亮的金发究竟是她们中谁的。正当我定神凝视时，眼前两个孩子的模样渐渐模糊起来，越退越远，最后，在那非常遥远的地方只剩下两张悲伤的面孔依稀可辨。他们沉默不语，却好像在对我说："我们不是爱丽丝的孩子，也不是你的孩子，我们压根儿就不是小孩子。爱丽丝的孩子们管巴特姆叫爸爸。我们只是虚无，比虚无还要空虚，不过是梦境。我们只是某种可能性，要在忘川河畔渺渺茫茫等待千年万代，才能成为生命，拥有自己的名字。"——于是，我恍然醒来，发现自己安安静静地坐在单身汉的圈手椅里，刚才不过是睡梦一场，只有那忠实的布丽姬特依然如故地厮守在我的身边——而约翰·兰——（又名詹姆斯·伊利亚）却永远地消失了。

1 maiden /'meɪdən/ n. 少女
2 recede /rɪ'siːd/ vi. 后退
3 Lethe 希腊神话中的遗忘河
4 bachelor armchair 兰姆终生未娶，故此
5 James Elia 詹姆斯·伊利亚，系兰姆给他哥哥约翰·兰姆起的名字

含英咀华

本文节选自兰姆最优秀的散文作品《梦幻中的孩子们：一段奇想》（Dream Children: A Reverie），它于1822年一月初次发表于杂志《伦敦》（London），当时兰姆的哥哥约翰刚刚去世不久。文章内容与作者孤独凄惨的身世息息相关，文中的爱丽丝影射作者曾经深爱的女孩安妮·西蒙斯。但安妮没有回应兰姆的爱，而选择嫁给了巴特姆。留给作者的就只剩下盼望和没达成的梦想。哥哥约翰的去世，更增添了作者的忧愁。留在兰姆身边的人就只有他精神失常的姐姐。兰姆是忧郁的，但赢得我们的并不是他的自我怜悯，而是作品跌宕起伏的结构和亦真亦幻、悲喜交织的梦境氛围所构成的艺术魅力。兰姆把个人的不幸身世升华为幽默隽永的文章，在娓娓道来之间透出一种向忧愁微笑的动人力量。

Virginia Woolf
维吉尼亚·吴尔芙

维吉尼亚·吴尔芙（1882—1941），英国小说家、评论家，被誉为二十世纪现代主义与女性主义的先锋。最知名的小说有《雅各的房间》（*Jakob's Room, 1922*）、《达洛维夫人》（*Mrs. Dalloway, 1925*）、《到灯塔去》（*To the Lighthouse, 1927*）。她对英语语言革新良多，小说创作上反对自然主义，强调"意识流"手法(*stream of consciousness*)，主张简洁的风格。散文写作以人物随笔和批评文学著称，见解独到卓越，感受真切。

On a Faithful Friend

记一位忠实的朋友

There is some impertinence[1] as well as some foolhardiness[2] in the way in which we buy animals for so much gold and silver and call them ours. There is something profane[3] in the familiarity, half contemptuous[4], with which we treat our animals.

I do not think that in domesticating our lost friend Shag we were guilty of any such crime; he was essentially a sociable dog, who had his near counterpart in the human world. I can see him smoking a cigar at the bow window[5] of his club, his legs extended comfortably, whilst he discusses the latest news on the Stock Exchange[6] with a companion. His best friend could not claim for him any romantic or mysterious animal nature, but that made him all the better company for mere human beings. He came to us, however, with a pedigree[7] that had all the elements of romance in it. The whole of the Skye-terrier[8] tribe — who, that is,

人们一掷千金购买动物，将它们据为己有，这种做法既有些匪夷所思又不免轻率。在我们对待爱畜亲密而又不乏蔑视的态度中，同样有亵渎之嫌。

我觉得在驯养我们已经失去的老朋友沙格的过程中，我们不曾犯下任何上述罪行。它天生是条善于交际的狗，在人类社会中也有着类似它这样的角色。我能想象得出它在自己的俱乐部的弓形窗下抽着雪茄，惬意地伸长了双腿，与一位同伴谈论着股票交易所的最新行情。它最好的朋友也说不出他有任何浪漫神秘的动物本性，可也正因如此，它只能成为人类更好的伙伴。然而，他是带着富有浪漫气息的纯种血统来到我们家的。整个斯凯狗祖系——也就是继承了父系特征的斯凯狗，不知何故在地球上消失殆尽。沙格是诺福克郡一个偏僻的小村子幸存的纯种斯凯犬唯一后裔，原属于一位出身低微的铁匠，但对主人极为忠诚，并着意显

1 impertinence /ɪmˈpəːtnəns/　*n.*　荒谬，不合理
2 foolhardiness /ˈfuːlhɑːdɪnɪs/　*n.*　蛮勇，有勇无谋
3 profane /prəˈfeɪn/　*adj.*　不敬的
4 contemptuous /kənˈtemptʃuəs/　*adj.*　表示轻蔑的，瞧不起的，藐视的
5 bow window　弓形窗
6 Stock Exchange　证券交易所
7 pedigree /ˈpedɪɡriː/　*n.*　家世，血统，出身
8 Skye-terrier　斯凯狗，一种苏格兰种长毛短腿猎犬

inherited the paternal[1] characteristics — had somehow been swept from the earth; Shag, the sole scion[2] of true Skye blood, remained in an obscure Norfolk village, the property of a lowborn blacksmith, who, however, cherished the utmost loyalty for his person, and pressed the claims of his royal birth with such success that we had the honour of buying him for a very substantial sum.

He was too great a gentleman to take part in the plebeian[3] work of killing rats for which he was originally needed, but he certainly added, we felt, to the respectability of the family. He seldom went for a walk without punishing the impertinence of middle-class dogs who neglected the homage[4] due to his rank, and we had to enclose the royal jaws in a muzzle[5] long after that restriction was legally unnecessary. As he advanced in middle life he became certainly rather autocratic[6], not only with his own kind, but with us, his masters and mistresses; such a title though was absurd where Shag was concerned, so we called ourselves his uncles and aunts. The solitary occasion when he found it necessary to inflict[7] marks of his displeasure on human flesh was once when a visitor rashly tried to treat him as an ordinary pet-dog and tempted him with

示自己的高贵出身，终于使我们深感荣幸地不惜重金买下了沙格。

沙格是一位十足的绅士，不屑于干捉老鼠这种粗俗的活儿，这本为我们最初买它的目的。但是我们觉得，它确实为家里增添了名声。每次外出散步，它都会惩罚那些对它的地位不敬的、无礼的中产阶级狗，我们就不得不用口套把它高贵的下巴套住，尽管在法律上这种约束是不必要的。步入中年后，它变得越发专横起来，不仅对它的同类，对它的男女主人也是如此。对沙格来讲，我们以主人自称是可笑的，所以我们就改称为叔叔阿姨。沙格仅有的一次觉得有必要在人类的肉体上留下标记以表明其内心的不快，是一位客人轻率地把它当做一只普通的宠物狗来对待，用糖块逗它，并给它换了个名字，用卑贱的哈巴狗的名字"法朵"称呼它。随后，沙格露出了我行我素的本性，拒绝了糖块，在那

1 **paternal** /pəˈtɜːnl/　*adj.*　父亲的，父系的
2 **scion** /ˈsaɪən/　*n.*　后裔，子孙
3 **plebeian** /pləˈbiːən/　*adj.*　卑贱的，粗俗的
4 **homage** /ˈhɒmɪdʒ/　*n.*　尊敬，敬意，崇敬
5 **muzzle** /ˈmʌzl/　*n.*　（动物的）口套，口络
6 **autocratic** /ˌɔːtəˈkrætɪk/　*adj.*　专横的
7 **inflict** /ɪnˈflɪkt/　*vt.*　施以

sugar and called him "out of his name" by the contemptible[1] lap-dog title of "Fido". Then Shag, with characteristic independence, refused the sugar and took a satisfactory mouthful of calf[2] instead. But when he felt that he was treated with due respect, he was the most faithful of friends. He was not demonstrative[3]; but failing eyesight did not blind him to his master's face, and in his deafness he could still hear his master's voice.

The evil spirit of Shag's life was introduced into the family in the person of an attractive young sheep-dog[4] puppy — who, though of authentic breed, was unhappily without a tail — a fact which Shag could not help remarking with satisfaction. We deluded ourselves[5] into the thought that the young dog might take the place of the son of Shag's old age, and for a time they lived happily together. But Shag had ever been contemptuous[6] of social graces, and had relied for his place in our hearts upon his sterling[7] qualities of honesty and independence; the puppy, however, was a young gentleman of most engaging manners, and, though we tried to be fair, Shag could not help feeling that the young dog got most of our attention. I can

1 **contemptible** /kən'temptəbl/ *adj.* 可鄙的，卑劣的，不屑一顾的
2 **calf** /kɑːf/ *n.* 小腿
3 **demonstrative** /dɪ'mɒnstrətɪv/ *adj.* 易动感情的，感情外露的
4 **sheep-dog** 牧羊犬
5 **delude oneself** /dɪ'luːd/ 自欺
6 **contemptuous** /kən'temptʃuəs/ *adj.* 蔑视的，傲慢的
7 **sterling** /'stɜːlɪŋ/ *adj.* 优秀的

人腿上心满意足地咬了一大口。但是，当它觉得自己受到了应有的尊重时，便会成为最忠实的朋友。它不会轻易表露情感，但虽然视力衰退，它仍能看见主人的脸；虽然两耳失聪，它也仍能听见主人的声音。

一条惹人喜爱的小牧羊犬来到家里后，沙格生命中邪恶的一面显露了出来。这条小牧羊犬虽然血统纯正，却不幸少了条尾巴，沙格对这一发现十分得意。我们自欺欺人地相信，这条小狗可以充当老沙格的孩子，并且它们也曾一度相安无事。沙格一直鄙视社交礼仪，而凭正直独立的优秀品质赢得在我们心目中的地位；然而，这条小狗却是个风度翩翩的年轻绅士。虽然我们尽量保持公平，但沙格还是不由觉得那条小狗最得宠。我看到沙格笨拙而羞怯地抬起僵硬衰老的脚爪让我握，而这是小狗邀宠的拿手好戏之一。沙格的举止让我差点落泪，虽然面带微笑，但我仍是忍不住想起李尔王。但是沙格太老了，学不会什么新的社交技巧了。但它绝不甘拜下风，于是它决定用武力来解决。因此，度过了剑拔

see him now, as in a kind of blundering[1] and shamefaced way he lifted one stiff old paw and gave it me to shake, which was one of the young dog's most successful tricks. It almost brought the tears to my eyes. I could not help thinking, though I smiled, of old King Lear[2]. But Shag was too old to acquire new graces; no second place should be his, and he determined that the matter should be decided by force. So after some weeks of growing tension the battle was fought; they went for each other with white teeth gleaming — Shag was the aggressor — and rolled round and round on the grass, locked in each other's grip. When at last we got them apart, blood was running, hair was flying, and both dogs bore scars. Peace after that was impossible; they had but to see each other to growl[3] and stiffen[4]; the question was — Who was the conqueror? Who was to stay and who to go? The decision we came to was base, unjust, and yet, perhaps, excusable[5]. The old dog has had his day, we said, he must give place to the new generation. So old Shag was deposed, and sent to a kind of dignified dower[6] house at Parson's green, and the young dog reigned in his stead.

Year after year passed, and we never saw the old friend who had known us in the days of

弩张的几周之后，它们终于打起来了。它们露出白晃晃的牙齿扑向对方——沙格先发制人——它们在草地上滚来滚去，咬成了一团。我们最终把它们分开时，只见鲜血淋漓，毛发乱飞，两只狗都落下了伤痕。自那以后，日子就不太平了，它们一见面就狂吠不已，腰身绷紧。可问题是，谁是胜者呢？谁该留下，谁该离开呢？我们作出的决定卑鄙、不公，但或许也是情有可原的。我们认为，老狗已经有过风光的日子，该让位给下一代了。于是老沙格被打发到了帕森公园一位颇为体面的寡妇家里。小狗取代了它的位置。

年复一年，我们再也没有见过我们年轻时彼此熟识的这位老朋友。但在夏日的假期里，我们外出，留下管家在家时，它再次登门了。时间就这样流逝，直到去年，可是我们事先并不知道，那是它生命中最后一个年头了。某个冬夜，一个令人讨厌、焦虑的时刻，

---

1 blundering /'blʌndərɪŋ/ adj. 笨拙的
2 King Lear 莎士比亚著作《李尔王》中的主人公，故事讲的是一个专制独裁的皇帝，由于刚愎自用而遭受了悲惨的结局
3 growl /graʊl/ vi. 怒吼
4 stiffen /'stɪfn/ vi. 变僵硬
5 excusable /ɪk'sjuːzəbl/ adj. 可原谅的，有道理的
6 dower /'daʊə/ n. 寡妇

our youth; but in the summer holidays he revisited the house in our absence with the caretaker. And so time went on till this last year, which, though we did not know it, was to be the last year of his life. Then, one winter's night, at a time of great sickness and anxiety, a dog was heard barking repeatedly, with the bark of a dog who waits to be let in, outside our kitchen-door. It was many years since that bark had been heard, and only one person in the kitchen was able to recognize it now. she opened the door, and in walked Shag, now almost quite blind and stone deaf, as he had walked in many times before, and, looking neither to right nor left, went to his old corner by the fireside, where he curled up[1] and fell asleep without a sound. If the usurper[2] saw him he slunk guiltily away, for Shag was past fighting for his rights any more. We shall never know — it is one of the many things that we can never know — what strange wave of memory or sympathetic instinct it was that drew Shag from the house where he had lodged for years to seek again the familiar doorstep of his master's home.

It was in crossing the road which leads to the gardens where he was taken for his first walks as a puppy, and bit all the other dogs and frightened all the babies in their perambulators[3], that he met his death. The blind, deaf dog neither saw nor heard a

厨房门外反复传来狗叫，那叫声包含着等着被放进屋子的意味。这种声音已经多年没有听到了，此刻厨房里也只有一个人还能辨认出那是沙格的声音。她一开门，沙格便窜了进来，就像它以往许多次进屋时一样，当时它近乎彻底又聋又瞎了。它没有左顾右盼，径直走到早先它在火炉边上的角落，蜷起身子，不声不响地睡着了。如果被这块地盘的新主人看见，它会像有罪似地溜走，因为沙格已无力为自己的权利战斗了。我们永远都无法知道——那是我们永远不知道的许多事情之一——是什么奇异的记忆的波澜或是令人同情的本能，把它从落脚多年的住所吸引过来，再次寻找熟悉的主人家的门阶。

在穿过通往花园的马路时，它迎来了自己的末日。那个花园，它还是一条小狗时就被带去那儿散步，在那里，它咬过所有的狗，吓坏过童车中所有的婴儿。如今这条又瞎又聋的狗，既看不见马车，也听不见车声。车轮从它身上碾了

1　curl up /kə:l/　蜷起身子
2　usurper /juːˈzɜːpə(r)/　n.　篡位者，篡夺者
3　perambulator /pəˈræmbjuleɪtə(r)/　n.　婴儿车

hansom[1]; and the wheel went over him and ended instantly a life which could not have been happily prolonged.

So we say farewell to a dear and faithful friend, whose virtues we remember — and dogs have few faults.

过去，立即结束了它即使活着也难以快乐地延续的生命。

就这样我们告别了一位亲爱的、忠实的朋友，它的美德我们铭记不忘——而狗类几乎没有什么缺点。

1 hansom /'hænsəm/ *n.* 马车

含英咀华

这篇随笔情深意浓，回忆了爱犬沙格的生前情形种种以及老年的凄凉与死亡，描写了一只狗一辈子对一个人、一个家的忠诚不渝，寄托了主人对忠实于她的朋友沙格的无限哀思，同时也让人感受到了作者的挚诚情感。

Kathleen Norris
凯瑟琳·诺里斯

凯瑟琳·诺里斯（1880—1966），美国小说家，1909年与作家查尔斯·诺里斯 (Charles Norris, 1881–1945)结婚。她在加利福尼亚大学接受了特殊的教育，著有许多广受欢迎的浪漫小说。其文风感伤、朴实、坦率。诺里斯是她那个年代里收入最高的女作家，她的许多作品至今仍有很高的地位。1910年以后，她开始向《大西洋》(Atlantic)、《美国杂志》(The American Magazine)、《麦克卢尔》(McClure's)等杂志投稿。

My Aunt Batty

贝蒂姨

Every time I think of Aunt Batty I laugh, and that, in itself, I think, is a tribute[1] to her memory. Every time the other girls and boys who grew up under her forceful influence begin to discuss her, her absurdities[2] and idiosyncrasies[3] and unreasonableness, and her sheer sweet goodness, they laugh, too. And sometimes they've been caught wiping their eyes after the laughter.

She was not really my aunt. Her mother's sister had been my grandfather's second wife, if anyone cares to work out the relationship from that. But she stood, by age and nature, in the position of an aunt. We were orphaned when scarcely out of childhood, six of us, and how we should have weathered[4] the storm at all without Aunt Batty nobody cares to imagine.

Not that she had money. She never had money. She was widowed, with four children to raise, when I remember her first, her one asset a large, shabby[5], bay-windowed[6] house in a sunshiny section of San Francisco. Here Aunt

每次想到贝蒂姨，我都会想笑，我想只这一点便足以让人怀念她了。深受她熏陶的其他女孩和男孩们，每次谈论她的可笑、怪僻、不讲理和她的慈爱时，也会笑起来。但是在他们笑过之后，你会发现他们会偷偷地擦眼泪。

其实，她并不真是我的阿姨。如果有人想弄清楚，我们之间的关系是这样的：她母亲的妹妹是我祖父的第二个太太。但是就年龄和实际情况来看，她就是阿姨。我们兄妹六个，几乎还没度完童年就成了孤儿。如果没有贝蒂姨，我们怎样应付得了那段苦日子，那将不堪设想。

并不是她有钱。她从来就未曾富有过。在我的最初印象中，她是个有四个孩子的寡妇。她唯一的财产是一幢破旧、窗子突出墙外的房子，坐落在旧金山一个阳光普照的地区。贝蒂姨把房间租给别人，替客人做饭，剪延命菊和山龙眼拿到妇女交易场所去卖，用一架旧四方钢琴教音乐，替别

---

1 tribute /ˈtrɪbjuːt/   n.   颂辞，称赞
2 absurdity /əbˈsɜːdɪti/   n.   荒谬，可笑
3 idiosyncrasy /ˌɪdɪəˈsɪŋkrəsi/   n.   怪癖
4 weather /ˈweðə(r)/   vt.   经受
5 shabby /ˈʃæbi/   adj.   破旧的
6 bay-windowed   窗子突出墙外的

Batty rented rooms, cooked for boarders, clipped[1] yellow marguerites[2] and banksias[3] roses to sell at the Woman's Exchange, gave music lessons at an old square piano and knitted[4] baby blankets on order. She never mentioned money as important, or seemed to worry about having it or not having it. It sounds ridiculous, but there are persons like that. Yet somehow they manage to do what they have to do and what they want to do.

In person she was completely unimpressive; small, stout, gray, bustling[5]. Only an inconspicuous[6] middle-aged little woman, yet there was something confident — indeed, royal — in her manner. When she said to a traffic officer, "I am leaving my car here, my man; just keep an eye on it!" he quietly went and got them. When she reached authoritative hands for a strange baby in a streetcar, the mother instantly surrendered the child. And the baby always stopped crying and stared at Aunt Batty as one bewitched[7], as possibly he was.

Aunt Batty loved life as no other human being I ever knew loved life. She never did things that didn't interest her, and she never had enough time for those that did. She never went to lunch or dinner parties or played cards. But she cooked and knitted and cared for everyone's

人编制婴儿毛毯。她从来不提钱的重要，似乎也不为有没有钱而担心。这听上去似乎很好笑，但是有些人就是这样。然而，这些人仍旧能设法做到他们必须做的和他们想要做的事情。

她的外表全无动人之处，矮矮胖胖的，灰色头发，终日忙个不停。虽然她只是一个平凡的中年小妇人，但她的举止仪态中，却自有一股自信高贵的气质。她对交通警察说："跟你说，我把车停在这儿，你替我照看一下！"警察会悄然从命。她在公车上向一个陌生的婴儿伸出那双有力的手，婴儿的母亲就会立即把孩子递给她。孩子的哭声也戛然而止，两眼望着贝蒂姨，就像着了魔一样——可能确实着了魔。

贝蒂姨热爱生活，我从来没有见过第二个像她这样热爱生活的人。她不感兴趣的事从来不做；她喜欢做的事情，做起来总觉得时间不够。她从不参加宴会或牌局，而是忙着做饭、编织、照料每一家的孩子。无论哪一家突遭病痛灾难都需要她的出现。在她的一生中，她热爱骑脚踏车；贴满了

---

1 clip /klɪp/ vt. 剪下
2 marguerite /ˌmɑːgəˈriːt/ n. 雏菊
3 banksia /ˈbæŋksɪə/ n. （植物）山龙眼（产于澳洲）
4 knit /nɪt/ vt. 编织
5 bustling /ˈbʌslɪŋ/ adj. 忙碌的
6 inconspicuous /ˌɪnkənˈspɪkjuəs/ adj. 不显眼的，不起眼的
7 bewitched /bɪˈwɪtʃd/ adj. 着了魔似的

baby. She was needed in every house where there was sudden sorrow or sickness. To the end she bicycled enthusiastically; pasted up endless scrapbooks[1]; gardened until she was earthy, perspiring[2], sunburned, ravenous[3] and cramped[4]. Her garden never had a completed look, but her stocky figure and battered[5] old hat were somehow an always pleasant sight among the weedy borders.

We came to depend upon her honesty as a very rock under our younger lives. Between Aunt Batty's quiet "You've got a sick baby there" and her equally quiet "Well, this little feller's[6] made up his mind to stay with us awhile" lay life's extremes of fear and relief for young mothers. Her saying, "The way to begin living this ideal life they talk about is just to begin," has stayed with some of those long-ago boys and girls as the very base of their philosophies .

She faced what came without flinching[8]. On one rainy afternoon she sat with her only brother in a hospital room; her fingers knitting, her voice serene[9]. She had answered his question; the essential question. Yesterday a strong healthy man, planning for his future and that of his motherless children, had been struck

---

无数的剪贴簿；在花园里修剪花木，直到满身泥土、汗流浃背、晒红了脸、饥肠辘辘、腰酸背痛为止。她的花园一辈子也整理不完，但是她矮矮胖胖的背影和破旧的帽子，在杂草丛生的花坛间永远是一幅赏心悦目的画面。

贝蒂姨的诚实是我们年轻时生活的基石，她轻轻的一句"你的小宝宝病了"或是"嗯，这个小家伙已经决定要暂时留在我们身边了"，就决定了年轻母亲们极度的惊慌和宽慰。她有句名言："想过大家谈论的那种理想生活，就立刻开始。"有些许多年前在她照顾下长大的男孩女孩们，一直把这句话当做他们处世哲学的根本。

不管遇到什么事她从不畏缩。一个雨天的下午，她坐在医院的病房中，陪着她唯一的兄弟；她双手不停地编织，说话的声音很平静。她回答了他的问题，这个至关重要的问题。昨天，他还是一个强壮而健康的人，计划着自己的前途和他几个失去母亲的孩子们的将来，可是一辆横冲直撞的货车把他撞倒了。今天他就完了。

---

1 scrapbook /'skræpbʊk/ *n.* 剪贴簿
2 perspiring /pə'spaɪərɪŋ/ *adj.* 汗流浃背的
3 ravenous /'rævənəs/ *adj.* 饥肠辘辘的
4 cramped /kræmpt/ *adj.* 腰酸背疼的
5 battered /'bætəd/ *adj.* 破旧的
6 feller's （俚语）fellow has
7 philosophy /fɪ'lɒsəfi/ *n.* 人生观，处世哲学
8 flinching /'flɪntʃɪŋ/ *n.* 退缩
9 serene /sɪ'riːn/ *adj.* 镇静的

down by a derelict[1] truck. And today was the end.

"You lie here for an hour and think it over," she said. "I'll give the children their supper and send them in to see you. You've had a good, full life, Peter."

"The girls?" he faltered.

"I'll see to[2] the girls. You needn't be afraid."

He looked long at her. To his eyes came sudden peace.

"Thank you, Bat," he said. "I'm not afraid."

Nor was he, from that moment. Simple middle-aged brother and sister saying good-bye to each other, there was a dignity, even magnificence[3], about the little scene.

Well, that was all there was to her, a blunt, busy, stubby-handed little widow who lived in a dilapidated[4] old house, married off sons and daughters, took children to circuses and beaches, made ginger-bread and trimmed Christmas trees, gardened, nursed the sick, welcomed every new baby as if it were the first in the world, and loved on Sunday nights to gather a group of young people around an old piano while she played sentimental[5] old songs that everyone knew.

Rising from a long, joyous lunch table

1 derelict /'derəlıkt/ adj. 横冲直撞的
2 see to 照看
3 magnificence /mæg'nıfısns/ n. 伟大
4 dilapidated /dı'læpıdeıtıd/ adj. 年久失修的
5 sentimental /ˌsentı'mentl/ adj. 伤感的，动情的

"你在这儿躺一个小时，好好想想，"她说，"我去照顾孩子们吃晚饭，然后再叫他们来看你。彼得，你的一生很好，很圆满。"

"女孩子们呢？"他讷讷地说。

"我会照顾她们。你不用担心。"

他望了她好久，慌乱的眼神突然间平静了下来。

"谢谢你，贝，"他说。"我不担心。"

从这一分钟起，他的确不害怕了。纯朴的中年手足互相道别，这一幕有着庄严甚至伟大的意味。

贝蒂姨就是这样一个人：一个心直口快、忙碌不停、手指精短、身材矮小的寡妇，她住在一幢年久失修的老房子中，帮助儿女结婚成家，带领孩子们去马戏团和沙滩，做姜饼，布置圣诞树，从事园艺，照顾病人，欢迎每一个新来的婴儿就像是世界上第一个婴儿似的，喜欢在星期日的晚上邀一群年轻人到家里去围着一架旧钢琴，她则弹一些人人知道的动情的旧歌曲。

一个星期日，漫长而愉快的午餐后，贝蒂姨从座位上站起

one Sunday, she leaned on her oldest son's arm.

"I think you'd better help me upstairs, Bucky," she said. She hadn't called Tom that since he was five years old. We sat in stricken silence, for I think we all knew, then.

For two days she lay looking at us serenely, fondly, only disturbed when the children were too much silenced in the halls. And she gave us in parting perhaps her finest gift, the last of so many! I mean the sharing of her own conviction that the stubby hands, the eager mind, the inexhaustible[1] love that was part of her were preparing themselves for new fields of labor.

来，倚在她大儿子的胳膊上。

"小伙子，我想你最好扶我上楼，"她说。自从汤姆五岁以后她就没有再以名字称呼过他。我们大家默默地坐着，心里十分难过，因为我想当时大家都有同样的预感。

之后两天，她躺在床上，安详宁静地无限怜爱地望着我们，只有当孩子们在屋子里静得出奇的时候她才显得不安。她给了我们临别的也许是她最好的礼物，无数礼物中的最后一份！我是指分享她的信念：生茧的手、热忱的心以及她无尽的爱，都将在我们身上延续。

---

1 inexhaustible /ˌinigˈzɔːstəbl/　*adj.*　无穷无尽的

含英咀华

　　在这篇文章中，作者回忆了远方亲戚贝蒂姨，是她不辞劳苦地收养了在幼年时就成了孤儿的作者及她的几个兄妹。她辛勤劳作，热爱生活，从不消极，她的爱感染了每一个人。